Philadelphia Furniture
& Its Makers

Cover illustration: Secretary, attributed to Thomas Affleck, circa 1760–1770. Primary wood is mahogany; secondary woods are pine, tulip poplar, white oak, white and red cedar. 107" high to top of moulding and 112" high including bust; 47" wide, 25" deep. *Photograph courtesy of Bernard and S. Dean Levy.*

ANTIQUES Magazine Library

Philadelphia Furniture
& Its Makers

Edited by John J. Snyder, Jr.

Main Street/Universe Books

New York

Articles included in this volume are printed exactly as they appeared originally in the following issues of *The Magazine* ANTIQUES:

Part I. Some Pennsylvania Furniture, May, 1924; Living With Antiques, The Pennsylvania Home of Mrs. J. Stogdell Stokes, November, 1956; An Early Philadelphia Desk, January, 1960; The Spice Cabinets of Pennsylvania and New Jersey, October, 1939; Irish Influence in Pennsylvania Queen Anne Furniture, March, 1961; Notes on Construction of Philadelphia Cabriole Chairs, October, 1950.

Part II. Benjamin Randolph of Philadelphia, May, 1927; More About Benjamin Randolph, January, 1930; Jonathan Gostelowe, Philadelphia Cabinet and Chair Maker, Part I, June, 1926, and Part II, August, 1926; Add to Gostelowe, July, 1930; Thomas Tufft, October, 1927; Early Pennsylvania Craftsmen, Thomas Tufft "Joyner," March, 1928; Adam Hains of Philadelphia, May, 1947; Aesop's Fables on Philadelphia Furniture, December, 1951; Philadelphia via Dublin, Influences in Rococo Furniture, March, 1961.

Part III. Daniel Trotter and his Ladder-Back Chairs, November, 1959; Sheraton's Influence in Philadelphia, April, 1953; William Haydon and William H. Stewart, Fancy-Chair Makers in Philadelphia, September, 1973, Joseph B. Barry, Philadelphia Cabinetmaker, January, 1975; Philadelphia Empire Furniture by Antoine Gabriel Quervelle, September, 1964; The Furniture of Anthony G. Quervelle, Part I, Pier Tables, May, 1973.

Part IV. A Labeled Card Table by Michel Bouvier, April, 1973; Finial Busts on Eighteenth-Century Philadelphia Furniture, December, 1971; A Philadelphia Desk-and-Bookcase from Chippendale's *Director,* January, 1973; George Henkels, Nineteenth-Century Philadelphia Cabinetmaker, October, 1973; Carved Chippendale Case Furniture from Lancaster, Pennsylvania, May, 1975.

First Edition

Introductory material copyright © 1975 by The Main Street Press

Original articles copyright © 1924, 1926, 1927, 1928, 1930, 1939, 1947, 1950, 1951, 1953, 1956, 1959, 1960, 1961, 1964, 1971, 1973, 1975 by Straight Enterprises, Inc.

Library of Congress Catalog Card Number 75-10932

SBN 0-87663-250-9, cloth edition
SBN 8-87663-921-X, paperback edition

Published by Universe Books, 381 Park Avenue South, New York City 10016. Produced by The Main Street Press, 42 Main Street, Clinton, New Jersey 08809.

Printed in the United States of America

Cover design by Helen Iranyi

Contents

Introduction

That *Philadelphia Furniture & Its Makers* should appear in the period of this country's Bicentennial is timely in two respects. First, it brings facets of Philadelphia's artistic legacy to public attention at the time when the city will be commemorating its key role in the American Revolution. Moreover, the book marks the first time in forty years that any comprehensive study of Philadelphia cabinetwork has been published.

In 1935 William Macpherson Hornor published his *Blue Book of Philadelphia Furniture*. Now a great rarity, Hornor's book has remained the most authoritative and definitive study of eighteenth-century Philadelphia furniture. For both the scope of its content and the general quality of its documentation, Hornor's *Blue Book* is still unsurpassed in its field. In many respects, *Philadelphia Furniture & Its Makers* cannot supplant Hornor's achievement; nor can it supply the footnotes to Hornor which many readers have sought in vain in his book. Instead, this book seeks to show the advances made in research in the field through a compilation of articles which have appeared *in The Magazine* ANTIQUES from 1924 to 1975.

In seeking to define what constitutes "Philadelphia furniture" appears the most fundamental difference between the perspective of 1935 and that of today. To Hornor and his contemporaries, the furniture worthy of the attention of the scholar and collector was that of the William and Mary, Queen Anne, Chippendale, Hepplewhite, and Sheraton periods. In the past twenty years, increasing awareness of the importance of Philadelphia Empire and Victorian furniture has expanded the temporal limits of the Philadelphia School to the era of the Centennial. Recent work has also expanded the spatial limits of the school. Forty years ago, it was believed that most, if not all, quality furniture from eighteenth-century Pennsylvania was produced in the Quaker City. Today it is realized that, in the 1700s, Philadelphia was the center of a complex and diverse regional school which reached from South Jersey to Maryland to inland Pennsylvania. Many articles from ANTIQUES which are included in this book have led the way in expanding the traditional definitions of the temporal and spatial bounds of the Philadelphia School. Possibly the most important contribution of this book will be to create recognition of this growing and changing concept.

In addition to establishing a new understanding of the extent of the Philadelphia School, it is hoped that *Philadelphia Furniture & its Makers* will serve as a useful reference work. By assembling in one volume many of the most important articles on Philadelphia furniture which were printed in ANTIQUES during fifty-one years, there is created a unified book which can save the reader many hours of otherwise tedious searching through back issues. The compilation of many articles in one volume enables the reader to make comparisons directly and immediately, which could not be done easily with a series of separate articles. Further, each article included in this book testifies to the role of ANTIQUES in publishing the most recent advances in research on American decorative arts.

From the William and Mary to Victorian periods, Philadelphia artisans adapted English design sources to create a distinct regional school. But the products of Philadelphia cabinetmakers' shops were more than reflections of English prototypes; they were a manifestation of the city's total culture. Thus, some knowledge of the historical and cultural background is necessary for understanding Philadelphia furniture.

When William Penn was made proprietor of Pennsylvania in 1681, he conceived his new colony as a "Holy Experiment" in which many of Europe's social and economic problems could be remedied. Penn encouraged settlement by many ethnic groups, ranging from England's persecuted Quakers to Germans from the Palatinate. This quality of ethnic diversity, plus an atmosphere which encouraged religious freedom, made Pennsylvania the most pluralistic of all the colonies in the eighteenth century. The mingling of sources from diverse national backgrounds enriched Pennsylvania's arts; English, Irish, French, and Germanic influence on furniture of the Philadelphia School will be illustrated in articles included here.

In 1682 Philadelphia was laid out with a grid plan and five open squares. The fact that the city was planned before any building took place, plus Penn's personal influence, provided an opportunity for introducing many of the ideas about city planning and architecture which had developed in London after the Great Fire of 1666. Hence, from its founding, Philadelphia was unlike many New England towns, where a strong, lingering medieval tradition persisted. Philadelphia's position at the junction of the Schuylkill and Delaware Rivers soon made it the leading port of the Middle Colonies. By the opening of the eighteenth century, the foundations of the great fortunes of Philadelphia's merchant families, including Norris, Shippen, Pemberton, and others, were firmly established. The combined factors of mercantile wealth, direct contact with England, and the city's role as Pennsylvania's seat of government gave Philadelphia the prerequisites for becoming a center of cultural and artistic activities.

The survival rate for Philadelphia art predating 1730 has been low. Most of the important architecture of the city's first half century, like the Slate Roof House and the Norris countryseat, Fairhill, were destroyed long ago. Save for the portrait of Johannes Kelpius of Germantown painted by Christopher Witt between 1704 and 1708, little remains of Philadelphia portraiture which predates the works executed by Gustavus Hesselius in the 1720s and the 1730s. Indeed, occasional pieces of silver and furniture in the William and Mary style constitute the mainstream of Philadelphia's artistic legacy from this period.

The years between 1730 and 1800 constituted Philadelphia's "golden age" in terms of its economy, culture, arts, and sphere of influence. By the middle of the eighteenth century, Philadelphia led all other cities in Britain's North American colonies. In the whole British Empire, only London and Bristol surpassed it in importance as a port. With a population of about 40,000 on the eve of the Revolution, Philadelphia was the third largest city in the English-speaking world, being exceeded only by London and Dublin. Therefore, it is not surprising that here the Continental Congresses convened, the Declaration of Independence was signed, and the United States Constitution was adopted.

Philadelphia's institutions complemented this picture of prominence and prosperity. In 1751 the Pennsylvania Hospital was founded and the cornerstone of its impressive building was laid four years later. Benjamin Franklin's Junto became the American Philosophical Society, and the College of Philadelphia, chartered in 1755, was the predecessor of the University of Pennsylvania. Under the influence of Quaker patronage, the city's charitable institutions grew famous, and the city's prisons were the most advanced in the country. Also noted were several early theaters, and the dancing assemblies.

In its appearance, America's metropolis was both urban and urbane; in fact, in 1786, Thomas Jefferson stated that, in his estimation, London and Paris were "not so handsome as Philadelphia." From the 1720s through the end of the eighteenth century, Philadelphia was the center of a strong regional school of Georgian architecture. Representative of the polarities of this school are two of its earliest extant products: Stenton, the countryseat of James Logan, built between 1728 and 1734, and Christ Church, erected between 1727 and 1744. Whereas the former represents the understated refinement often regarded as typical of Quaker taste, the latter reveals an exuberance of baroque forms and ornament achieved under Anglican patronage. A synthesis of these two strains may be perceived in the Pennsylvania State House (Independence Hall) of c. 1730-1748, in which a plain exterior is contrasted with an elaborate interior. This aesthetic polarity, expressed in the contrast between the elegantly simple and the richly ornate, may also be seen in many pieces of Philadelphia Queen Anne and Chippendale furniture. Contemporary with the greatest works of Philadelphia Chippendale are some of the masterpieces of Philadelphia's mid-Georgian architecture, including countryseats like Cliveden (1764) and Mount Pleasant (1761), townhouses such as the Stedman-Powel House, and the works of Philadelphia's leading architect-builder, Robert Smith.

From the 1740s through the end of the eighteenth century, most of the leading artists of the colonies and young republic worked in Philadelphia. Before 1750, Robert Feke painted the portraits of some of the city's leading citizens. He was followed by John Wollaston,

the young Benjamin West, the Claypoole family, William Williams, and many others. After the Revolution, Philadelphia was the chief residence of the remarkable Charles Willson Peale and his brother James, who were the progenitors of America's most noted family of artists.

Among the famed silversmiths who worked in Philadelphia in this period were Philip Syng and the Richardson family. Several years before the Revolution, the short-lived firm of Bonnin and Morris produced America's first porcelain in Philadelphia's Southwark area. Hence, it is evident that in the seven decades following 1730, Philadelphia was the leading center of artistic activity in America.

In 1790 Philadelphia became the capital of the new country, in addition to continuing its role as Pennsylvania's seat of government. Throughout the following decade, the city enjoyed that cosmopolitan and somewhat international sensibility which is always associated with a national capital. The city's position of commercial and cultural preeminence only heightened its role of administrative leadership. Moreover, by this time Philadelphia had acquired a strong sense of its own identity. Some idea of Philadelphia's brilliant society may be gleaned from the words of Sally McKean, who described one of Martha Washington's Friday-evening drawing rooms as "brilliant beyond anything you could imagine" with "a good deal of extravagance" and "much of Philadelphia taste in every thing." In this same decade a French visitor noted that Philadelphia's ladies were dressed "to the tip of French fashions."

Philadelphia's best architecture in the Federal period often was the most avant-garde in the country. The Woodlands, countryseat of the Hamilton family, was the earliest example of fully developed Adamesque architecture in the country when completed in the late 1780s. The Bank of Pennsylvania, erected between 1798 and 1801 from designs by Benjamin Henry Latrobe, was the first large building in America to employ a Greek order; thus it heralded the Classical Revival. Other notable examples of Federal style architecture in Philadelphia included Lemon Hill, William Bingham's townhouse, and Robert Morris's never-completed French-style residence.

As the national capital, Philadelphia attracted important artists, among them being Gilbert Stuart, Adolph Ulrich Wertmuller, and various members of the ever-growing Peale family. Graceful pieces of silver of neo-classical inspiration were wrought by Christian Wiltberger, John McMullin, John Germon, and many others. The city's cabinetmakers produced elegant furniture to grace the interiors of many important houses. As was the case elsewhere in America, the published designs of Hepplewhite and Sheraton influenced most high-style furniture. However, in the 1790s, Philadelphia produced a few pieces of painted seat furniture in the Louis XVI style; the most notable examples of this style are the twelve open armchairs and sofa made for the Burd family, some of which have been exhibited at Lemon Hill in Fairmount Park. In adopting French sources, Philadelphians were in advance of the rest of the country, where the influence of French designs became important somewhat later.

In 1800 the national capital left Philadelphia for Washington; a year earlier, Pennsylvania's capital had moved inland to Lancaster. Both removals were due to political pressures from the West and the unfavorable memories of yellow fever epidemics which had ravaged the city. With the loss of its position as the center of two governments, Philadelphia also lost some of its national stature. Nonetheless, it remained the country's largest city and leading port. Not until near the end of the first quarter of the nineteenth century did New York outrank it in both population and commercial importance. Despite these losses, Philadelphia remained one of the country's leading seaports, and throughout the nineteenth century it grew as a center of manufacturing. The secure position of the city's cultural and educational institutions, upheld by the fortunes of its established aristocracy, endowed Philadelphia with an aura of refined, stable gentility as the nineteenth century progressed.

In the first half of the nineteenth century, the quality of Philadelphia's art and architecture remained high. At the very time when Bouvier and Quervelle were making what is now the best-known Philadelphia Empire-style furniture, the city's architecture was partaking of the eclecticism which then was prevalent. For example, William Strickland's Second Bank of the United States of 1818-1824 was an adaptation of the Parthenon, whereas John Haviland's Eastern State Penitentiary of 1823-1836 was built in the fortress-like Norman style. Elaborate pieces of Empire style silver, often showing strong French influence, were made by Harvey Lewis, Anthony Rasch, and Simon Chaudron. In the twelve years following 1826, William Ellis Tucker's factory produced porcelain reflecting European styles. And for almost three quarters of the nineteenth century, Phila-

delphia was home to America's leading romantic portrait painter, Thomas Sully.

As Philadelphia prepared to host the nation's Centennial in 1876, its focus of attention was by no means concentrated solely on its own past. Among the city's important Victorian architects were Samuel Sloan, Joseph Hoxie, and Frank Furness. In addition to the venerable Thomas Sully and later members of the Peale family, Philadelphia artists of the second half of the nineteenth century included still-life painters like John F. Francis, William Harnet, and John F. Peto. At present, too little is known about decorative arts of Victorian Philadelphia to permit any sweeping statements. This book's one article about Victorian furniture from Philadelphia can only suggest that a very fertile field remains to be explored.

The furniture discussed in this book covers almost two centuries of Philadelphia's cabinetmaking artistry. There is no one common denominator by which all this diverse assemblage might be evaluated unless it is in the degree of success by which the respective pieces and styles reveal something about those who created them. With this standard of judgment, it is believed that *Philadelphia Furniture & Its Makers* will prove that the furniture of this city encompasses more in both quality and quantity than most people ever imagined.

Lancaster, Pennsylvania
June, 1975

John J. Snyder, Jr.

I The William & Mary and Queen Anne Styles

In studying Philadelphia furniture, the words "Queen Anne" might well evoke the image of a graceful cabriole leg chair to most connoisseurs, but the same people might well be at a loss to recall one great piece of William and Mary furniture made in that city. This reaction constitutes a revealing insight into the state of knowledge of Philadelphia William and Mary furniture. In the 1924 article reprinted as the first in this book, Homer Eaton Keyes illustrated several Pennsylvania William and Mary chairs, but in the following fifty-one years, the publication of the signed 1707 Edward Evans escrutoire constituted the sole notice of a piece of Philadelphia William and Mary furniture whose maker could be identified. The quality of the Edward Evans escrutoire, plus the scope of the early pieces seen in the J. Stogdell Stokes collection, can only indicate that Philadelphia artisans created many fine pieces in this style. Perhaps the poverty of knowledge about this period is due to the loss of many pieces.

The William and Mary style commenced in England in the last two decades of the seventeenth century. Through its proficiency of design and execution, the 1707 Evans escrutoire indicates that the style was well known in Philadelphia by the first decade of the eighteenth century. In both England and America, the new style was marked by the change from the framed, panel-type construction of the earlier Jacobean style to boarded construction which gave large, flat surface areas which could be left plain or ornamented with veneers or inlays. Generally, it appears that Philadelphia craftsmen favored relatively plain surfaces on William and Mary pieces, although a distinctive type of vine and berry inlay was developed in nearby Chester County. A Philadelphia or Chester County dressing table dated 1724, now at the Philadelphia Museum of Art, indicates the strength of the William and Mary style through the 1720s. Indeed, in provincial areas, some aspects of this style lasted until after the middle of the eighteenth century.

Regarding the source of its name, the Queen Anne style owes little to the monarch who was the last of the Stuart line. Indeed, many of the pieces which Americans term "Queen Anne" would be called "Early Georgian" in England. One all-important characteristic distinguished the Queen Anne style from its predecessors: the use of the "S" or cyma curve. This curve, which Hogarth called the "line of beauty," influenced every element of furniture design, including the cabriole leg, chair splats, and scroll pediments. Hornor, in his *Blue Book,* stated that the earliest documentary reference to this style in Philadelphia occurred in 1742. However, it is likely that the Queen Anne style was introduced about 1730; for ex-

ample, a Delaware Valley cabriole leg dressing table, believed to date 1732, was exhibited at the Newark Museum in 1958. Although the Queen Anne style certainly was fading in Philadelphia by the mid-1750s, vestiges of it remained into the closing years of the century.

That some distinctive qualities of Philadelphia Queen Anne furniture are derived partly from Irish sources is demonstrated in the article by David Stockwell in the March, 1961, ANTIQUES. The spice cabinets of southeastern Pennsylvania and adjacent areas, discussed in another article by Stockwell, may be regarded as a regional form. Today it is believed that many of these small cabinets were used for storing small valuables. Further, Stockwell's article on the construction of cabriole leg chairs marked the first time in which detailed illustrations were used to illustrate structural techniques in Philadelphia chairs. The reader wishing to know more about chair construction should consult John Kirk's excellent book, *American Chairs—Queen Anne and Chippendale* (1972).

In view of the just acclaim received by the masterpieces of Philadelphia Queen Anne furniture, it is surprising that few signed or labeled pieces have been reported. Among the makers of documented examples are Joseph Armitt, John Elliott, and William Savery. It is to be hoped that future research may reveal the identities of more of the cabinetmakers who fabricated this very elegant and graceful furniture.

Fig. 1 — WAINSCOT ARM-CHAIRS

a. Walnut chair, perhaps once the property of Jacob Winchell in his old house, erected 1711, near Sycamore Mills. Exact dates are not easily assignable to such pieces; but the strongly beveled paneling and the character of the turnings suggest a period 1680–1700. In English chairs of the seventeenth century the low front stretcher is usually considered to be earlier than the type which is raised toward the middle of the legs. *Owned by J. Watts Mercur.*

b. Walnut chair. Native walnut appears to have been used in the Pennsylvania country with much the same freedom as characterized the use of maple in New England. It was plentiful, worked well, and offered a satisfactory substitute alike for oak and for mahogany. The similarity of the crestings in this and in the previous example is noteworthy. General proportions, however, are more slender. *Owned by Arthur Scott.*

c. Walnut chair with drawer. A cruder piece than either of the preceding. Stiles of the back extremely narrow and arms similarly restricted. As a result the supports are cut away in a curious manner, a device not uncommon in English analogues. The overhanging drawer lip and the two knobs so located as to infringe upon the legs of the occupant suggest the possibility that this part of the chair is a renewal.

Some Pennsylvania Furniture

By THE EDITOR

(Illustrations by courtesy of Clarence W. Brazer from collections as noted.)

JUST why Pennsylvania furniture, even that which seems to owe nothing to the German affiliations of its makers and owners, should be different from that which pleased the early New England taste, it would be impossible to say. Little as we know of the early cabinet-makers of New England and the influences which shaped them and their productions, we know still less of those who settled in Pennsylvania, in New Jersey, and along the shores of Chesapeake Bay in Maryland.

The Pennsylvanians may have come from a different section of England from that whence emigrated their New England brethren. They may have brought with them across the Atlantic provincial prejudices and habits of workmanship peculiar to their communities of origin. Or their new environment may have affected them in one way while the New England environment was operating in another.

It is worthy of note, for example, that the seventeenth century type of wainscot chair is of infrequent occurrence in New England. Mr. Nutting suggests that hardly more than half a dozen are known.* Yet in Pennsylvania perhaps a dozen such pieces have been marked by students of early furniture. On the other hand the turned Brewster and Carver types of chairs are so infrequently discovered outside of New England that their occurrences in other districts suggest a presumption of New England origin. This may, in part, be due to the fact that a settled society was of earlier occurrence in New England than in Pennsylvania, and that it resorted to turned chairs of a style which had become out of date at the period of the Pennsylvania immigration. Yet such explanation is far from completely satisfying.

The personal requirements of the users of furniture, furthermore, may well have had something to do with the characteristics evolved to meet them. The traditional conception of Uncle Sam was derived from generally accepted notions of a New England type, tall and spare, and longitudinally restricted. The fatter counties to the south may

*Wallace Nutting, *Furniture of the Pilgrim Century*, Boston, 1921, p. 180.

Fig. 2 — WAINSCOT CHAIRS

a. Walnut side chair. The truss support of the seat rail is interesting. The cresting and the terminals of stiles are closely similar to those of *Fig. 1, a and b*, and suggest a common origin. *Owned by Clarence W. Brazer.*

b. Walnut chair. The lower turnings are rather embryonic. While the back stiles are of normal width, the narrow arms have necessitated a whittling back of the supports. *Owned by T. VanC. Phillips.*

c. Walnut chair. Vigorous turnings. Flat panel with unusually wide moulding. The complete absence of the carving which was so characteristic of English wainscot chairs constitutes a peculiarity of these Pennsylvania examples. *Owned by J. Watts Mercur.*

Fig. 3 — PENNSYLVANIA CHAIRS

a. Banister back, imposed cresting. Called a "square cut Queen Anne," but comparable with a chair in *Furniture of the Pilgrim Century*, p. 283, which is assigned to the period 1711–1720. *Owned by Clarence W. Brazer.*

b. Carver type, found in Delaware. This may be a New England piece, yet it displays peculiarities which suggest that it was made in the locality where it was found. *Owned by Mrs. Thomas W. Cahill.*

c. Banister back chair. Quite different from the New England type, which usually exhibits turned stiles. Attributable probably to the first quarter of the eighteenth century. *Owned by J. W. Mercur, Jr.*

13

Fig. 5 — "Windsor" Settee

Oak spindles, gumwood seat, walnut and maple stretchers. Reported once to have been in the old Court House at Chester. Exceptionally fine spindles and characteristically bold and vigorous volute termination to the arms. Probably of first half of the eighteenth century. While generalizations are dangerous, it seems worth while here to suggest an important point of difference between the Windsor settees of Pennsylvania and those of New England. Fine examples of the former are quite likely to display a remarkable array of elaborately turned spindles supporting back and arms, while legs and stretchers are more summarily treated. New England types, on the other hand, seem to indicate preference for plain tapering back and arm spindles, whose simplicity is offset by impressive turnings of legs and stretchers. *Owned by T. VanC. Phillips.*

Fig. 6 — Eighteenth Century Chairs

a. One of a pair of maple chairs of Queen Anne type (*c. 1720*) showing unusual recessed curved stretchers, strongly reminiscent of certain Dutch types. The splayed toes, apparently derivations of the earlier "Spanish foot" seem to be more characteristic of Pennsylvania and New Jersey than of New England. It is more fully exemplified in Figure 6c. *Owned by T. W. Scattergood.*

b. Chippendale type. Of mahogany (*c. 1760*). Attributed to William Savery. The low seat, and the heavy apron, which shortens the proportions of the legs, suggest affinity with the lowboys and high chests of that Philadelphia craftsman. The elaboration of the carving is likewise notable. A generously ample chair, unusual in the shape of arms at joining with seat frame. *Owned by Francis D. Brinton.*

c. Queen Anne chair. Formerly in Governor Keith's dining room at Grahme Park. Made of walnut and said to have been imported from England about 1722. The restricted dimensions of the seat may be in part accounted for by the dining-room use. *Owned by Mr. and Mrs. Arthur Scott.*

Fig. 4 — PENNSYLVANIA CHAIRS

a. Wainscot oak chair. Traditionally, certain oak chairs of Pennsylvania were brought from England about 1682. It would, perhaps, be difficult to prove the case either way. The absence of carving and the placing of the cresting well down between the stiles suggest American handiwork. *Owned by J. Watts Mercur.*

b. Oak chair, Cromwellian (*c. 1650*). Said to have been brought from England by the Savage family. Quite possibly English and displaying some subtlety in the taper of the back; but, in general, heavier than many contemporary English examples. *Owned by Mrs. George T. Worrell.*

c. Wainscot chair of oak, with Victorian needlework on horsehair seat and back. Said to have been brought from England previous to 1681*, but exhibiting singular similarity of cresting to that in various preceding examples. *Owned by T. VanC. Phillips.*

have produced more ample citizens. William Penn is represented as broad of beam. His Quaker followers were, many of them, well fleshed. Residence in Philadelphia gave Ben Franklin a galaxy of chins and an exuberant waist line. This may be no better than a fanciful comparison; but it is undeniable that, in general, Pennsylvania furniture conveys an impression of larger scale, of more generous proportions, often of greater sturdiness, than does the greater part of that encountered in New England. Here and there, in the latter district, one encounters broad bottomed Windsors, and, from the period of the earliest settlements, quite cavernous armchairs, that must have been fashioned for the greater comfort of massive citizens. But these seem not so much the general rule as is the case in Pennsylvania.

The point is fairly well illustrated in the selection of examples, here illustrated, chosen from the loan exhibition of Pennsylvania types which was held last October by the Delaware County Historical Society in the old Colonial Court House at Chester, Pennsylvania. This ancient Court House, erected in 1724, is said to be the oldest public building in the United States continuously in use for public purposes. Only recently it was vacated as the City Hall and

was restored to its original condition under the architectural supervision of Clarence W. Brazer of New York and Chester. Mr. Brazer likewise arranged the exhibition, and to his courtesy ANTIQUES is indebted for the accompanying photographs. Acknowledgment is likewise due to those who have allowed publication of pieces in their personal possession.

The examples here illustrated by no means exhaust a field of great extent, variety and richness. In fact they serve merely as a kind of informal introduction to a subject deserving of far more detailed study and original investigation of sources than it has hitherto received. Such specific commentary on the illustrations as seems, for the time being, pertinent will be found included in the legends which accompany them. But in the absence of information necessary to fully satisfactory conclusions, whatever is said should be considered very tentative and liable to further revision.

*The territory known as Pennsylvania was granted to William Penn by Charles II in 1681. Penn crossed the ocean one year later. On his arrival he found the west bank of the Delaware already occupied by about 6,000 Swedes, Dutch and English.

15

BY ALICE WINCHESTER

Living with antiques

*The Pennsylvania home of
Mrs. J. Stogdell Stokes*

SOME PEOPLE COLLECT ANTIQUES as appropriate furnishings for an old house. The house shown here illustrates the opposite process: recently built, it was designed especially for the antiques that furnish it. They are the cream of a lifetime collection.

Mr. J. Stogdell Stokes was long interested in American antiques, especially those of the Pennsylvania and New Jersey of his ancestors. Over the years he and Mrs. Stokes acquired a large and distinguished collection of local furniture of the seventeenth and early eighteenth centuries, and also of pottery, ironwork, lighting devices, glass, fractur work, and wood carvings. Views of their pre-Revolutionary farmhouse where these things were gathered were shown in ANTIQUES for February 1942, and many individual pieces are illustrated in Nutting's *Furniture Treasury*. Some of these antiques are now in the Philadelphia Museum of Art, of which Mr. Stokes was president for many years; others have been dispersed. A choice selection furnishes the small house in Bryn Mawr which Mrs. Stokes had built after her husband's death. Picking out her favorite pieces, she engaged the architect Sydney E. Martin to design a setting expressly for them and for her. It is of stone, the typical material of the region, and in exterior appearance and interior detail has the character of the eighteenth century, though it is not an exact reproduction. In this felicitous setting Mrs. Stokes' fine antiques are perfectly at home.

In the entrance hall a rare Pennsylvania William and Mary walnut lowboy whose trumpet-turned legs are joined by a flat, scrolled, cross stretcher is flanked by a pair of late seventeenth-century high-back chairs with heavy semicircular crest typical of Pennsylvania. These match an armchair formerly in the Stokes collection and may have originally accompanied a matching daybed. The Pennsylvania chest is of the rare type painted with unicorns as well as floral motifs. In the far corner a slat-back chair with big mushroom armrests, made close to 1700, is partially visible.

One of the most unusual, and charming, pieces in the house is the Pennsylvania Queen Anne lowboy whose shaped contour seems almost akin to the blockfront developed in Newport a generation or so later (Hornor, *Blue Book of Philadelphia Furniture*, Plate 22). This admirably designed piece is of walnut and has its original engraved brasses. On it are displayed three rarities from the Stokes collection of Pennsylvania lighting devices, each more interesting than the others. From the turned wood screw standard in the center hang two iron betty lamps whose covers have little roosters for handles. The cup-shape iron lamp on the left swings on a wrought-iron standard with graceful scroll handle. The device on the right, standing on high scrolled feet, supports a crusie which may be raised or lowered by means of a shaft and key in the standard. Various other early lamps and candleholders may be seen about the house, and the electric lights are worth noting as well: some are made from early Pennsylvania slipware jars, some from brass or iron candlesticks and early lamps.

The arched fielded panels and narrow mantel shelf on the chimney breast, the heavy bolection molding framing the fireplace opening, the deep window embrasures with raised panels below, and the moldings of cornice and other woodwork, though new, are all in the early eighteenth-century tradition of Chester County. Gathered about the fireplace are a Spanish-foot wing chair, probably of New York origin, a Philadelphia Queen Anne armchair, Pennsylvania gate-leg table, turned stretcher stool, William and Mary armchair (one arm and post visible in foreground), and a sturdy upholstered oak bench made in the late seventeenth century. The slipware plates on the mantel and the bowls and mortar on the table beside the Schimmel eagle are only a part of the Stokes collection of Pennsylvania pottery. The wrought-iron candelebra on the mantel are Pennsylvania; the central carved figure group is Continental European.

One of the most important pieces in the house is the Pennsylvania walnut secretary in the living room, whose upper case is double-domed and has arched paneled doors; these early eighteenth-century features are rare in American furniture. Beside it are a banister-back armchair and an unusual turned stretcher stand with strongly raked legs. The turned chair with panel splat and seat and pierced heart in the scrolled crest is a Chester County type. Above it hangs the illuminated penwork birth record of Hannah Stokes.

17

On the dining-room chimney breast hangs a painting of *Penn's Treaty with the Indians* after West's painting, which was known through engravings. The rare tin sconces are painted dark red. There are excellent Pennsylvania windsors here; that at the right has the stretchers surprisingly at right angles to the usual arrangement, that at the left has carved arm supports The dresser is garnished with colorful English earthenware—gaudy Dutch, Prattware, and pieces from Clews' blue-printed *Dr. Syntax* series. Partially visible at the right is the ornamental wrought-iron hanger which served as the cover design for ANTIQUES for August 1956.

A Queen Anne side chair in a living-room corner has a high shaped back, compass seat, and crisply carved trifid feet, its splat outlined with unusually lively scrolls. Distinguished in form and detail is the Queen Anne walnut five-drawer dressing table with arched front, beside it. The mirror with brass candleholders attached to the frame bears the label of John Elliott of Philadelphia. The sconce with pierced reflector, on the dressing table, is of brass, as is the large eighteenth-century bowl. The flat-top tall clock visible beyond is by Peter Stretch of Philadelphia (1670-1746). Through the door to the dining room, at the right, may be seen a walnut corner cupboard of the early 1700's, whose raised panels, dentil cornice, and molded base served as models for the new woodwork in this room. The arched slat-back chair is a Delaware Valley type.

Early Pennsylvania chairs of various sorts are used in the dining room, with gate-leg tables. Pennsylvania fractur work and an embroidered sampler give color on the white plaster walls. Numerous hooked and braided rugs are used in the house, and short curtains with small printed patterns. Here again are interesting lighting devices—the iron candlestand with toggle arms, and the elaborately wrought chandelier. The small paneled door provides easy access to the kitchen for serving; its Pennsylvania iron latch and tulip hinges are old.

A windsor bench in the upper hall has many features to appeal to the collector: eight turned legs, turned stretchers and posts, shaped seat, molded back rail with well-carved knuckles. The Pennsylvania slat-back chair beyond is perhaps the most delightful of several in the house, with its very high back, six undulating slats, and ball-turned stretcher. Typical of Pennsylvania in its broad proportion, though none the less a rarity, is the broad William and Mary walnut chest-on-frame, its turned legs joined by scrolled flat stretchers. *Photographs by Cortlandt V. D. Hubbard.*

19

An early Philadelphia desk

BY JOHN M. GRAHAM II, *Director of collections, Colonial Williamsburg*

A PHILADELPHIA SECRETARY-DESK found in England in 1958 is one of the most important acquisitions made in Colonial Williamsburg's search for American furniture. The piece is in the William and Mary style, with fall front and ball feet, and is made of walnut with secondary woods of red pine and white cedar. Stamped in the cedar base of one of the interior drawers are the name Edward Evans and the date 1707. Evans is recorded as a "joiner" in Philadelphia; contemporary records reveal that he made "an Ovell Table" July 4, 1703, and a coffin in 1714 (Hornor, *Blue Book, Philadelphia Furniture,* page 3). So far as is known, this desk is the earliest signed and dated piece of Pennsylvania furniture extant, and the only surviving example by this craftsman.

This Pennsylvania piece is in a remarkably good state of preservation, retaining the original hinges of its fall front and its original ball feet. One small interior drawer was missing, as were the original brasses. The lettering of the inscription on the back as well as that of the stamped

Earliest known signed and dated piece of Philadelphia furniture: William and Mary fall-front secretary desk of walnut, pine, and cedar, with brand *Edward Evans 1707.* The torus molding of the cornice conceals an extra drawer. *Colonial Williamsburg.*

Brand of Edward Evans (Philadelphia, w. 1703-1714),
stamped in the base of one of the small drawers of the upper section
of the desk shown on facing page.

mark conform to those in use during their respective periods.

The desk was brought to my attention by Robert Wilberforce of Bath, England, who wrote of a discovery which his wife made, "quite by chance, among some of the furniture which she had inherited from her father's family, the late Mr. Schuyler N. Warren of New York. In one of the drawers of an old American bureau she found the name Edward Evans 1707 branded into the wood."

The desk was acquired and when it arrived in Williamsburg a faint inscription in black ink was found on the back, which, when photographed with infra-red, proved to be *Rev⁴. E. Grant/ Bedford/ W. Chester Cᵒ./ New York.* Through the West Chester County Historical Society it was learned that the Reverend Ebenezer Grant was a Presbyterian minister of the Bedford church from 1804 until his death in 1821. Grant was a graduate of Queens College, now Rutgers University, and was ordained on November 13, 1800, at Shrewsbury, New Jersey, where he remained for four years. He was buried in Bedford. Further research revealed that he was the son of the Reverend Thomas Grant of New Jersey and a brother of Catherine Grant who married Abraham Schuyler Nielson in New Brunswick, New Jersey.

The desk descended in the family from Mrs. Abraham Schuyler Nielson to Mrs. Wilberforce, a great-granddaughter. Thus its history since the early 1800's is clear, but who its first owner was, where it spent its first hundred years, and how it came into Ebenezer Grant's possession may have to remain unknown.

Editorial note

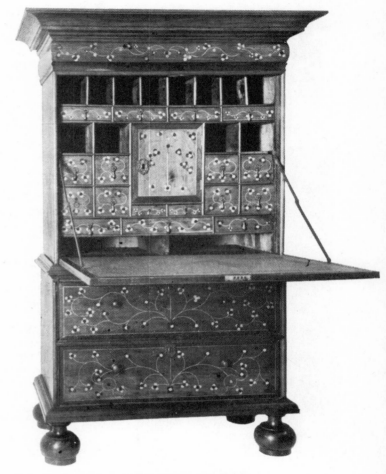

Cedarwood secretary with inlay of beech and walnut; c. 1690-1700. Handed down through eight generations of the Brinckerhoff family of New York.
Museum of the City of New York.

THE FALL-FRONT desk-on-chest (called scrutoire, scriptoir, or scriptor in contemporary English records) came to America from England, but the form did not originate there: fall-front cabinets were made in Italy during the Renaissance, and they occur in Spanish, French, and Dutch furniture as well. In England the forerunner of the type seems to have been a cabinet-on-frame which appeared during the Restoration and developed into the more stable desk-on-chest later in the seventeenth century (Symonds, *Veneered Walnut Furniture*, Plates 6, 7, 20, 21). The English versions were usually elaborately decorated with marquetry or fancy veneers (Macquoid and Edwards, *Dictionary of English Furniture*, rev. ed., Vol. 1, Figs. 27, 28, 29); some have bracket instead of bun feet, but these seem to be later replacements.

The form is extremely rare in American furniture. Perhaps the earliest approach to it known in this country was the cabinet-on-frame believed to have been brought here from Holland by Kiliaen Van Rensselaer, in which the accounts of the Manor of Rensselaerswyck were kept for generations (Morse, *Furniture of the Olden Time*, Illus. 94, 95). The inlaid Brinckerhoff secretary illustrated here, a New York piece, clearly shows the Dutch influence.

A walnut and oak desk-on-chest almost exactly like the Williamsburg piece is illustrated in Cescinsky and Hunter (*English and American Furniture*, p. 164, right) and in Miller (*American Antique Furniture*, No. 775). Miller credits this piece to the Metropolitan Museum of Art, but it is not now in the museum's collections and its present location is unknown. Apparently it differs from the Evans secretary only in the number and arrangement of pigeonholes and small drawers in the upper section, and in having two small and two large rather than three large drawers in the lower.

THE SPICE CABINETS OF PENNSYLVANIA AND NEW JERSEY

By DAVID HUNT STOCKWELL

WHAT lore of clipper ship, what tale of spume-flecked southern sea and hard-run race to distant eastern port, that does not evoke cargoes of legendary glitter and the tantalizing pungency of spice? In the old full-flavored days, beneath slim decks, jewels and spice seemed rightful associates, equally precious. Through several centuries our European forebears vied with each other to discover a shorter path to the East where they might obtain these valued articles of trade; our American ancestors, too, were involved in more than one serious argument over the right to trade with the spice islands. For us to understand, however, why spice was treated with the same fine respect that was accorded bullion and jewels, we must reconstruct in our minds that period of economic scarcity, when only the wealthiest could afford spices now available to the poorest among us. And as evidence of our ancestors' high regard for exotic stimulants of the palate, we may contemplate the little cabinets of exquisite workmanship which they constructed for the safekeeping of those rare delicacies.

The finest of these spice cabinets were used throughout the eighteenth century and even earlier, in rural districts within a radius of about seventy-five miles of Philadelphia, and more seldom in the great houses of Philadelphia, Salem (New Jersey), and other urban sections. Sometimes they took the form of a miniature highboy with trumpet-turned or cabriole legs (*Figs. 2, 3*); sometimes, a rectangular case with elaborate scroll top, not unlike the head of a tall clock (*Fig. 4*). The more usual form, however, was the plain rectangular case mounted on ball, straight bracket, or ogee bracket feet (*Figs. 5, 6, 7*). Cabinets found in rural districts, particularly in the Pennsylvania German country, are occasionally embellished with inlay, or attempt to follow the plan of the sophisticated scroll top with less well-balanced results than the example of Figure 4.

A few spice cabinets are initialed and dated. One example, with intertwined tulip inlay, bears on the door the inscription *E W 1731;* it shows unmistakable German influence, though it is known to have descended in the White family of Chester County. Figure 5 is marked *A M 1747*. Figure 6 is known to have been made in 1774 for Mary Martin who married Joseph Brinton in that year; her initials *M B* appear on an inner drawer. An inventory of James Claypoole's "great house," one of the

FIG. 1 — EARLY SPICE CABINET (*c. 1680*)
Of oak, with pine interior. The treatment of sunken geometric panels and applied spindles is akin to that of certain contemporary New England chests; probably both derived from the same English prototypes.
From the author's collection

FIG. 2 — SPICE CABINET (*c. 1700–1710*)
A miniature William and Mary highboy, in walnut. Heavy moldings; hinged doors with fielded panels; three small drawers in lower frame.
From the Metropolitan Museum of Art

FIG. 3 — SPICE CABINET (*c. 1730–1740*)
A miniature Queen Anne highboy, in walnut. Dainty slipper feet. Note the large center drawer, presumably for holding lumps of loaf sugar.
From the collection of Mrs. William du Pont Jr.

FIG. 4 — SPICE CABINET, OPEN AND CLOSED (c. 1750–1760)

Of cherry, combining decorative features found on various furniture items. Similar in proportions and details to the head of a contemporary tall clock. Note inset fluted corner columns, heavy pediment molding, rather overpoweringly large finials and rosettes, and well-shaped ogee feet. The gouge work of the interior center panel is similar to that found on fine Philadelphia mantels of the period.
From the collection of S. H. du Pont

assigned to it — seventeenth-century England?

In my limited survey of English cabinets suggestive of our spice containers I have been drawn to the conclusion that the Englishman demanded such small, lockable storage space, not for spices, but for jewels and valuable trinkets, luxury articles which left no lingering pungency in their wake, for none of the English cabinets that I have seen retain the slightest aroma. The few cabinets of the first quarter of the nineteenth century found in Pennsylvania and New Jersey reveal the same lack, and also the same lack of daily wear exhibited by earlier English prototypes. It is, therefore, within the realm of probability that Pennsylvanians had by that late date found other means of storing the increasingly abundant spices and relegated their cabinets of small drawers to their original English usage.

Made from finely selected woods, most often walnut, spice cabinets were placed in the parlor or dining room, where they were not only convenient for household use, but where they provided a proper complement to other fine pieces of furniture. They were fitted with single or double doors and a lock, for the dual purpose of preserving the full richness of the spice and of protecting it from theft. The key

largest houses appearing in the original plan of Philadelphia, mentions a "boxe for contaening spice." This record, found in the files of the Pennsylvania Historical Society and dated *1686*, is undoubtedly one of the earliest mentions of the spice cabinet.

The small cabinet of Figure 1 is one of the earliest that has come to my attention. Another, in the Metropolitan Museum of Art, and one in the collection of Henry F. du Pont exhibit similar panels and split turnings. These examples, characteristic of the Pilgrim Century, impel one's gaze in the direction of New England. Is it possible that a few early cabinets were produced there and after a decade or so ceased to be made, reappearing later in Pennsylvania? Or is it more likely that these three pieces are isolated examples; that the spice cabinet's true place of origin is even farther beyond the Pennsylvania and New Jersey boundaries

to the door was kept by the good dame of the house on a chain around her waist, so that the sweet-toothed child or servant could not indulge a clandestine taste.

The nests of small drawers held most of the spices we know today, while the usual large central drawer may have contained either mortar and pestle, or the highly prized loaf sugar cut into appropriate size for table use. This drawer was seldom large enough to accommodate the full-size, cone-shaped loaf, which stood some eight or ten inches tall, but it could easily have held a small mortar and pestle or a spice mill, ready to hand for grinding the spice into usable form. And when family and friends would gather at the large, round tea table of an afternoon, the little spice cabinet would be unlocked. Soon pleasant, aromatic odors would permeate the warm brew and the atmosphere, and, if credence

FIG. 5 — SPICE CABINET, CLOSED AND OPEN (*dated 1747*)

Of walnut. The ball feet and heavy moldings are reminiscent of a somewhat earlier period than is indicated by the inscribed date. The initials *A M* presumably refer to the original owner. This piece has several secret drawers, one under the top molding in front, three in the back.
From the collection of Miss Mary E. Speakman

may be placed in novels about the eighteenth century, conversation would sparkle and scintillate.

Some of the more elaborate spice cabinets that I have examined reveal an arrangement of concealed drawers and secret paneling reminiscent of similar intricacies found in desks of the period. The explanation of these is purely conjectural, of course, but it has been suggested that the lady of the house and her daughters kept their valuable trinkets there, rather than using the entire cabinet for such a purpose, as was the practice abroad. Equally plausible is the suggestion that they were a repository for the very rarest spices. At any rate, it is evident that the same pride of workmanship which led to the construction of sliding panels and secret places in the contemporary desk contributed to their presence in the spice cabinet.

One of the most interesting facts concerning these little cabinets, a fact which at first seems somewhat baffling, is that of their complete limitation within the boundaries of Pennsylvania and New Jersey. In both the north and the south we find an article of equivalent usage, but with wide variations in construction. The New England equivalent took the form of a crudely dovetailed, soft-wood box divided into tiers of small drawers, with no door and not often with a lock. In the south, we find the sugar and spice chest, a desklike affair with some small drawers and a roomy storage space, described in ANTIQUES for April 1934 (*p. 140*).

Apparently the eighteenth-century New England housewife, with her relatively small house and often with no servants, had little use for an elaborate cabinet with door and lock. Consequently her spice box was made to hang by the fireplace on the kitchen wall, within easy proximity of her own hands. The reverse was true of the mistress of the southern plantation. Her house was large, her servants were numerous, and the distance to town or trading post was long. She needed ample storage space and a strong lock against the sly thievery of her darkies. She could not have found room for a quarter of her month's sugar and spice supply in one of the little cabinets and boxes which served their purpose so effectively in Pennsylvania and New England.

In this brief comparison it is possible to glimpse the economic situation that undoubtedly contributed to the form of the spice containers in each locality. In Pennsylvania and New Jersey, where dwellings were neither so small as in New England nor so large as in the south, and where neither dearth nor plethora of servants was apparent, the necessity was supplied with a spice container that, while suggesting some qualities of both the others, developed unusual characteristics of its own. The final environmental factor that undoubtedly contributed to the exquisite cabinetwork of the Pennsylvania and New Jersey spice cabinet was the local influence of the great artisans of Philadelphia.

That these cabinets are not more generally known and admired today is doubtless due to their scarcity. Even in the states to which they are indigenous, comparatively few are brought to light. We can guess that they were far from inexpensive in their own time, and we can also guess how easily so small an article could be discarded and destroyed after the original necessity which called it into existence had been removed. Bearing us out in the matter of cost, painted, soft-wood nests of drawers, similar to the type found in New England, are occasionally discovered in the kitchens of smaller houses in Pennsylvania and New Jersey. This seems to indicate that the fine little cabinets and the crude nests of drawers were, figuratively speaking, made side by side, and that not every family could afford the price of the former.

I have purposely referred to these small case pieces as spice *cabinets* to differentiate them from the spice *box* of the north and the spice *chest* of the south. Anyone who examines their structure and design will, I think, find them not unworthy of the name; and, though a labeled piece has never been discovered or an attribution risked, several of them are thoroughly worthy of the great Philadelphia cabinetmakers.

Irish influence
in Pennsylvania Queen Anne furniture

BY DAVID STOCKWELL

A CHARACTERISTIC PROFILE in certain furniture of the Philadelphia region after about 1720 is seen in the type of cabriole leg which has a carved "sock" formed of one or more ridges extending upward from a trifid, slipper, or club foot. The carved sock and other details of this Queen Anne furniture have long been considered unique to the region influenced by Philadelphia and its craftsmen. In recent years, however, travelers in Ireland have been observing marked similarities between early eighteenth-century Irish furniture and that of the Philadelphia region. In the early Georgian period the Irish cabriole leg also appears with a carved sock, in varying combinations with trifid, slipper, and club feet. This is only one of numerous similarities between the two schools, which in some instances are so close that it is necessary to refer to the secondary wood and methods of construction to determine the country of origin.

We have frequently remarked the influence of the English, German, Dutch, and, possibly, Spanish, on American furniture, and explained it by the presence of groups of settlers from these countries in specific regions. Though we scarcely realize it today, there was a large group of Irishmen among the earliest settlers of Pennsylvania. Belated though it may be, it seems fitting that we acknowledge their presence and their influence. Their contemporaries did. In the year 1729, Mayor and part-time Governor James Logan of Philadelphia sat in his study overlooking the Delaware and observed:

It looks as if Ireland is to send all her inhabitants hither: for last week not less than six ships arrived and every day, two or three also arrive. The common fear is THAT IF THEY CONTINUE TO COME, they will make themselves proprietors of the Province. (*Logan Papers.*)

This was quite a statement for Logan, who was himself born near Belfast in Ireland.

Albert Cook Myers in his volume *Immigration of Irish Quakers to Pennsylvania 1682-1750* estimates that between fifteen hundred and two thousand Irish Quakers

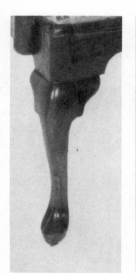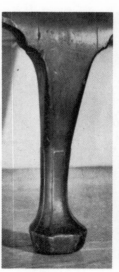

Philadelphia and Irish cabriole legs with "socks," c. 1720-1750. *Left to right*: Slipper foot, Philadelphia armchair; *collection of Mr. and Mrs. Kenneth Chorley.* Slipper foot, Irish drop-leaf table; *privately owned.* Trifid foot, Philadelphia armchair; *author's collection.* Trifid foot, Irish slab-top table; *privately owned.* Club foot, Philadelphia sofa; *Winterthur Museum.* Club foot, Irish tea table; *collection of Mr. and Mrs. Thomas Grasselli.*

landed in this region during the first sixty-eight years of the colony. From Ulster and Leinster came yeoman farmers who for the most part settled in the country. From Waterford, Cork, Limerick, Wexford, and Dublin came artisans who settled in and about Philadelphia where they could find work. As early as 1682 an Irish Quaker family, Dennis Rochford and wife, came with William Penn on the ship *Welcome*. Names well known in Pennsylvania history appear among those of the Irish Quaker immigrants, from James Logan on through the Hollingsworths, Pembertons, Claridges, Barclays, Pennocks. Among them, too, was Thomas Holmes, who drew the first formal plan of Philadelphia for William Penn.

Philadelphia armchair with slipper feet, c. 1740-1750.
Collection of Mr. and Mrs. Kenneth Chorley.

Irish drop-leaf table with slipper feet, c. 1720-1730.
Privately owned.

Philadelphia armchair with trifid feet, c. 1730-1740. *Author's collection.*

Irish slab-top table with trifid feet, c. 1720-1740.
Collection of Lord Talbot of Malahide Castle.

Records of Irish Quakers are well preserved, but rarely do they indicate crafts or trades. According to Myers, the craftsmen named below either were Irish or intermarried with people of Irish lineage. (The terms carpenter and joiner often referred to a maker of furniture in the seventeenth and early eighteenth centuries.) These men must have influenced furniture design in the Philadelphia region where they worked, and there were probably more.

1682 Thomas Coburn	Carpenter	Chester and Chester Township
1683 William Bates	Carpenter	Philadelphia and West Jersey
1701 Benjamin Chandlee	Clockmaker	Philadelphia and Chester County
1708 John Miller	Joiner	Chester County
1725 Isaac Jackson	Clockmaker	Chester County
1734 Isaac Jackson	Clockmaker	New Garden and Chester County
1735 Joseph Tatnall	Carpenter	Chester County
1739 Charles Bush*	Cabinetmaker	Wilmington
1746 John Jackson	Clockmaker	Philadelphia and Chester County
1750 Benjamin Chandlee Jr.	Clockmaker	Nottingham and Chester County

* Charles G. Dorman, *Delaware Cabinetmakers and Allied Artisans, 1655-1855.*

Philadelphia side chair with club feet, labeled by William Savery, c. 1740-1750. Colonial Williamsburg.

Irish side chair with club feet, c. 1720-1740. Privately owned.

Through the mist of two centuries, it is difficult to tell whether the style of a piece of furniture was determined by the artisan who made it or was demanded of him by the customer who ordered it. Perhaps it was often a combination of both. It remains a fact that Irish Quakers came to Pennsylvania early enough, and in sufficient numbers, to account for the marked similarity in detail between certain eighteenth-century furniture of the Philadelphia region and Irish furniture of a like period.

For helpful suggestions concerning Irish Quakers in Pennsylvania my thanks are due to Bart Anderson, Chester County Historical Society; R. Norris Williams, Pennsylvania Historical Society; Robert Raley and John Sweeney, Winterthur Museum; and Valentine Massey, Dover, Delaware.

Irish card table with club feet, c. 1730-1740.
Collection of Mr. and Mrs. William Glasgow Reynolds.

Irish tea table with club feet, c. 1730-1750.
Collection of Mr. and Mrs. Thomas Grasselli.

NOTES ON CONSTRUCTION OF
Philadelphia Cabriole Chairs

By DAVID STOCKWELL

THERE HAVE BEEN from time to time articles published on the regional characteristics of American furniture. Usually these articles draw certain distinctions between the furniture of one region of colonial America and another through the identification of certain outward details of design, proportion, or carving. That there are many inward or constructional details, which in conjunction with the outward ones make this identification even more interesting and convincing, should not be overlooked. In this series of photographs I have tried to point out recognition points both in construction and design, but with special emphasis on construction, of Philadelphia Queen Anne and Philadelphia Chippendale cabriole chairs. These roughly span the years from 1730 to the Revolution.

It goes almost without saying that no reading material or photograph could attempt to provide an adequate substitute for the experience of seeing and studying the furniture first-hand: nevertheless, this presentation may provide some clues that will help the reader later on in actual experience.

FIG. 1—PHILADELPHIA QUEEN ANNE ARMCHAIR. *Construction detail:* (A) No joint in curved front of seat rail as leg is pinned into it. (B) Quarter-round edge at top of seat frame is usually applied. *Stylistic detail:* (A) Back legs are stump. (B) Back legs show pronounced rake. (C) Front feet are trifid or drake type. (D) Splat has rather elaborate profile and is "spooned," or shaped, to fit the human back. (E) Hoop-type arms not typical but found in Philadelphia region.

FIG. 2—THE SAME PHILADELPHIA QUEEN ANNE ARMCHAIR (with slip seat removed). *Construction detail:* (A) Seat rails very heavy, often with less wood cut away than here, leaving square rather than shaped opening inside frame (as shown by dotted lines). (B) Seat frame constructed in four sections (1). (C) Front legs pinned or projected through curved front rail with 1-inch tenon (2).

FIG. 3—THE SAME PHILADELPHIA QUEEN ANNE ARMCHAIR (rear view). *Construction detail:* (A) The ends of the two side rails of the seat frame show clearly (1). There is a slot or *mortise* cut right through the back legs into which the end or *tenon* of the side seat rails is fitted. When it shows this way, it is called a "bare-faced tenon." (B) Two small pins (2) show on inside of leg opposite the bare-faced tenon. They hold the concealed or "blind tenons" of the back rail of the seat in place.

FIG. 4—TRANSITIONAL PHILADELPHIA QUEEN ANNE CHAIR. *Construction detail:* (A) Joints in square front and sides of seat rails show front leg has now become integral part of seat frame. (B) Quarter-round edge at top of seat frame is now carved from the solid wood of the rail and not applied as in Figure 1. *Stylistic detail:* (A) Back legs are stump. (B) Back legs still have pronounced rake in profile. (C) Front feet are trifid or drake type. (D) Splat has elaborate profile and is distinctly curved but not "spooned." (E) These lively and elaborately curved arms and arm supports are most typical of all the better Philadelphia chairs before 1780. They occur both on pure Philadelphia Queen Anne chairs and pure Philadelphia Chippendale ones, as well as on this transitional type.

FIG. 5—TRANSITIONAL PHILADELPHIA QUEEN ANNE CHAIR (view from beneath inside seat frame showing front and back corners). *Construction detail:* (A) Large quarter-round soft pine or poplar blocks (1) fitted into corners for strengthening frame. They are often 3 inches long and usually in one, two, or three sections so that they will fit snugly around the leg. (B) Rough inside section of front leg (2) shows beneath soft wood block. It has become an integral part of seat frame and is mortised to it. (C) Thickness and solidity of rails still apparent though not so heavy as those in pure Queen Anne curved- or balloon-seat types.

Answers to Questions Often Asked Concerning Philadelphia Cabriole Chairs

ON CONSTRUCTION:

1. Can the bare-faced or exposed tenon shown through back legs be considered typical?

Yes. In the rare instances where it occurs elsewhere in colonial America, it is through Philadelphia influence. It also occurs occasionally on some English provincial chairs.

2. Could a chair that does not have a bare-faced tenon showing through the back legs be a Philadelphia chair?

Yes, it could if it shows other Philadelphia characteristics of construction. However, the hidden or "blind-tenon" construction is not usual.

3. Is pinning of tenons into the mortise with little wooden pins typical of Philadelphia exclusively?

No, this was a habit practiced by many cabinetmakers throughout the Colonies and abroad.

4. Are there always large soft-wood, poplar or pine, corner blocks used inside the seat frame of Philadelphia chairs?

Yes.

5. Are the corner blocks the same size?

No, there is considerable variation in size, shape, and number used. They are generally larger than in other Colonies. These blocks often dry out and fall off. If they are missing, there should still be evidence of their use in the chair originally.

6. Is more wood used in construction of Philadelphia chairs than elsewhere?

Much wood is used, more than in most of the other Colonies. Chairs are heavier in weight.

7. Is it true that the Quaker cabinetmakers emphasized the grain of the wood?

Yes, especially in the Queen Anne period, wood was most carefully selected to use finest grains where they would show to best advantage. This is a definite characteristic of Philadelphia chairs.

8. Were Philadelphia chairs ever veneered?

Queen Anne chairs were very occasionally veneered on splat and seat frame to show fine graining.

ON STYLE:

1. Were oval or octagonal stump back legs the only type used in Philadelphia chair design?

They are usual and considered a typical form but there are rare exceptions. A shaped back leg is found on several of the famous Randolph "sample" chairs now owned by the Philadelphia and Metropolitan Museums. Other examples are known but they are definitely rare.

2. Were stretchers used on Philadelphia cabriole chairs?

Yes, occasionally, but only on Queen Anne chairs. These stretchers were flat with pleasingly shaped profile rather than round and turned as in New York and New England where turned stretchers continued in use into the Chippendale years.

3. Were other types of foot terminations than the trifid or drake foot found in Philadelphia Queen Anne chairs?

Yes. Slipper, Spanish, pad, biscuit, and web feet *without* emphasized toes were all used on the front legs of Philadelphia Queen Anne chairs; however, the trifid or drake foot *with* emphasized toes seems to be a particularly characteristic local design.

4. Do the splats of Philadelphia Queen Anne chairs show a more sophisticated profile than those of the other Colonies?

Yes, as a whole they do. The elaborate "parrot" splat employing cyma reversa curves in the most pleasing form is found on most urban Queen Anne chairs. Even in rural types the splat is likely to have scalloped shoulders rather than the simple "Dutch" shoulders seen so often north of Philadelphia.

5. What other differences in design may be noted between Philadelphia chair splats and those of other regions?

The Philadelphia splat both in Queen Anne and Chippendale years is either curved or spooned to fit the back. It never resembles a flat board with holes punched in it as is often true of chairs from other regions.

6. Are Philadelphia chairs larger than elsewhere?

Yes, most of them in this period are larger. The backs are taller, the seats wider in front, narrower in back. Later Philadelphia Chippendale cabriole chairs are lower in the back and wider, with no ears. They conform more closely to the more available English designs in the years just preceding the Revolution.

7. Was the carved cockleshell motif used on both Philadelphia Queen Anne and Chippendale chairs?

Yes, it was, with elaborations and variations. Later Philadelphia Chippendale carving shows vigorous and elaborate flower and acanthus motifs employed with variety and imagination on many surfaces.

FIG. 6—PHILADELPHIA CHIPPENDALE CHAIR (view from above; slip seat removed). *Construction detail:* (A) These seats are all identical in construction to Figures 4 and 5. (B) Seat frame is in six sections (visible inside): two side rails (1); front and back rail (2); and two front legs (3). The back legs could be included also as two more parts though there is little of them visible inside the seat frame. (C) The front legs (3) are rough behind the strengthening soft-wood corner blocks inside the frame. Outside they are slightly rounded and finished to form the corners of the seat. (D) The soft wood, pine or poplar, corner blocks (4) are fitted around the two rough sides of each front leg. In this chair they are in two sections about 3 inches long. (E) The soft-wood blocks, rear (5), are single quarter rounds.

FIG. 7—PHILADELPHIA CHIPPENDALE CHAIR. *Construction detail:* (A) The front corners of seat are the finished outside of the legs. They are mortised and tenoned and usually pinned with small pins as an integral part of the seat frame. *Stylistic detail:* (A) Rear legs in ovoid stump form. (B) Rear legs raked. (C) Ball-and-claw foot front legs with slightly flattened ball. (D) Splat curved rather emphatically. (E) Much fine carved detail of a quality and vitality found seldom in other regions.

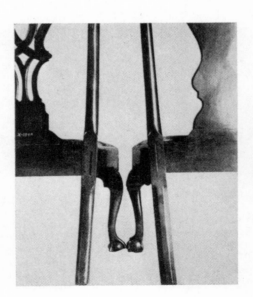

FIG. 8—PHILADELPHIA CHIPPENDALE AND PHILADELPHIA TRANSITIONAL CHAIRS (rear view). *Construction detail:* (A) Bare-faced tenon of seat rails shows very clearly. *Stylistic detail:* (A, Right) A cross section of stump back leg would show octagonal treatment. (B, Left) A cross section of stump back leg would show ovoid treatment.

FIG. 9—PHILADELPHIA CHIPPENDALE WING CHAIR (with stripped frame; rear view). *Construction detail:* (A) Seat frame mortised and tenoned through back legs. (B) Large pine or poplar blocks used to strengthen legs under the seat frame. (C) Large amounts of poplar and pine used in construction of frame under upholstery. (D) Back seat rail is chestnut, also side rails; white oak, ash, or chestnut sometimes used in parts of frame subject to unusual stress. *Stylistic detail:* (A) Ovoid stump rear legs. (B) Ball-and-claw feet, exhibiting slightly flattened ball. (C) The arms of Philadelphia wing chairs have developed the cyma curve, under their upholstery, to the same lively and pleasing degree seen in the fine arms of the so-called "wooden" chairs *(Fig. 4)*. The pronounced vertical roll (1) in contrast to the emphatic horizontal one (2) can be clearly seen here.

II The Chippendale Style

The term "Philadelphia Chippendale" conjures the image of an opulent scroll-top highboy with rich applied carving. Although this image is an accurate symbol for the products of Philadelphia's cabinetmakers in the second half of the eighteenth century, it also highlights some of the complexities of defining what the term means. The fact that the highboy (then called a high chest of drawers) reached such a sophisticated development testifies to the individuality of American decorative arts before the Revolution, for no comparable form then existed in English high-style furniture. On the other hand, the word "Chippendale" betrays the indebtedness of American art to English sources. Indeed, "Chippendale" may convey two distinct meanings: it may refer to designs published by Thomas Chippendale, or it can connote Anglo-American interpretations of the rococo in the decorative arts.

Thomas Chippendale, a London cabinetmaker, published the first edition of *The Gentleman and Cabinet Maker's Director* in 1754, but it can not be proved that this edition was known in Philadelphia. However, it is known that the third (1762) edition was used there. Although the *Director* exerted tremendous influence on the ornamental details of furniture, relatively few pieces of Philadelphia cabinetwork were copied directly from its plates. The designs from various printed sources apparently influenced some of the most elaborate pieces. In addition to Chippendale, other English designers whose publications probably influenced American cabinetmakers included Thomas Johnson, Matthias Lock, and Robert Manwaring.

In a broader context, Chippendale may be considered as a term for many English adaptations of the French rococo style. Although the rococo originated as a court style in France in the second decade of the eighteenth century, it did not flourish in England until the late 1730s. The style was soon introduced to Philadelphia, as is witnessed by an elaborate rococo silver service by London's Paul Lamerie ordered by by Philadelphia's Franks family between 1743 and 1745. According to some authorities, the portrait of that eminent Philadelphian, Mrs. Charles Willing, done by Robert Feke in 1746, may be the earliest extant American painting showing rococo influence. That the rococo made a strong impact on Philadelphia decorative arts is evident in the silver teakettle on stand, now in the Garvan Collection at Yale, made for the Plumstead family by Joseph Richardson before 1755. Cabinetmakers may have been slightly slower than painters and silversmiths in adopting this new style, but, by the early 1760s, it was evident in both interior woodwork and furniture. In

working in this general context of the rococo, the cabinetmakers and carvers in Philadelphia created some pieces of striking originality and refinement. Their finest products, like the backs of some of the "Sample Chairs" attributed to Benjamin Randolph, possess that unity of form and ornament which epitomizes the spirit of the rococo. Although the Chippendale style was giving way to neoclassical influences in the 1780s, some elements, such as the favored use of fluted quarter columns in the corners of case pieces, occasionally appeared as late as the opening years of the nineteenth century.

Of the hundreds of artisans who produced Philadelphia's furniture in the second half of the eighteenth century, it is likely that a relatively small number made the masterpieces. Some of the most famous cabinetmakers, including Benjamin Randolph, Jonathan Gostelowe, Thomas Tufft, and Adam Hains, are discussed in the articles reprinted in the following chapter. A key person not included in this section is Thomas Affleck, the cabinetmaker to Governor John Penn; he worked on Second Street from the 1760s until his death in 1795.

Meyric Rogers' article on possible Irish sources for some Philadelphia work, and David Stockwell's article on themes from Aesop's Fables in Philadelphia carving, illustrate the complex nature of Philadelphia's artistic climate in the third quarter of the eighteenth century. While America's metropolis was part of international cross-currents of style, it was also capable of creating art characterized by remarkable independence in conception and execution. By 1775, Philadelphia's cabinetmakers had achieved such a degree of confidence in their skills that one of them, John Folwell, proposed publishing his *Gentleman and Cabinet Maker's Assistant,* containing more than two hundred plates. It is believed that the outbreak of the Revolution prevented the publication of Folwell's book, which *could* have been the first American book of furniture designs.

Fig. 1 — Two of the Six Sample Chairs

These chairs, now quite definitely attributed to an American maker, belong in a group representing the highest achievement of Philadelphia furniture makers.

Owned by Howard Reifsnyder.

Benjamin Randolph of Philadelphia

By S. W. Woodhouse, Jr.

I. Philadelphia, Leading City of the Colonies

IT is interesting to remember that pioneer collectors called a certain type of high chest of drawers a *southern highboy* until there was discovered, in Baltimore, a walnut lowboy with the label of William Savery, of Philadelphia, in the bottom of the upper drawer. This piece was afterwards purchased by Luke Vincent Lockwood for the Colonial Dames at Van Cortland Manor, New York. Thereupon dealers and collectors, in the flush of discovery, styled all fine American Chippendale furniture *Savery*.

Though there were, undoubtedly, good makers in Annapolis, Baltimore, and Charleston, comparatively little important furniture was, as a matter of fact, produced in the South.

Philadelphia, however, in the latter half of the eighteenth century — larger than New York or Boston — was, for some time, the centre of wealth and luxury in America. As late as 1765, New York had not progressed far beyond the position of a Dutch trading post; and Boston was a small town of prim and Puritanic character — certainly not a place where luxury prevailed. Concerning Philadelphia, on the other hand, it should be remembered that there were men of wealth amongst the early settlers in Pennsylvania. Their numbers were later increased by the advent of younger members of distinguished English families who, thanks to the opportunities afforded in the new land, were, in due time, able to emulate the elegant and refined surroundings to which they had been accustomed at home.

The significance of the fact that Philadelphia always boasted an important group of fashionables — spoken of as "World's people" in distinction to the plain Friends or Quakers — has not been sufficiently appreciated. During the years prior to and during the Revolution, many Tories, Quaker pacifists, and so on, lived in Philadelphia; and, though the city was occupied by the British, relatively little was destroyed during the war. Hence it is easy to understand why the major part of the choice American furniture that follows a style which, in a loose way, we may call *Chippendale*, has come to light in Philadelphia — as is indicated by the Pendleton collection at the Rhode Island School of Design, and the Palmer and Myers collections in the Metropolitan Museum.

II. The Six "Sample Chairs"

Twenty-five years ago "Jimmy" Curran heard rumors, hunted up and bought a fine chair. It was one of six that old wives' tales had frequently referred to as "the six sample chairs." By judicious efforts the entire six were ultimately unearthed, though one still remains in the family of original ownership.

The first was bought by the Doyen of American collectors, Henry W. Erving, of Hartford. He found it in Curran's treasury one hot summer's day as he was returning from his son's commencement at Johns Hopkins. Of this chair Luke Vincent Lockwood says, "It is the best chair that has been found in this country."* Three others of the six, one wing and two side chairs, are in the collection of Howard Reifsnyder, of Philadelphia.

Fig. 2 — The Wing Sample Chair
The largest chair of the group. This was discussed at some length by Herbert Cescinsky in Antiques, Vol. VIII, page 273 *et seq.*
Owned by Howard Reifsnyder.

Other pieces of furniture showing points of resemblance are the fine chair illustrated on page 91 of Lockwood, now owned by Mrs. Ingersoll of Hartford;† the chairs from the Charles Wharton house;‡ the Cadwalader card table and console table.§ The question which has constantly lain before all collectors is: are these pieces of American or English make? The great connoisseurs have vaguely suggested American, perhaps English; or English, perhaps Philadelphia; and we get nothing more definite.

After the publication of the Metropolitan Museum *Bulletin* (Vol. XIII, No. 12, 1918) in which my friend,

*Luke Vincent Lockwood, *Colonial Furniture in America*, New York, 1926, Vol. II, p. 92.
†Formerly in the Bulkeley Collection.
‡Exhibited at the Pennsylvania Museum.
§Metropolitan Museum, American Wing.

R. T. H. Halsey rescued the name of one of Philadelphia's brilliant galaxy of cabinetmakers, all were naturally searching for a clue to some of the others, or seeking to discover which of the various kinds of furniture following the general fashion of Chippendale was made by which individual of this group. The next considerable contribution to our information came in the form of the very splendid engraved business card of Benjamin Randolph.* Yet from that time until a chair was discovered bearing Randolph's actual label, we were still at sea, though there had been various efforts to connect the "six sample chairs" with this maker.

III. Benjamin Randolph, Cabinetmaker

Little has been published about Randolph. He was supposed to have come from New Jersey, and it was known that, when he retired, he went to his place *Speedwell Mills*, on Wading River, near Burlington, in that state.

Gradually, however, I have acquired some data concerning this interesting cabinetmaker.† He first married, February 18, 1762, Anna Bromwich, only daughter and sole heiress of William Bromwich, stay maker of Sassafras Street. As William Bromwich was buried in Christ Church graveyard, November 19, 1763, it would seem that, by his marriage, Benjamin Randolph came into close association with "World's people."

In his early transactions he is noted as "joiner." He possessed one horse, some cattle, and one servant, and paid a tax of £42.16 in the Middle Ward. Soon, however, we find his taxes increased, and he styles himself "cabinetmaker" in 1768.

By regular progression he climbs in the scale as a "carver and gilder," and then as "merchant," until, in 1786, he pays a tax of £176.11, and has property in the High Street Ward, in the Mulberry Ward, in the Middle Ward, in the Northern Liberties, and out in Abington. He is now pos-

*See Antiques, Vol. VII, p. 121, where this card is reproduced.
†Records in the Genealogical Society of Pennsylvania.

sessed of two horses, cattle, and one negro. Finally, at the time of his retirement, he styles himself "gentleman," a term not lightly used in the eighteenth century. It would be well to remember that Benjamin Randolph was a cabinetmaker in such a position as to secure Thomas Jefferson's patronage, and, as Jefferson states, to make for that statesman the desk on which the Declaration of Independence was drafted.*

Several of Randolph's old property transfers are very interesting, and shed further light on our maker of fine furniture.† In 1767, when purchasing his shop in Chestnut Street from one Thomas Shoemaker, a carpenter, Randolph, we find, acquired a lot twenty-four feet wide by one hundred and seventy deep, "through to the lots on High Street," with a seven-foot cartway at the side, adjoining the property of Henry Mitchell, "joiner." We observe that these men, most of them woodworkers, were meticulously accurate, for this deed expressly states "to be paid in dollars — that is to say sixty-six Spanish milled dollars commonly called milled silver pieces of eight, each piece weighing seventeen pennyweights, six grains, fine coined silver and eleven-sixteenth parts of a dollar." So shin plasters, currency, depreciations, and what-not may come and go, but Thomas Shoemaker, Quaker carpenter in Philadelphia, is certain to receive full value in silver bullion.

In 1781, Randolph purchases property, adjoining Benjamin Franklin's lot, for £775 "in gold and silver coins." Of more interest than the fact of sale is the quaint phraseology of the deed when he transfers some of the old Bromwich property on Sassafras Street. It begins:

TO ALL THE PEOPLE, I BENJAMIN RANDOLPH, Carver and Gilder send greeting. Know ye that the said Benjamin Randolph in consideration for £100 gold and silver coins do sell on the north side of Mul-

Fig. 3 — THE FIRST OF THE SIX CHAIRS
Said to be the finest chair yet found in America.
Owned by Henry W. Erving.

berry Street "formerly belonging to William Bromwich." William Bromwich died intestate, leaving his only issue a daughter named Anna, upon whom the same descends as heiress at Law, who intermarried with me, said Benjamin Randolph, and by whom I had issue two daughters named Mary and Anna, now living and in their minority and my said wife Anna some years ago died intestate, whereby her estate in the premises descended to my said two daughters, Mary and Anna as co-partners and Heiresses at Law, subject to the life estate of me, the said Benjamin Randolph as tenant by courtesy, — .*

IV. HERCULES COURTENAY, CARVER

We find that in 1767 the witness to one of the many real estate transactions of Benjamin Randolph is Hercules Courtenay. Now what do we know of Hercules Courtenay? He married Mary Shute, May 18, 1768, at "Old Swedes," Gloria Dei church. He advertises from his house in Front Street between Chestnut and Walnut, where he paid taxes in 1769, at that time styling himself "carver." The advertisement reads:

Hercules Courtenay, Carver and Gilder, from London, INFORMS his Friends and the Public, that he undertakes all Manner of CARVING and GILDING, in the newest Taste, at his House in Front-Street, between Chestnut and Walnut Streets. N. B. He is determined to be as reasonable as possible in his Charges, and to execute all Commands with the utmost Diligence."†

After the Revolution, apparently, he gave up his artistry and became a "tavern-keeper."

Now we enter the field of conjecture. One seldom goes far out of his way to hunt up a witness to his signature. It would seem probable, therefore, that Hercules Courtenay was in the employ of Benjamin Randolph at the time of delivery of the previously mentioned deed. It is even more probable that, when young Courtenay came out from London, as his advertisement states, he was employed by Benjamin Randolph. Yes, you may say, but what reason is there for connecting Benjamin Randolph

---

*Now in the Library of Congress.
†Recorder of Deeds, Philadelphia.

*Deed Book, D-19, p. 514.
†Alfred Coxe Prime, *Colonial Craftsmen*, from the *Pennsylvania Chronicle*, 8/14/1769.

with six elaborate sample chairs? — To discover that we must follow the story of Randolph's second marriage.

V. ESTABLISHING A LINE OF DESCENT

Benjamin Randolph, after his retirement, married Mary Wilkinson, widow of William Fenimore. Benjamin Randolph's will, dated 1790 recites:

Whereas there was a verbal agreement between me and my wife, Mary, previous to marriage, that neither of us would claim any right in any property of the other, in consequence I have not meddled in her real or personal estate, therefore I bequeath to my said wife, Mary, £20.*

Such ante-nuptial agreements were common usage.† The supposition that Benjamin Randolph came from the Fitz-Randolphs of New Jersey is strengthened by the fact that his only surviving daughter, Anna, after her father's death, went to live in Morristown, New Jersey, in which vicinity the name of Fitz-Randolph is prevalent.

Randolph's second wife, Mary Wilkinson Fenimore, survived him by some years. In her will, dated June 1, 1816, in the fifth paragraph, occurs the statement: "All the remainder of my household goods I give unto my son, Nathaniel Fenimore" (her son by her first marriage). By the second clause of the first paragraph, her daughter Priscilla is to have a home with her brother Nathaniel Fenimore as long as she remains single. Nathaniel Fenimore, who inherited under this will, married Rebecca Zelley, and had a daughter Rebecca Zelley Fenimore, who was born in 1831, and eventually married her cousin Samuel Stockton Zelley.

Five of the six sample chairs have been purchased from the descendants of Nathaniel Fenimore, stepson of Ben-

*At Trenton, New Jersey.
†Information of Dr. and Mrs. Satterthwaite, genealogists, at Trenton, New Jersey.

jamin Randolph. Benjamin Randolph was living with Mary Wilkinson Fenimore Randolph at the time of his death, and, though his will makes no mention of his personal effects, it seems reasonable to suppose that these prized pieces of household gear — the six chairs — remained in possession of his widow. From her they would naturally, by descent, pass to her heirs, after Benjamin Randolph's only surviving daughter Anna had gone to live in another part of the state; for, in those days of poor roads, one endeavored not to transport household furniture over long distances.

VI. THE ARGUMENT FOR AMERICAN WORKMANSHIP

It has generally been accepted that chairs of the latter half of the eighteenth century showing rounded, stump rear legs, or those so constructed that the seat rails completely pierce the stiles at the back, are, by those signs, to be classed as products of Philadelphia craftsmanship. Some of our six sample chairs display these characteristics; some do not. On that point, more presently.

In proportion the six chairs follow English rather than American precedent — the precedent of the *Director*, Plate XVI. American chairs tend to be smaller

Fig. 4 — THE SECOND OF THE SIX CHAIRS
The splat so broken as to engage the stiles of the back is an unusual feature. The lion's-paw feet should be compared with those shown in Figure 2 and with the feet in Figures 7 *a, b,* and *c. Privately owned.*

in the seat than English chairs, especially narrower at the rear of the seat. American chairs, however, have higher backs than contemporary English pieces.

The fact that our specimens follow English precedent in proportions is by no means evidence of English manufacture; though it does argue close regard for English methods. It is, therefore, to be noted that, in the Pennsylvania Museum, there is a very simple chair, bearing the label of Benjamin Randolph, which follows English proportions and in which the seat rails do not pierce the stiles. While the carving and structure of the splat of this chair are fine, they are extremely simple, for this is a much less elaborate type of chair than those pictured in the *Director*.

The only plates in the *Director* showing chairs with the splat spreading widely to connect with the sides are the three with ribbon-backs, and those in Gothic and Chinese taste. Mr. Erving's chair (*Fig. 3*), in its essentials, resembles the ribbon-back. The carving of all is of a peculiarly soft, rounded character, which has been spoken of as French carving. The second sample chair (*Fig. 4*), closely resembling Mr. Erving's piece, has the back splat widening at its upper third so as to become attached to the stiles. Very similar, again, is a hall chair exhibited by the late John D. McIlhenny at the Pennsylvania Museum in the Chippendale Show of 1924.

The two latter chairs present so many features in common that their close study is well warranted, though the modern upholstery of the sample chair quite alters lines that are intensified by the wooden seat in this superb example of Mr. McIlhenny's.

The Erving chair has rear legs following the English fashion; the two Reifsnyder side chairs, previously referred to as part of our sextette, have back legs with rounded Philadelphia stumps; the second

Fig. 5 — THE SIXTH CHAIR

The least ornate of the group. Designed in the Gothic style. The rear stump legs and their relationship to the lines of the chair-back should be compared with those of Figure 4. *Privately owned.*

chair has back legs with rounded Philadelphia stumps; the sixth chair likewise shows the Philadelphia stumps. In the chair at the Pennsylvania Museum the side rails do *not* pierce the stiles; in the two Reifsnyder chairs, the side rails do *not* pierce the stiles; in the second sample chair, the rails *do* pierce the stiles; in the sixth sample chair, the side rails *do* pierce the stiles.

Study of the illustrations will make it clear that the leg of the Cadwalader card table is merely the leg of the second chair elongated. The carving of the skirt of the card table and of the skirt of this second chair are virtually identical, and show, further, close similarity to that of the skirt of the Erving chair. Very similar handling is revealed in the carving of the Cadwalader pier table in the Metropolitan Museum, the Washington sofa in Independence Hall, and the Louis Myers pie-crust table in the Metropolitan Museum, the pier tables in the Pennsylvania Museum, the Pendleton collection at the Rhode Island School of Design, and, lastly, with the less ornate chairs from the Charles Wharton house. Mrs. Ingersoll's chair and Miss Esther Morton Smith's,* in varying degree, exhibit the same construction, timber, and carving.

It is interesting to note the English professional point of view as embodied in the opinions of Herbert Cescinsky, who states that, in English chairs, one seldom finds the side rails of as heavy timber as in American analogues; that the rounded stump legs do not occur in fine English furniture of the second half of the eighteenth century; that the side rails of our sample chairs are of heavier timber than is customary in English pieces; and that the bracing of these pieces is done in a manner peculiar to Philadelphia.†

In his advertisement, Benjamin Randolph not only draws attention to the fact that he makes all these fine things, but likewise does "Carving, Gilding, etc., performed in the Chinese and modern taste." As Hercules Courtenay seems either to have been in Randolph's employ or to have enjoyed specially friendly relations with him, I do not think we go too quickly in suggesting that all these chairs — as well as other similar pieces — were probably carved by Hercules Courtenay.

At least five members of the Carpenters Company of Philadelphia were possessed of Swan's *British Architect*, published in 1745. The third edition of Chippendale was bought by the Philadelphia Library Company in 1762. The

---

*Exhibited at the Pennsylvania Museum, December, 1920.
†*British American*, London, June and July, 1925.

Loganian Library had a copy of Battie Langley's *Treasury of Building and Working Men's Designs*, published in 1745. When Benjamin Randolph bought his shop in Chestnut Street, Smithers, who engraved his business card, was working in Philadelphia. There is no doubt that this engraver had access to the copy of the *Director* owned by the Library Company, or, more probably, to one of the several copies that I believe were in the possession of individual craftsmen in the city. It is significant that where we do find Philadelphia-made Chippendale furniture, it is from plates in the third edition, the copy owned by the Library Company.

Whatever the place which history ultimately reserves for Benjamin Randolph or Hercules Courtenay, it is quite certain that these six chairs, now considered together for the first time in more than one hundred years, are outstanding examples of work in the Chippendale fashion, and have undoubtedly had their home on the banks of the Delaware since before the Revolution.

Fig. 6 — THE CADWALADER CARD TABLE
The leg of this table is little more than an extension of the chair leg of Figure 4. The two skirts are almost identical.

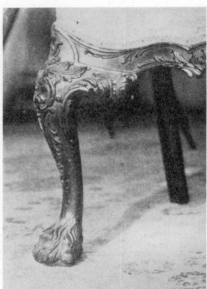

Fig. 7 — DETAILS
   a. Leg from the wing chair shown in Figure 2.
   b. Leg from the Washington sofa in Independence Hall.
   c. Leg from the second chair, shown in Figure 4.

More About Benjamin Randolph

By Doctor Samuel W. Woodhouse, Jr.

THE cabinetwork of Benjamin Randolph was first brought to the attention of collectors by an article in the Pennsylvania Museum *Bulletin* for January, 1925. As later research uncovered further information concerning this interesting cabinetmaker, the consequent alteration of former judgments resulted in an article in ANTIQUES, for May, 1927.

Still later, in arranging the recent exhibition in the State Museum at Trenton, held in connection with the two hundred and fiftieth anniversary of the city's settlement, I found some walnut chairs bearing the first *complete* label of Benjamin Randolph which has been discovered (*Fig. 4*), though Francis P. Garvan has, for some time, owned a chair with a partial label (*Fig. 5*). Conclusions drawn from a study of these fully labeled chairs, together with contemporary newspaper items, and from an examination of some portraits by Charles Willson Peale, have induced the publication of these additional notes.

In my article in AN-TIQUES, I assigned the celebrated six sample chairs to Randolph. Authorities seldom agree, however, and the cited instance proved no exception to the rule. I was, therefore, not surprised to see the elaborate ribbon-back chair owned by Henry W. Erving presented in a recent publication with the caption: "One of the sample chairs *thought by some* to be the work of Benjamin Randolph." The italics are mine.

Under the circumstances it seems advisable to recite the reasons for believing the sample chairs to be American; for if one is of native make, so are they all. While scholarly

Fig. 1 — The Cadwalader Card Table and Its Owners (*detail*)
Portrait of General John Cadwalader and his wife, Elizabeth Lloyd, with their child Anne (*born 1771*) seated on the table.
Painted by Charles Willson Peale in 1775.
By permission of John Cadwalader, Jr.

articles have appeared on the sources of the design of these notable pieces of furniture, no full statement as to their construction and material has been placed before the public.

The large wing chair, formerly in the Reifsnyder Collection, and now owned by the Pennsylvania Museum, has a frame of chestnut, a wood not used in English construction. The timber employed in the rails of all six chairs is heavier than English makers seemed to fancy, and the mahogany is certainly a variety commonly used on this side of the water, but not found in English work of the period.

As the master himself tells us, the cabinetmaker may emulate Chippendale's most extravagant designs; or he may indulge in such simplifications of the original theme as will reduce the cost of the finished work. Mr. Garvan's straight leg chair, here illustrated, undoubtedly represents an effort to produce a handsome, yet unelaborate chair at a suitable price. But the sample chairs, as their name indicates, would normally be more highly ornamented specimens, from which, by a process of eliminating costly decorative elements, reasonably priced pieces might be derived to meet the general demand.

It has been urged that, since, in America, no other chairs have as yet come to light at all comparable in florid elegance to Mr. Erving's, or, for that matter, to the late Mr. Reifsnyder's three chairs, or to the second chair of the six, now owned by Thomas A. Curran (*Fig. 3*) — that the famous group never served as working models. Mr. Garvan's chair does not approach their ornateness, though it resembles them in the fundamentals of design and handling.

Fig. 2 — THE CADWALADER CARD TABLE
By permission of Mrs. John Cadwalader

The Cadwalader card table, however, the skirt of which is identical in variety of wood and in handling with the skirt of the Curran chair, vitiates the negative argument (*Fig. 2*). The appearance of this table in the portrait of General John Cadwalader, painted by Charles Willson Peale, in 1775, proves that the piece was in the possession of an American citizen at a time contemporary with its

Fig. 3 — SKIRT OF SECOND SAMPLE CHAIR
The pattern of the carving is the same as that of the table pictured above.
By permission of Thomas A. Curran

production. It is important to observe that a drawer at the back of this table is built of poplar and yellow pine — woods, in so far as we know, not used in British-made furniture of the eighteenth century.

A companion portrait depicts Lambert Cadwalader, brother of the General, leaning on the back of a chair which is closely similar to the second sample chair, the chief difference between the two being that the sample is carved on the stiles, while the chair in the portrait is fluted (*Fig. 9*). This would indicate that the former piece served as a pattern for the furnishings purchased by the Cadwaladers. Be it noted, further, that, as the General, his brother, and their father, Doctor Thomas Cadwalader, all signed the Non-Importation Agreement, they are most unlikely to have bought imported household goods.

It is commonly believed that, in American-made chairs of Philadelphia type, the rails always completely pierce the stiles, so that the end of the tenon is visible at the back. Though, in many instances, this is true, I should like to emphasize the fact that this piercing is merely less skilful joiner's work, and should not be accepted as an infallible mark of specific local authorship. The chairs bearing Randolph's labels in the Trenton exhibition are made of walnut, and the side rails do *not* completely pierce the stiles. On the other hand, among the six sample chairs, the very elegant specimen belonging to Mr. Curran exhibits the visible tenon. The same thing is true of the sixth and plainest of the sample chairs. The two latter are the only examples of Randolph's work known to me which possess this feature. All of the Randolph chairs so far examined are beautifully finished at all points, even to the rounded stump leg, and the more sophisticated English foot, where the latter occurs. With Randolph, simplicity never implied crudeness.

It is common American practice to leave the timber of the stile in the form of a heavy rectangle at the point where rail and stile join. In Randolph's work, the careful modulation of these stiles, in their transition from the round to the rectangular member, is notable. Many Philadelphia craftsmen made the curve at this point abrupt and the rectangular section unnecessarily long. Randolph seems to have avoided this awkwardness.

While the walnut chairs of the Trenton exhibition are considerably more elaborate than Mr. Garvan's chair, we may assume that they are not representative of Randolph's

Fig. 4 — Randolph Chair and Label (*one of six*)
By permission of their owner, the great-great-granddaughter of Anne Gillingham and George Brearly

full capabilities in this direction. They are certainly made in America. Were they English, they would not be constructed of Pennsylvania red walnut. Yet the weight of their timber and the method of its handling are similar to what we find in the mahogany sample chairs. Should Mr. Erving's chair be given a British pedigree, it would be the only English piece of my acquaintance made of this variety of mahogany and handled in such a fashion.

In view of the established authorship of the walnut chairs, it would be well to study closely the mahogany chair formerly belonging to Mr. Reifsnyder and recently loaned by Matthew S. Sloan for the Girl Scouts Exhibition (*Fig. 6*). In handling, proportion, and design, this chair is so close to the Randolph chairs as to justify the belief that it is the product of the same master craftsman.

Concerning Benjamin Randolph's personal affairs, I have found his first documented appearance as a woodworker, in 1766, when he furnished sash for the new Alms House at Tenth and Spruce Streets, Philadelphia. That he was of the patriotic party is implied in his letter to General Wayne, written from Speedwell Mill in 1777, and the following advertisement published in the Pennsylvania *Evening Post*, May 6, 1777:

Holsters, pistols, carbines, swords for the Light Horse wanted immediately. Inquire of Benjamin Randolph in Chestnut Street.

This is succeeded, November 5 and December 7, 1782, by Randolph's advertisements for the sale of his own very considerable city real estate, in the course of which, he says he is "intending to leave the state."

In May, 1927, I was unable to supply any exact data connecting Randolph with his supposed New Jersey origin. It now transpires that he was the son of Isaac Fitz-Randoph of Monmouth County, New Jersey, a descendant of Edward Fitz-Randolph of Nottingham, England, who, in 1634, came to Scituate, Massachusetts, and, thirty-five

Fig. 5 — Randolph Chair Bearing Partial Label
*Loaned to the Pennsylvania Museum from the collection of
Francis P. Garvan*

Fig. 6 — Chair Attributed to Benjamin Randolph
*Formerly owned by the late Howard Reifsnyder.
From the collection of Matthew S. Sloan*

years later "for greater freedom," removed himself to New Jersey.

On April 17, 1783, appears the following advertisement describing property in New Jersey which Benjamin is selling as an executor of the estate of James Fitz-Randolph, his brother, who has recorded himself as "yeoman of Sketer Cove":

BENJAMIN RANDOLPH   Property for Sale

To be Sold (and entered on immediately)

That pleasantly situated house and gardens in the city of Burlington West New Jersey, on that well-known and beautiful spot called Green Bank, on the River Delaware . . .

For particulars apply to Benjamin Randolph in Philadelphia, or Joseph Bloomfield, esquire, adjoining the premises.

Likewise a Plantation in East New-Jersey situated at Mosquito Cove on Tom's River — containing about 350 acres. Containing . . . salt works, a very good fishing &c.

For particulars apply to
Benjamin Randolph
in Philadelphia   ⎫
or   ⎬ Executors of James Randolph
Tobias Hendrickson   ⎭ Late of New Jersey.
in East New Jersey

On October 10, 1783, the Pennsylvania *Gazette* prints still another advertisement of James Randolph's property

in New Jersey. Perhaps his brother's illness had prompted Benjamin's temporary retirement to New Jersey.

BENJAMIN RANDOLPH

Freehold, New Jersey, October 10, 1783.

Whereas the subscribers, executors of the last will and testament of James Randolph (having advertised that all who are indebted should come, etc.) the executors now being determined to settle the whole of that estate, give public notice that they will attend at the house of Tobias Hendrickson in Freehold from the first of November next to the first of March ensuing, and after that day they do not intend to receive any account whatever against said estate, it being inconvenient for Benjamin Randolph to attend so far from home.

The executors have for sale belonging to the estate a farm (400 acres) on Tom's River, a number of lots of good cedar swamp, a lot of one acre on Red-Bank in Shrewsbury, an excellent stand for a store and boat for the New York trade. The whole will be sold for cash or bonds against the estate.

B. Randolph
Tobias Hendrickson, Executors.

Attention has been called to the fact that woodworkers in Philadelphia were thoroughly conversant with the art of Chippendale and that they were anxious to produce furniture equal in quality and similar in character to that devised by the master minds of London. It has, further, been abundantly demonstrated that the most elegant and elaborate American cabinetwork following the Chippendale style was produced in the Delaware valley, and that it

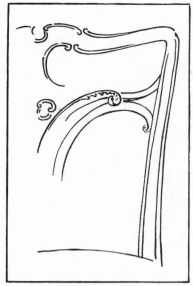

Fig. 7 — Sketch Showing Rectangular Joining of Chair Rail and Stile

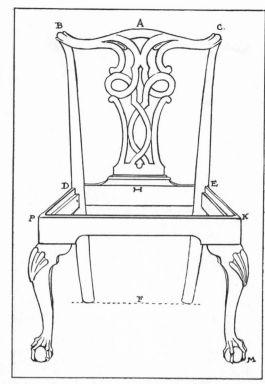

Fig. 8 — Comparative Chair Measurements

The table below gives the point to point dimensions of the sample side chairs, the Garvan chair, and the Trenton chairs. The proportions are virtually the same as those found in Plate XV of Chippendale's *Director* (third edition).

	Sample Chairs	Garvan	Trenton
B to C	22½"	23"	21½"
A to H	21	21	21
D to E	18	19	18½
K to M	17½	16½	18
P to K	22½	23	22½
E to K	17½	19	18½

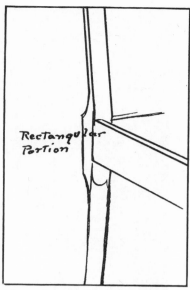

Fig. 9 — Sketch of Chair in Lambert Cadwalader Portrait

remained for Philadelphia to be the one hither-seas town projecting the issue of an edition of Chippendale's *Director*, though the Revolution put a quietus on this scheme.

Through Benjamin Franklin, the Library Company of Philadelphia acquired the third edition of the *Director* at the time of its publication, in 1762; and we have reason to believe that this book, which was available for consultation by any of the local artisans, was not the only publicly owned copy in Philadelphia. The Carpenters' Company possessed a number of standard English works: Swan's *British Architect*, *Ornaments in the Palmyrene Taste*, Swan's *Stairways*, *A Book of Designs for Chimney Pieces*, and *The Builders' Companion*, by William Paine.

It is enlightening to observe the similarities between the design and workmanship of Benjamin Randolph and those of James Gillingham. As yet we have found no evidence that the two men were directly associated, but their relationship is, perhaps, not unlike that existing between Chippendale and Hepplewhite, inasmuch as the work produced by Hepplewhite, or published in his book, is of extreme refinement and delicacy, while Chippendale's is

frequently more robust. In much the same way Randolph leans to vigor; Gillingham to lightness. That Gillingham was acquainted with Randolph's accomplishments seems, however, certain beyond a doubt. The labeled Randolph chairs, one of which is illustrated in Figure 4, are believed to have been made for Joseph Gillingham of Lower Makefield Township, Bucks County, Pennsylvania, who married, at Falls Meeting, May 25, 1768, Elizabeth Harvey of Falls. This Joseph was a brother of James Gillingham, who left Bucks County to carry on the trade of chairmaker in Philadelphia, where, at the Arch Street Meeting, he married Phoebe Hallowell, and is mentioned as "being a Joiner by trade." He died, February 1, 1781.

It is an odd circumstance that Joseph should have ordered his chairs from Randolph rather than from his own brother. As for the history of these pieces, they passed to Anne Gillingham, daughter of Joseph and Elizabeth, and thence to the present owners. So far as is known, they have never been out of the adjoining counties — Bucks in Pennsylvania and Mercer (formerly Hunterdon) County in New Jersey.

NOTES

a, For the drawings accompanying this article, I am indebted to Edward Warwick of the Pennsylvania Museum and School of Industrial Art, whose teachings and writings on furniture are well known.

b, The splat of the labeled walnut chairs which constitute the basis of this discussion, though by no means elaborately carved, is beautifully handled. A subtlety which might easily escape the casual eye is the weaving of the ribbon-bow of the splat alternately over and under its

four supporting scrolls. However, these chairs, as a whole, are treated with the utmost sophistication, not the least evidence of which is their adherence to the proportions laid down in the *Director*.

c, According to Horace Wells Sellers (grandson of Charles Willson Peale), the painter of the Cadwalader portraits frequently speaks, in his diary, of taking meticulous care to paint accessories and details only as he actually saw them. His rendering of the furniture in the above-mentioned portraits may therefore be relied upon as authentic.

Fig. 1 — HIGH STREET, WITH THE FIRST PRESBYTERIAN CHURCH, PHILADELPHIA
Jonathan Gostelowe's last shop, at 66 Market Street, was the two-story building east of the double three-story house, with entrance at Number 68.
From an engraving by W. Birch & Son.

Jonathan Gostelowe

Philadelphia Cabinet and Chair Maker

By CLARENCE WILSON BRAZER, *Architect*

THE QUEST

SEVERAL months ago, in a corner of the private office of the Associate Director of the Pennsylvania Museum, I was permitted to see an important serpentine walnut bureau that instantly commanded my admiration for its beauty of design and excellence of workmanship (*Fig. 2*). Great was my surprise to be shown, on the center front of a partition dividing the interior of the top drawer, the maker's label! Pieces of early Philadelphia furniture still bearing their original labels are very rare; for of the much heralded William Savery (1720–1787) only five labeled pieces are so far known — although I have just discovered a sixth. But this label was not that of Savery. In a space about two and one-half inches high by four inches long, it bore the following legend:

JONATHAN GOSTELOWE,
Cabinet and Chair-Maker,
At his shop in CHURCH ALLEY, about midway between
Second and Third-Streets,
BEGS leave to inform his former Customers, and the Public in general, That he hath again resumed his former occupation at the above mentioned place: A renewal of their favours will be thankfully received; and his best endeavours shall be used to give satisfaction to those who please to employ him.

"Now who, can you tell me, was Jonathan Gostelowe?" I asked; for, until then, I had no recollection even of having heard the name. Little did I realize that this Gostelowe would prove to be a Philadelphia cabinetmaker quite as important as the already famous Savery, and that I should discover him to have been the maker of some of the fine furniture now accredited to Savery.

44

Several months later, while on an antique hunt one Saturday afternoon, I bumped into a duplicate of that Pennsylvania Museum walnut bureau at that delightfully located old house of *The Cheyneys*, on the banks of the Springfield reservoir near Media.

No doubt of its being Philadelphia made, for nowhere else in America was ever such large and masculine appearing furniture produced as in that early metropolis. It was a type of furniture thoroughly at home in houses built of brick or heavy local stone, with their resultant deep window reveals. Thin wooden frame walls were virtually unknown among the plain and stolid folk of Pennsylvania, in whose substantial dwellings a light or delicate New England chair would seem as much out of place as would this bureau in the small scale wooden houses of the northern country.

But to return to the bureau. More grandiose and massive than the one in the Museum, it was the largest and most important bureau I had ever seen, a giant, yet decorated with most delicate detail (*Fig. 3*). With two very minor exceptions it still retained all its original ornate hardware, peculiarly French in its Louis XV style. And crowning it was a most delightful serpentine dressing glass of exquisite workmanship — though, alas, the mirror was missing, and none knew what had become of it. The top drawer of this stand was elaborately partitioned into tiny lidded compartments. The intertwined initials *J.G.* and *E. T.*, formed with cut-steel pins, adorned a central white satin pincushion. The full importance of this detail did not then dawn upon me; but, as my research developed, I found this monogram to be the equivalent of documentary evidence concerning the maker (*Fig. 4*).

Here, then, was a second specimen of the work of Jonathan Gostelowe. I must learn more about the man. The surname was new to me: in fact to this day it is virtually unknown, at least in the neighborhood of Philadelphia. What was its nationality? Whence came its possessor? What kind of man was he? What other works did he produce?

A few weeks later I was told where, as a collector, I might be able to obtain a pair of circular mahogany card tables. I jotted down the meager address, far out in Chester County, and more weeks passed before I found myself in that vicinity. After several hours' search, I finally discovered the old farmhouse and its occupants, and the tables, which, however, were not just then for sale. While I was meditating about my woeful waste of time, my attention was drawn to a large oval mirror with a roughly fashioned frame of white plaster. In spite of its crudity, I was at once attracted by its unusual, classic design. Several dealers, I was told, had seen the piece but had passed it by. To me it seemed that, under the crude plaster covering, which could possibly be removed, there might be hidden a more or less beautiful ornament. I took a chance and bought the piece. Later I laboriously picked and brushed off that plaster covering, no doubt applied by some conscientious Quaker to hide from view the ornate carving. When I had finished, I was amply rewarded by contemplating the beauty of a chaste and classical Adams woodcarving.

During the conversation which accompanied my buying of the mirror, I enquired about the former owners of this fine specimen so unexpectedly found on a country farm. And then came the story. According to tradition, this mirror had descended from an ancestor, an heir of Jonathan Gostelowe, cabinetmaker of Philadelphia — and it had never been out of the family. The name startled me. Here, in an out of the way country corner, might be the answer to my quest for news of the urban craftsman. Were there any old Bibles containing family records? There were; and I was invited to search in the lean-to of a dark attic. After long prying into a far corner among boxes of old books, I found the Bibles; but the pages of vital statistics had long since been removed.

Then an old carpetbag, bearing the silver name plate of Robert Evans, and bursting with papers, caught my eye. Curiously I picked up the bag and unfolded the topmost paper. It was a document bearing the name of JONATHAN GOSTELOWE! Forthwith I begged the loan of bag and contents, and great was my satisfaction at their faith in me, a stranger, when the owners consented to let me carry it off.

Late that night, and for many nights thereafter, I pored over the contents of my strange find — old deeds, letters, wills, inventories, and what not else. The clues which they furnished have led me through months of research; and, in the crossing and recrossing of their tangled lines, I have picked up many life threads not only of Jonathan Gostelowe but of other famous craftsmen of his time.

Gostelowe's Birth and Parentage

Jonathan Gostelowe was born probably at his father's house at Passȳunk — then in the far southern part of Philadelphia County — in 1744 or 1745.* A gravestone, which he erected jointly to the memory of his mother, wife and brother in old Christ Church Yard at Fifth and Arch Streets, Philadelphia, bore an inscription — recorded before the years had rendered it illegible — which read as follows:

Lieth Lydia wife of George
Gostelowe Senʳ of Northampton shire
of old England died the 28th of
Decʳ 1771 Aged 57 years.

Whether it was the mother or her husband George who was "of Northampton shire of old England" is not entirely clear from the phraseology of the inscription. It is by no means unlikely that the mother is meant. George Gostelowe Senior was probably an immigrant from Sweden. He appears to have come to this country about 1729, and as a yeoman tilled a farm in Passȳunk. He died April 15, 1758, aged fifty-seven years, and was buried in Old Swedes (*Gloria Dei*) Church Yard in Wicacoa — now at Swanson Street below Christian Street, Philadelphia.

The spelling of the name Gostelowe and the fact of George's connection with the Swedish Church are both indicative of a Swedish origin. *Gösta*, I am told, is a Swedish Christian name for *Gustav*, and is pronounced *Jesta*. The appendage *lowe*, *low*, or even *lo*, as sometimes found

*This date is based on the age given in Gostelowe's obituary published at the time of his death. There are some reasons for believing that it should be set ten years earlier.

recorded, is not explained. Another reason for believing that George Gostelowe may have come to America directly from Sweden is discoverable in the fact that search of a dozen parish records in Northamptonshire fails to reveal any name even remotely resembling Gostelowe. As Lydia was thirteen years younger than her husband, it seems likely that the two met and were married in this country sometime after 1735 — probably about 1742.

Besides Jonathan, who was the eldest, George and Lydia Gostelowe had three children: George Junior, born 1750–1751, who died October 8, 1773, "aged twenty-two years"; James, born June 27, 1752, who appears to have died in infancy; and Hannah, who, after the death of the mother, probably resided with Jonathan, at least until the time of his second marriage.

Jonathan Gostelowe's name appears in the Philadelphia tax lists of 1754, but without indication of his trade affiliations. He was, however, a resident of the Chestnut Ward in the same square as "William Savery, joiner".* Whether he was apprenticed to Savery or ever worked with him, we may not surmise. Some other master joiners and chairmakers established at the time were Samuel Austin, Joseph Armit and Stephen Armit, David Cane, George

Jonathan Gostelowe was twice married. His first wife was Mary Duffield, a niece of Edward Duffield, the clockmaker, who will be remembered as Benjamin Franklin's sole executor. Edward Duffield was a vestryman of Christ Church, Philadelphia, from 1756 until 1772, in which latter year he moved to the country. It was during this period of Edward Duffield's urban residence that Jonathan Gostelowe met the niece Mary. It is not unlikely

Fig. 2 — Walnut Serpentine Bureau (c. 1783)
Bears the label of Jonathan Gostelowe, shown at the left. The handles are of recent date. The escutcheons are original.
Courtesy of the Pennsylvania Museum.

that Gostelowe had previously made acquaintance with the clockmaker in his trade capacity of cabinetmaker, and that he had produced cases for some of the Duffield clocks.

The married life of Jonathan and Mary was brief. Within less than two years from the date of his marriage, June 16, 1768, the bride, aged twenty-six, was dead and had been laid away in Christ Church Yard, Philadelphia. To her husband, Jonathan Gostelowe, she left a tidy estate in the form of houses and land, inherited by her from her paternal grandfather. Thus, comparatively early in life, Jonathan Gostelowe came into some wealth, which no doubt greatly assisted him in maintaining a position in the community.

By this time, however, he was already well established as a master "joiner" as he was termed in a deed of 1770. We find him, November 19, 1772, taking an apprentice, one Jacob Crawford, for the term of eleven years, eleven months and eleven days. The requirements of the appren-

Claypoole, Henry Clifton, Jeremiah Cresson, John Elliot, Thomas Gant, John Gillingham, Joseph Jones, Patrick O'Neal, Jedidiah Snowden, Francis Trumble, and William Wayne. With any one of these Jonathan Gostelowe may have been associated. I have the names of some twenty-seven other contemporaries but not all were established with shops.

---

*At this time the "City" was only eight squares in area. Its northernmost limit was Vine Street. Cedar Street was its southern bound. Westward from the Delaware River houses were built only to Seventh Street, beyond which lay the country. The Chestnut Ward, where Gostelowe and Savery dwelt, consisted of an active city square which extended from the north side of Chestnut Street to the south side of High (Market) Street, and from the west side of Front (First) Street to the east side of Second Street.

Fig. 3 — WEDDING BUREAU OF JONATHAN GOSTELOWE
A serpentine walnut bureau with dressing glass made by Gostelowe as a gift to his bride, April 19, 1789. The mirror frame, here shown still covered with plaster, was originally gilded to match finials on the walnut supports.
Length, 4' 6''; height, 3' 5''; depth at center, 26''.
Courtesy of "The Cheyneys."

ticeship were probably never fulfilled. The Revolution must have annulled many such contracts. Meanwhile, however, we find Gostelowe increasing his working force by the addition of Thomas Jones, from London, for a four-year period of service. This was in October, 1773.

The care of his household, following the death of his wife and subsequently of his mother, Gostelowe apparently left to an indentured servant, Mary McQuaid, Jr., possibly under direction of his surviving sister Hannah. It was the custom of the time to maintain dwelling and cabinet-making shop together. Evidently Jonathan Gostelowe was supervising a considerable establishment. On December 30, 1773, he added to his real estate by securing from the Province of Pennsylvania a warrantee of Land in Northumberland County, one hundred and twenty-five acres in all — further evidence of thrift and prosperity.

At this time Gostelowe was still a resident of the Chestnut Ward where we find him, in 1769, assessed for the Proprietary Tax, and, in 1774, for the Provincial Tax, which latter called for the substantial payment of three pounds fifteen shillings.

THE REVOLUTION

Then came the Revolution. In Pennsylvania a committee of safety was constituted under the presidency of Benjamin Franklin, who, after his departure for Europe, was succeeded by David Rittenhouse, the clockmaker. Presently Philadelphia became the arsenal of the Colonies. Every effort was made to develop the manufacture of saltpeter, an important ingredient of gunpowder. Among those lending their aid in experimenting to improve methods of production, Jonathan Gostelowe appears, no doubt as an assistant to Robert Towers, Sr., first Chief Commissary of Military Stores. In June, 1777, Gostelowe was one of the first to sign the test oath of allegiance to the new independent State.

Thus, early in the strife we find Jonathan Gostelowe and Robert Towers, Sr., associated. Towers was, at the time, a druggist with a shop at 66 Market (High) Street — an establishment which, years later, Gostelowe was to transform to his own uses. The two men became fast friends and, eventually, kinsmen.

Fig. 4 — WALNUT DRESSING GLASS
This dainty stand crowned Gostelowe's wedding bureau. The frame of the looking glass has been covered with plaster to hide the gilded carving. In the cushion of the drawer may be seen parts of the initials wrought in cut-steel pins. Some of the pins have been removed, but the impression of the complete cypher *J. G.-E. T.*, as shown at the left, remains. These are the initials of Jonathan Gostelowe and Elizabeth Towers.

Later, in the summer of 1777, when a corps of Artillery Artificers was raised in Philadelphia and placed under command of Colonel Benjamin Flower, we find Jonathan Gostelowe commissioned its first major. Throughout the war, our former joiner served as staff officer in Philadelphia with the title of Commissary of Military Stores. Companies of his regiment were stationed at Philadelphia and Carlisle — their duties being those of casting cannon, boring guns, and preparing munitions for the army. Major Gostelowe was, most probably, the C. M. S. who, in September, removed from their steeples the Liberty Bell and chimes of Christ Church to preserve them from British desecration. In 1779 we find him assessed as a resident of the South Ward, and also in the Walnut Ward, no doubt due to the destruction of his former shop and home by the King's soldiers.

CIVIL LIFE

After the return of the army to Philadelphia, Jonathan was elected a member of Masonic Lodge Number Two, and was very regular in attendance at meetings except when out of town on army business. He served repeatedly in the office of Senior Deacon for several years. In July, 1780, he was one of two selected to secure a painted hanging to be placed at the back of the Worshipful Master; but, after 1785, he seems to have tired of lodge attendance.

In 1781 and 1782 he was assessed as a resident in the western part of the township of Northern Liberties — probably for the house in which he died — on a farm on the east side of Ridge Road north of Hickory Lane (now Fairmount Avenue).* From his tax assessments we gather, further, that he was, at that time, executor for Joseph Donaldson's large estate.†

*See P. C. Varle, *Map of Philadelphia and its Environs,* in Pennsylvania Historical Society.

†Between his active participation in war activities and his occupancy of the Northern Liberties Farm, Gostelowe's domicile appears not to have been firmly fixed. In 1779 he was assessed for taxes in the Walnut Ward which closely adjoined his old residence in the Chestnut Ward. If, as seems not unlikely, the Chestnut Street property had been damaged or destroyed by the British, the farm establishment in Northern Liberties may have been granted to him in compensation for the loss. On a British campaign map the farmhouse appears labeled *Rumstead.* On the P. C. Varle map of 1796 a large house in precisely the same position is labeled *Mrs. Gostelowe.*

Upon retirement from the Continental army Jonathan, in May, 1783, became a Captain in the Third Battalion of the State Militia and served with apparent willingness in various minor capacities until 1789. He was so ardent a patriot that, during this time, he also served three years in the Volunteer Artillery Battalion until, the Federal Government being firmly established, he laid his uniform aside and began courting a new bride — the daughter of his best friend, Robert Towers, Sr.

In Jonathan Gostelowe we evidently have a man of parts, a dependable executor and organizer with clearly pronounced mechanical abilities. Recognition of his solid qualities was not confined to the army. He was likewise active in church affairs and a vestryman of Christ Church. But he was apparently devoid of ambition to attain notable preferment.

Ownership of the Northern Liberties Farm does not imply that Gostelowe had abandoned urban residence. His label in the Pennsylvania Museum chest of drawers announces his resumption of the business of furniture-making in Church Alley. And in Church Alley he remained until 1790, when, as his advertisement of October 21 informs us, he removed to the late Robert Towers' old shop at 66–68 Market Street (*Fig. 1*). Previous to the Revolution he had been simply a joiner. Now, however, in the first published *Directory* of Philadelphia, in 1785, he appears as a cabinetmaker.

By 1788 there were established in Philadelphia two organizations of cabinetmakers: the Gentlemen Cabinet and Chair Makers, a title possibly inspired by the title of Chippendale's book, and the Journeymen Cabinet and Chair Makers. Jonathan Gostelowe was chairman of the former. In 1795 the latter issued a "second edition corrected and enlarged" of the *Philadelphia Book of Prices*, superseding a former book, no doubt inspired by the more elaborate *The Journeymen Cabinet Makers' London Book of Prices*, issued in 1788, and illustrated by Shearer and Towes. This was shortly followed, on March 4, 1796, by the institution of the Philadelphia Cabinet and Chair Makers, an association of the Masters, who, in their turn, issued a *Book of Prices*. It was not until years later — November 8, 1806 — after Gostelowe's death, that the Pennsylvania Society of Journeymen Cabinet Makers of the City of Philadelphia was instituted. This Society was incorporated May 20, 1825.

Gostelowe was a prominent member of the first Gentlemen Cabinet and Chair Makers and, as a former Major in the Revolution, was most naturally named Chairman of the Company for its part in the public procession in honor of the establishment of the Constitution of the United States, held in Philadelphia July 4, 1788.

On the preceding day, as well as on the Fourth, Jonathan inserted the following notice to his fellow Master craftsmen in the daily paper:

The Gentlemen Cabinet and Chair Makers are requested to meet in Church Alley To-morrow Morning, the 4th of July at 8 o'clock, to proceed from thence to join the Federal Procession. Every Master will inform his Journeymen that their Company is expected; likewise furnish their apprentices with the Badges agreed on for the Day.
July 3.   Jonathan Gostelowe, Chairman.

Thus we see him leading his brother craftsmen, gathered in front of his own shop so conveniently located to the formation of the procession on Third Street.

Ten states had at that time ratified the Constitution, and were represented in the parade advertised to start "precisely at Eight o'clock in the Morning of Friday, the fourth of July 1788, proceeding along Third Street to Callow-hill Street; thence to Fourth Street, down Fourth Street to Market Street; thence to the grounds on the Union Green in front of Bush Hill where James Wilson Esq. will deliver an Oration suited to the day, after which a Collation will be prepared for the Company."* Bush Hill was close by Jonathan's own home on the Ridge Road.

This Federal Procession was probably the longest and most impressive Fourth of July Parade so far held in the states. About five thousand marched in line, and seventeen thousand partook of the "collation." Companies of the Militia and Volunteers with bands of music were interspersed with the various patriotic bodies.

Third among the trades and professions, but thirty-second in line, came "Mr. Jonathan Gostelowe at the head of the Gentlemen Cabinet and Chair Makers, carrying the Scale and Dividers, insignia of the craft, followed by Jedediah Snowden with the Rules of Architecture; four of the oldest Masters; Mr. James Lee, attended by three Masters bearing the standard, or cabinet makers' arms, elegantly painted and gilt on a blue field, ornamented with thirteen stars, ten of which were gilt, the other three unfinished; below the arms, two hands united. Motto, *By unity we support society*. . . The masters, six abreast, wearing linen aprons, and bucks tails in their hats. The workshop, seventeen feet long by nine feet eight inches wide, and fourteen feet high, on a carriage drawn by four horses; at each end of the shop ten stars; two signs inscribed *Federal cabinet and chair-shop*, one on each side; Mr. John Brown, with journeymen and apprentices, at work in the shop."†

Then came other trades including Carvers & Gilders, Upholsterers, Turners & Windsor Chair Makers, Clock & Watch Makers, Silversmiths, etc., etc., and ending with the Plasterers, seventy-third in line. Finally came more soldiers heading the civil and military officers of Congress then in the City, and His Excellency the President and the Supreme Executive Council. Such was the first model Independence Day celebration, faithfully continued with little variation, in every town in this locality at least, until very recent years.

SECOND MARRIAGE AND AFTER

For nearly nineteen years following the death of his first wife, Jonathan Gostelowe had remained a widower. But, on April 19, 1789, he made a second venture in matrimony, his bride being Elizabeth, daughter of the druggist Robert Towers. The groom was now forty-five years of age; his wife was thirty-one. If we may judge anything from their signatures affixed to a bond of 1789 both of them were precise, orderly and thriftily disposed (*Fig. 5*). Elizabeth

*Pennsylvania Packet and Daily Advertiser, July 3, 1788.

†Scharf and Wescott, *History of Philadelphia*, Vol. I, p. 449. For a note on a similar procession held in New York City nearly three weeks later, see ANTIQUES for January, 1926 (Vol. IX, p. 19).

Towers brought to her husband further accretions of property. In 1788 Jonathan had acquired four city lots at the southeast corner of Eleventh and Walnut Streets; but for a year after this second marriage he and his wife continued to reside above the Church Alley shop.

Close to this shop stood Christ Church, of which our prosperous cabinetmaker was a member, and to which he donated both a baptismal font and a communion table — the work of his own hands.* Under date of January 22, 1789, we find a resolution of thanks to "Mr. Gostelowe for his generous gift of a mahogany communion table and the making of a fount for Christ Church." Upon the cover of this font, lost or mislaid since 1841, was inscribed:

THE GIFT OF
JONATHAN
GOSTELOWE,
CABINET MAKER,
PHILADELPHIA
to
CHRIST CHURCH,
JANUARY, 1789.

As we have already observed, in 1790 Gostelowe and his wife moved from their Church Alley abode to a final location at 66 Market (High) Street. Robert Towers had just died, to be survived barely a month by his widow. His shop was vacant; furthermore, in December 1788, he had deeded the property to his daughter, Eliza-

Early in 1793 Gostelowe seems to have determined to retire from business, as is indicated by the following advertisement in *Dunlap's American Daily Advertiser* for January 16 of that year:

Inquire of Jonathan Gostelowe, at No. 68, Market Street-Who has on hand, a few Mahogany Bureaus, Dining and Pembroke Tables, Mahogany Bedsteads, and a handsome Set of Chairs, which he will sell cheap for cash.

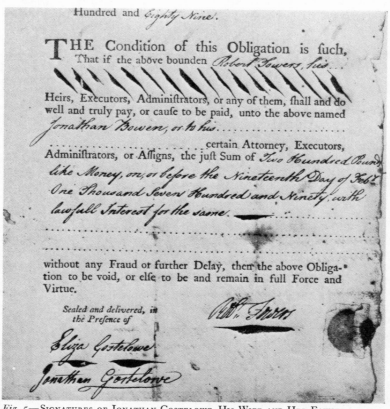

Fig. 5—SIGNATURES OF JONATHAN GOSTELOWE, HIS WIFE AND HER FATHER
A bond signed in 1789 just prior to Towers' death is here in part reproduced.
Figures 5 and 6 by courtesy of the heirs of Eliza Evans Towers.

By May of the same year, he apparently accomplished his purpose, as the following advertisement in the *Independent Gazetteer* of May 11 implies:

Jonathan Gostelowe, Having declined business, Will sell at Public Auction, On Monday, the 20th inst. at 10 o'clock in the forenoon, At his Cabinet Shop, No. 66 Market street... A Quantity of Mahogany and other Furniture, Consisting of 10 neat Mahogany chairs — fan backs, covered with sattin hair cloth and brass nail'd, Dining tables, End tables for ditto, *Circular Card tables*, Square ditto, Pembroke or Breakfast ditto, Wash-hand stands, Mahogany bedsteads, Button wood ditto, Likewise work benches, tools and The remaining Stock on hand.

Why, at forty-nine years of age, Jonathan Gostelowe should retire from business is perhaps something of a mystery. Yet he had

beth Towers Gostelowe, who now by her father's will received an equal share with her sister Sarah in the drugs and shop furniture and in a house and lot adjoining the shop. Jonathan Gostelowe was executor of the will.

The change in his location Jonathan made publicly known in an advertisement in the *Independent Gazetteer* for October 21, 1790. In the following year the *Directory* lists him as a cabinetmaker, located at 66 High Street, next door but one east of the Presbyterian Meetinghouse. Whether in Gostelowe's mind any important difference attached to the words *cabinetmaker* and *joiner* it is hard to tell. Previous to the Revolution he had termed himself a joiner. In the post-Revolutionary directories he, as well as the other furniture craftsmen, appears as cabinetmaker; but, as late as November 5, 1792, we find the signature of *Jonathan Gostelowe, joiner*, appended to a mortgage as well as to a joint bond for eight hundred pounds as security for the debt.

led an active life, had accumulated a competency, and, in view of the comparatively early demise of his parents—both at fifty-seven years of age — he doubtless felt that his own expectation of life must needs be limited. Nevertheless, he was not at the time in poor health. The yellow fever which drove most of the well-to-do folk of Philadelphia into the country in the summer of 1793 left Gostelowe unscathed. And, on the twenty-third day of April, 1794, we find him as executor of the will of his late father-in-law, Robert Towers, petitioning the Orphans Court to be appointed guardian that the property inherited by his niece and nephews from their grandfather Robert Towers might be safeguarded until they came of age. The three children were the offspring of Gostelowe's wife's sister, Sarah Towers Evans. It was through the eldest of the three, Robert T. Evans, who outlived his younger brother and sister, that the documented furniture of Gostelowe descended to the present heirs.

*These will be illustrated in a succeeding chapter.

DEATH

Gostelowe's period of retirement was unbroken by any other event of importance; but it was a period almost pitifully brief. Apparently he removed to his Ridge Road home, and here, on Tuesday, February 3, 1795, he died. Two days later he was buried in Christ Church burying ground. These facts we learn from a short newspaper obituary, which, further, gives the age of the deceased as fifty-one years.

'Tis odd — no gravestone can be found for so important a patriot and a vestryman of the Church among whose parishioners he sleeps. Neither can one be found for his friend Robert Towers, Chief Commissary and also a vestryman; nor in fact, are monuments discoverable for several signers of the Declaration of Independence whose interment in this same yard is recorded. Can it be that Fate decrees obliteration of the mementos of restless spirits whose patriotic ardors have endeared them to posterity, while the stones for obscure and peaceful souls like Jonathan's mother, brother and two wives still endure? Perhaps there is something of compensating justice in the preservation of some record of those who otherwise would remain forever unknown—since no engraved stone is necessary for those who have carved their own records in history.

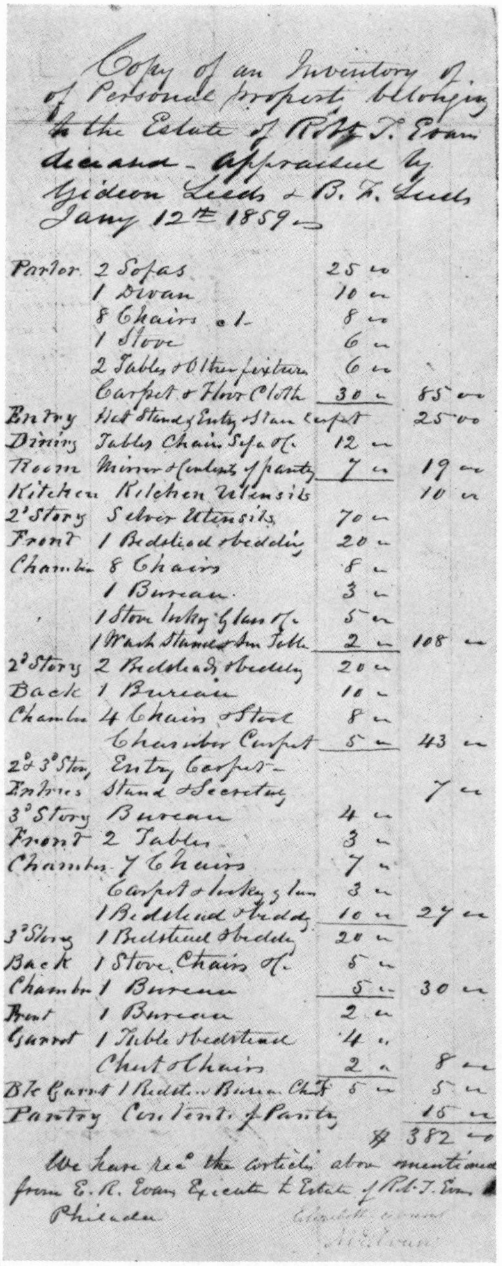

THE GOSTELOWE HERITAGE

With the passing of Jonathan and his maiden sister Hannah, who died the following year, the name of Gostelowe seems to have moved entirely into oblivion, for no modern bearer of the name has yet been found. The master's will in which he termed himself "cabinet and chair maker," was written August 20, 1789, soon after the second marriage, and was probated February 21, 1795. In this document he left all his property to his wife Elizabeth, who, it may be observed, subsequently made provision for Jonathan's surviving sister Hannah. Precisely how long the widow Gostelowe mourned her departed husband, unreconciled, we cannot say. But at some time undetermined, between March, 1798, and September, 1803, she took a second husband,

Fig. 6 — INVENTORY OF HOUSEHOLD FURNITURE
In the Philadelphia residence of Robert Towers Evans after his death. Note the two tables in the parlor, the mirror in the dining room, the looking glass in the second story front chamber, and the bureau in the second story back. These are items now known, and discussed in these articles on Gostelowe.

Matthew Locke, probably from Salisbury, North Carolina. Short-lived were these women. Elizabeth Gostelowe Locke died June 23, 1808, aged fifty-seven years and nine months, and was buried in Christ Church Yard.

And this brings us to the line of descent of the Gostelowe furniture. It will be remembered that Elizabeth had a sister Sarah Towers Evans, mother of three children, two boys and a girl. To this sister, Elizabeth bequeathed her entire property. Sarah, in turn, died about 1815. She had outlived her daughter and her second son. So it came about that Robert Evans, eldest son of Sarah, Jonathan Gostelowe's sister-in-law, became the sole heir of Jonathan Gostelowe.

Robert was married October 6, 1803, to Eliza Ridgway. For a time he was a farmer at Paoli, Chester County, Pennsylvania; but following the death of his wife, in 1835, he removed his residence to North Ninth Street, Philadelphia, where he lived with his four daughters and his two sons, Robert, Jr. and Edward. On the death of this Robert Evans, in 1858, the household effects of his Philadelphia residence were appraised before they passed to his daughters Elizabeth and Martha (Fig. 6). At the death of Elizabeth, her portion passed to Martha.

The next shift of the household goods came at Martha's death, in 1895, when it was found that she had willed all her possessions in that category to an adopted niece, Eliza Ferguson Evans. Eliza married John Fraser, and the couple took up their abode on a farm in Brandywine Manor, where, January 10, 1920, Eliza died. Her estate passed to her children, three daughters and two sons, who disposed of the furniture.

Briefly summed up, the pedigree of this furniture is as follows:

Jonathan Gostelowe d. February 3, 1795
Willed to wife Elizabeth (later married to
    Matthew Locke) d. June 23, 1808
Willed to sister Sarah Evans (who died
    intestate) . . . d. circa 1815
Only heir, son Robert Towers Evans
    d. December 1858
Willed to daughter Elizabeth Evans . . . . d. August 15, 1860
    and to daughter Martha P. Evans . . . d. February 5, 1895
Willed to Eliza (Ferguson) Evans Fraser . . . d. January 10, 1920

(The work of Gostelowe will be discussed in a subsequent issue)

Jonathan Gostelowe

Philadelphia Cabinet and Chair Maker, Part II*

By CLARENCE WILSON BRAZER, *Architect*

AS we have learned in the previous chapter of this study, Robert Towers Evans became the residuary legatee of the Gostelowe furniture, which came to him from his aunts, who, oddly enough, had, in each case, survived the males of the family. He had no need to buy anything new, though, when the city house was renovated for his marriageable daughters about 1849, he did indulge in some furniture of the style of the day, as is evidenced by the original bills found in that old carpetbag. These accretions of a decadent style do not, however, interest us; and, more to the point, occasion no confusion with the Gostelowe pieces.

THE WALNUT CHEST-ON-CHEST

Of these Gostelowe heirlooms which have descended through the long line of spinsters and widows—with only one male recipient along the way — the oldest is a walnut chest-on-chest, or clothespress, as it was anciently called (*Fig. 7*). While this chest is not specifically identifiable in the Evans inventory of house furnishings, it may quite possibly have come from the Paoli home, of which a separate inventory was made.

So far, this is the only piece which we may feel fairly sure was made by Gostelowe before the Revolutionary War. It may have been turned out for his wedding to Mary Duffield, in 1768; but, of course, this is only conjecture. There are, however, several characteristic details which distin-

Fig. 7 — CLOTHESPRESS, OR CHEST-ON-CHEST (*c. 1768*)
Of walnut, a bonnet top example with scrolled pediment and interesting carved shell in upper middle drawer. The brasses are all original. Of pre-Revolutionary descent through Gostelowe's heirs.
Courtesy of "The Cheyneys".

guish this clothespress from others of its time, and which are similar to those of Jonathan's authenticated later work.

First, let us note the cock bead glued and pinned to the edges of the drawers rather than run on the carcase surrounding the drawer, as was sometimes the custom of William Savery. Other Philadelphia joiners of the period prior to the Revolution followed a custom prevalent after 1720, and usually cut an ovolo lip molding on the solid of the drawer front. The cock bead had, however, been used in England comparatively early in the century.

Secondly, we may observe even here Gostelowe's penchant for ornate hardware, evidenced by his use of pierced plates, instead of the solid ones usually found on contemporary work. Jonathan, being an Episcopalian, and having, thereby, perfect freedom to follow worldly fashions, usually chose hardware of more elaborate English design than was customary on furniture made for plain Quakers, or for those influenced by long years of Friendly environment. The English type of hardware used on this chest-on-chest is identical with that on Harry H. Flagler's Philadelphia highboy of about 1765, illustrated in *Furniture of the Olden Time.**

This clothespress, by the way, bears a strong resemblance to the highboy in question, and its design was, no doubt, strongly influenced by that of the latter; but the detail of the drawer mold is not the same in the two pieces. The general form of the broken scroll pediment is similar in both of them, as well as the flame finials and the shell-carved drawer front, whence much of the applied scroll carving has disappeared with the hard usage of time. The carved shell, while in design resembling the so-called Savery type, is apparently the work of another hand. This clothespress, however, has a bonnet top, or curved roof, flush with the top of the scrolls — the roof on the left being broken. Virtually none of the so-called Savery type of highboys has a bonnet top. Such pieces do, however, have similar scroll pediments with a circular daisy form of rosette, while Gostelowe's later work follows closely the architecturally correct form of level cornice with broken pediment.

Certain other details of this double chest, such as the simple molded bracket feet and the coved base molding surmounting it, while not identical with Gostelowe's post-Revolutionary work, are strongly suggestive of it. The use of fluted quarter columns on the corners, while quite usual on Philadelphia pieces of the time, runs true to Gostelowe's favorite later style of fluted corners. But, in this case, the columns have a true architectural entasis, or taper, which is very rarely found. It indicates that the designer had a very thorough training in the essentials of architectural proportions. All in all, this piece, which with the wedding bureau is, I am told, to be presented to the Pennsylvania Museum, possesses a graceful and noble proportion. It might well have been made by one who formerly worked upon similar Savery highboys. The possibility would tend to support the prior surmise that Gostelowe may have been employed by Savery as early as the 1754 tax list.

The Labeled Bureau

Next, in chronological order of Gostelowe's documented work, comes the labeled walnut serpentine bureau in the

Pennsylvania Museum (*Fig. 2*).* From the wording of the label this piece would probably date from about 1783, when, after laying aside his major's uniform, the cabinetmaker had reopened his shop in Church Alley.

This type of serpentine bureau, of which he must have made many, seems to have been his favorite form, and the one later adopted for his masterpiece. Quite similar chests of drawers with canted corners, sometimes carved with fretwork, were current in England about 1760. Such a specimen is shown in John C. Rogers' *English Furniture.*† Shearer, in *The Journeyman Cabinet-Makers' London Book of Prices,*‡ illustrates a fluted cant corner to a serpentine front, with similar coved base moldings. Still other and similar pieces of English origin are to be found in Philadelphia today. Whether or not they had been imported sufficiently early to have served as inspiration for Gostelowe, it is nevertheless certain that our cabinetmaker's work follows English precedent in such details as the cock bead molding on the drawers — moldings more delicate than those generally found on the work of other Philadelphia joiners — and, lastly (especially in his later work), the exquisitely fine dovetailing characteristic of the best London cabinetwork. Either Gostelowe studied and learned from the latter, or he had more than one (Thomas Jones, from London) good English cabinet journeyman in his employ.

This Pennsylvania Museum bureau, which bears the only Gostelowe label so far found, is three feet, nine and one-half inches wide on the carcase, and the top and base project one inch more on each end. It is one foot, seven and one-half inches deep on the plain end surface; and the extreme width of the top at the center of the bow measures two

Fig. 8 — Baptismal Font (1788-1789)

Made of mahogany by Jonathan Gostelowe and presented to *Christ Church, Philadelphia*, where it now stands. The flat top, or cover, which transforms the piece into a credence, doubtless supersedes a wooden lid similar to that crowning the font in St. Paul's. The base is filled with sand to supply ballast.
Courtesy of the Reverend Louis C. Washburn.

*For Figures 2, 3, 4, 6, see Antiques for June, 1926 (Vol. IX, pp. 387, 388, 389, 392).
†London, 1923, Figure 108.
‡London, 1788, Figure 1, Plate 2.

feet, one and one-half inches. The canted corners carry five flutes each and are two and five-eighths inches wide. The height of the piece above the floor is three feet, one inch. Of the original ornate hardware only two escutcheons now remain. The top drawer is divided by a partition lengthwise in the center. The two sections are again divided into five equal and nearly square compartments. On the face of the long central partition and directly in the center of the front compartment may be seen the all important label of the maker.

The molded bracket feet, nearly always used by Gostelowe, in the style of an earlier period, appear somewhat clumsy in comparison with the generally refined design of the other more dainty details. For this the canted corner is largely responsible. A more broken and interesting cutting of the fetlock would have afforded needed scale and lightness. We find in this piece the delicate single cove and fillet base molding which appears typical of this master's later work. Worth observing, too, is the beaded board foot pad, which not only adds a definitive touch but serves to bind the several pieces constituting the foot into one solid and practical bearing, whose various parts are, in consequence, less liable to split off under unequal pressure. This bottom bead, frequently found on Gostelowe's work, is not usual to other Philadelphia cabinetmakers.

BAPTISMAL FONT IN CHRIST CHURCH

During the year 1788, Jonathan decided to make, and to donate to Christ Church, a new mahogany baptismal font (*Fig. 8*). This supplanted an older and plainer walnut font from which Bishop White was christened, and which has now been restored to present-day use. According to the late Reverend Benjamin Dorr, former Rector of Christ Church, Gostelowe's font was in use in 1841, and carried on its lid a brass tablet bearing the donor's name. This lid must have been removed and mislaid when the earlier font was restored to its original

Fig. 9 — BAPTISMAL FONT
In St. Paul's Church, Philadelphia. Sufficiently similar to the font made by Gostelowe for Christ Church to suggest identical authorship.
Courtesy of Philip Wallace.

duty, and when the addition of a table top transformed Jonathan's font to use as a credence beside the altar. In such condition the font has remained for many years, for a photograph taken prior to 1898 shows it, at that time, precisely as it appears today. At a later period its carved mahogany was temporarily painted white to match the pulpit; but, as the paint proved to be an unsuccessful finish for so small an article of furniture, it was subsequently removed.

As it now stands, this font measures three feet, six inches in height and fourteen inches in diameter. The base is loaded with sand to steady it against an undignified fall. The proportions are not very graceful, and Gostelowe must have wrought his design without recourse to the best books then available. The font designs illustrated by James Gibbs[*] as early as 1728 and 1739, or Batty Langley[†] in 1756, would have shown him more beautiful and well-proportioned examples. The curved surfaces of the base and top were, no doubt, meant to harmonize with the sweeping curves of the beautiful white and gilt pulpit installed in the church in 1770. To show how Gostelowe's font probably appeared with its top, we illustrate in Figure 9 the font in St. Paul's Church on Third Street south of Walnut, which, it would appear, was either designed by Gostelowe or inspired by his font in Christ Church.

Whoever designed and made the pulpit (*Fig. 10*) wisely kept close to good precedent, for it is a clever combination of the parts of five different pulpit designs invented by Batty Langley in 1739, and published, in 1756, in his book *The City and Country Builder's and Workman's Treasury of Designs.*[‡] There is hardly a detail of this pulpit, plain or carved, that cannot be found among these five plates! The

[*]James Gibbs, *A Book of Architecture*, London, 1739, Number 148, Plate 146.
[†]Batty Langley, *The City and Country Builder's and Workman's Treasury of Designs*, London, 1756, Plate CL.
[‡]London, 1756, Plates 113 to 117 inclusive.

carved fretwork beneath the cap molding is a touch of the ornament so favored by Gostelowe in his later chest-on-chests. According to Doctor Dorr, Watson the annalist, and as shown in old engravings, the pulpit once boasted a beautiful sounding board—now missing—and the whole edifice stood in the center of the chancel overlooking Gostelowe's communion table.

To return to our rare and unusual Christ Church font, however ungraceful its three major parts of equal size, it is, in detail, just what we might expect of Major Gostelowe, the artillery artificer. Here we again find the beveled or octagonal fluted form with small moldings, which convey a sense of nobility and scale. Three varieties of carved moldings provide us excellent opportunity to become familiar with the maker's choice of ornament; and, whatever we may think of the general form of the font, these moldings are well composed, especially the base moldings just below the fluted octagonal stem.

THE COMMUNION TABLE

Jonathan's mahogany communion table (*Fig. 11*) was, on the other hand, exceptionally plain, if we may judge from a reproduction from the only obtainable photograph. Naturally, when the pulpit, which had been designed as a focal climax to the interior of the chancel, was removed to the nave, this simple table failed as a satisfactory substitute. It is not strange, therefore, that a

Fig. 10 — PULPIT IN CHRIST CHURCH, PHILADELPHIA (*c. 1770*)
Compare with Batty Langley's *Designs*, Plates CXIII, CXIV, CXV, CXVI, and CXVII.
Courtesy of Philip Wallace.

larger and more dominating altar was sought. But why a stone design, entirely out of harmony with the beautiful Colonial architecture of the building, should have been permitted is beyond comprehension. And—indignity upon indignity—the time-honored mahogany table was completely encased in stone and entirely obliterated from view! Only a small round hole, about three inches in diameter, in each end of the new stone altar, permits one to thrust in his arm amidst the dust, to feel and make sure that the old table is still confined within its sacred prison.

One's sense of touch reveals, as the only old photograph does not, that the legs are tapered and fluted on the two exposed sides only, and that the anciently called *stone*, or *astragal*, bead molding about the skirt of the apron is sharply carved with a regular leaf-bud similar to the uppermost carved molding on the font. Of course, this communion table, when in use, was probably laid with a fine linen cloth, and, as is still the custom in England, was completely veiled with heavy frontal and superfrontal hangings, such as would have rendered useless a more elaborate frame. The main value of this table to our research is the revelation of Jonathan's usual fluted and tapering leg and the same general Adam character of design, which prevailed throughout his post-Revolutionary work.

The communion table which may still be seen in St.

Peter's Church at Third and Pine Streets is very similar to Gostelowe's table in Christ Church. As St. Peter's was a chapel of Christ Church, of which Gostelowe was a vestryman, it is quite probable that he also made the St. Peter's table, especially as it still displays carved scroll brackets at the top of the legs, a feature which Gostelowe was fond of using. A similar table, semielliptical in form, may be seen in old St. Paul's Church on Third Street.

THE WEDDING BUREAU

Shortly after the official acknowledgment of his gifts by Christ Church Vestry in January 1789, Jonathan began work upon a present for Elizabeth Towers, his future bride. It took the form of a nobly proportioned, serpentine walnut bureau with superimposed dressing glass. This, in so far as size, workmanship, and perfection of detail can make it, is the masterpiece of this cabinetmaker's documented work (*Fig. 3*). The length of this bureau is four feet, six inches on the carcase. The greatest width in the center of the top is two feet, two inches — the canted and fluted corners being two and one-half inches wide, and the plain ends twenty-three inches deep. The height above the floor is three feet, five inches. This bureau, therefore, is nine inches longer, and three inches higher than the similar labeled bureau in the Pennsylvania Museum. The details of feet, moldings, and the like, are, however, identical with those upon the smaller piece, and thus impart a nobility of scale and proportion that is almost majestic.

Here the feet are not too large, and appear correct for the support of so heavy a mass. Note the beaded foot pad, coved base mold, five-fluted cant corner, cock-beaded drawers, the unusual molding on the edge of the top, the general serpentine form, and the highly decorative hardware — all precisely as they are found on Gostelowe's labeled bureau. The hardware is somewhat exceptional in the use of pheasants for post roses and escutcheons — love birds, as they were sometimes called among the German settlers, and most appropriate on a bridal gift. The only difference in design between the two bureaus under comparison is the improvement made in the later one by dividing the large upper drawer space into two units, thereby agreeably intensifying the scale of the masterpiece. For greater ease in shifting the heavier bureau, it is equipped at each end with large brass handles.

Fig. 11 — COMMUNION TABLE, CHRIST CHURCH, PHILADELPHIA (*1788-1789*)
Like the font, made and presented by Jonathan Gostelowe; subsequently sealed within a stone altar which still hides it. This old and inferior photograph gives small conception of the piece.
Courtesy of the Reverend Louis C. Washburn.

Similar but smaller brass handles have also been applied to the sides of the surmounting dressing glass, for the sake of harmony as well as to facilitate lifting (*Figs. 3, 4*). This stand is eighteen and one-half inches long and twelve inches deep on the ends, with an extreme width, across the widest part of the serpentine curve, of thirteen and one-half inches. The height of the case above the bureau is seven inches, but, measured over the top of the mirror posts, it is seventeen inches. The hardware of the dressing stand is different from that of the bureau, but it shows an ornamental pattern. Note also the same use of the cock-beaded drawer edges, the coved base molding, and the usual design of the fetlock on the molded bracket feet, to which, however, due to the lighter weight, there was no need for adding the beaded foot pad. The workmanship of the divisions of the top drawer into bone-capped lidded compartments is exceptional and gives evidence of a loving care and pride in perfection of detail. The intertwined pin pattern initials *J. G.* and *E. T.* are gracefully formed in script monograms, but unfortunately some of the old and short bead-headed pins of which the letters are made, are gone (*Fig. 4*).

The mirror and its elaborate frame are shown here as they were found. Since then the desecrating plaster has been removed, disclosing a beautifully carved Adam style chain of leaf-buds with bead and reel in the solid wood. It is justifiable to assume that this elaborately carved frame was originally gilded, thus stimulating Quaker righteousness to insist upon the plaster of Paris covering. The top finials of the supporting posts are still gilded. The leaf work and surmounting lamp and flame appear coarse and heavy in the photograph because the plaster obscures all details. While the original pivot supports are missing, the mirror still just fits into the form of the supports and balances nicely when supported on new horizontal pinions. The original mirror itself measures eight by eleven inches and the carved frame over all is twelve by twenty-five inches.

That this wedding bureau has always been considered the finest one in the family may be seen from the 1859 inventory of the city household furniture, made for the purpose of settling the estate of Robert T. Evans (*Fig. 6*). This bureau stood in the second-story back chamber, which, with its cheerful western exposure, was apparently the main bedroom of the house. The front chamber on this floor appears to have been used in the customary manner as a private sitting room. But (just think of it!) the appraisal of Jonathan Gostelowe's masterpiece at that time was the lowly sum of ten dollars! Compound interest cannot compare with the increased value of a fine antique, for even computing the sixty years since 1860 the original ten dollars would now only amount to $467.72, whereas this masterpiece is easily now worth many times that sum. But even so, the value placed on this piece in the inventory was two and a half times that allowed on the other bureaus in the list.

Mirror Carving

The similar but larger mirror shown in the Frontispiece is probably the looking glass listed at an appraisal of five dollars, with the stove, etc., in the second-story front chamber of 320 North Ninth Street, Philadelphia, in 1859. Here again, are the characteristic Adam chain of leaf-buds and bead and reel carving with surmounting lamp and flame. The scroll at the base is entirely gone except for the supporting stick, which shows its former size. Although this frame was, like the smaller one, ignominiously treated with plaster, and therefore requires regilding, the glass is original and in exceptionally good condition. This glass is eighteen inches wide and twenty-three inches long; the frame measures twenty-three inches wide by forty-four inches high over all.

There can be no doubt that the smaller oval frame was carved to fit into the supports of Jonathan's dressing glass. And the great similarity of its design and the execution of its carving to those of the larger mirror frame offers conclusive evidence that both pieces are the work of the same hand. Gostelowe no doubt ordered — and probably designed — the smaller mirror to be made by his regular carver and gilder. The latter, thus provided with a fine example of Gostelowe's taste, and wishing to give his employer an appropriate wedding gift, probably reproduced the small design at twice the size for that purpose. For, inscribed in pencil and neatly written vertically with the grain of the wood, may be seen, with the aid of a glass and a little imagination, the signature *James Reynolds of Philadelphia*. The first name is quite clear, but the latter is barely decipherable.

James Reynolds, carver and gilder, on January 5, 1769, moved his shop "from between Walnut and Chestnut streets, in Front Street, to nearly opposite the London Coffee House in Front Street." We shall recall that Jonathan Gostelowe was, at the time, established in the adjoining square. After the war was nearly over, on April 11, 1781, Reynolds "removed from Front Street to Third Street, between Market and Arch streets, directly opposite the house of Mr. John Wilcocks" and therefore within a stone's throw of the shop in Church Alley where Gostelowe established himself after the war. These men had thus been close neighbors south of Market Street before the war, and, after the war, had reëstablished themselves north of Market Street in even closer proximity.

Both of the carved mirrors are made of American woods. They are, therefore, not imported pieces but were carved here. Before the war Reynolds advertised that he had imported "A very large and genteel Assortment of LOOK-ING-GLASSES, in carved and white, carved and gilt frames, etc." After the war he makes no mention of importations but he "also executes the various branches of carving and gilding, in the newest and genteelest taste." Verily, these mirrors fully live up to that advertisement!

A Mahogany Card Table

Last of all the five pieces of Gostelowe furniture that remained until recently in the family of his heirs is the circular mahogany card table, one of a pair, shown in Figure 12. This pair is probably that advertised for sale in May 1793, and bought in for family use. There were formerly, in the same family from which this table was obtained, four "neat Mahogany Chairs — fan backs, covered with sattin hair cloth and brass nail'd" — no doubt the same four chairs listed in the inventory of the "2nd Story Back Chamber", in which room stood the fine bureau. They were obtained by an antique dealer a number of years ago. Possibly the remaining six of the ten advertised were sold in the sale as a set.

Among other notable articles of family furniture that may have been made by Gostelowe and that were obtained by the same dealer, were the mahogany sewing stand, inventoried with a secretary at seven dollars, and an elaborate carved mirror, with an eagle on the top and ornamental cords at the side, inventoried in "the Dining Room with contents of the Pantry at $7.00." I wonder whether this elaborate mirror could have escaped the plaster of Paris covering which modified the sinful contours of the two mirrors already shown.

The table illustrated is one of the "two tables" listed in the 1859 inventory with "other fixtures" at a value of six dollars. This piece and its mate have the standard diameter of three feet but, due to shrinkage across the grain, they measure thirty-five inches in the other direction, and stand twenty-nine and one-half inches above the floor.

The "Marlbro" legs are tapered from one and two-thirds to one and one-eighth inches, and are fluted on each of three sides with three tapered flutes. They project one-quarter inch beyond the three and one-half inch veneered rail. The frame is well constructed of hard yellow pine dovetailed at the corners and joined in the center of the arc with a dovetailed spline one and seven-eighths inches by three-quarters of an inch. All angles are reinforced with glue blocks of yellow pine. The fly foot frame and its five knuckle pivots are, however, of heavy oak one and three-eighths inches by three and three-eighths inches. The two rear legs are "fly foot", and each one folds out to align with the spacing fixed by the front legs — a refinement not possible with only one fly foot. The tapered foot plinths are glued to the legs.

The edge of the three-quarter inch top folding leaf is worked with "two beads and a hollow", and the underside of the lower, or stationary, leaf has a "hollow on the under edge of the top" and a one-quarter inch astragal, or stone molding, about the bottom of the rail. All of these details became standard construction two years later, in 1795, when the Journeymen Cabinet Makers issued their *Philadelphia Book of Prices*. The unusual and unpriced feature here distinctive of Gostelowe design is the carved scrolls filling four inches of the joining angle between the legs and the apron. Scrolls similar, yet different in detail, are found on English tables of the time, but on few, if any, examples of furniture made by other Philadelphia masters. In fact, tapered fluted legs and neatly tapered plinth feet are equally rare on such circular tables. But this corner bracket thus executed is a characteristic Gostelowe detail by which his work may be identified. In other respects the details of this table resemble those of the Christ Church communion table, thereby giving us corroborative evidence as to Gostelowe's general style of work.

Remembering that Jonathan Gostelowe was chairman of the Gentlemen Cabinet and Chair Makers in 1788, and that these circular card tables were probably made in the early part of 1793, it is interesting to note the prices given in the Journeymen's *Philadelphia Book of Prices* of 1795 in comparison with the resultant Masters' *Book of Prices* of 1796; and also *The Journeymen Cabinet Makers' London Book of Prices* of 1788, all based approximately on the standards illustrated by this mahogany table:

A CIRCULAR CARD TABLE

Three feet long, the rail veneered, one fly foot, a square edge to the top, plain Marlbro' legs, two beads and a hollow on the edge of the top.

	An astragal, or hollow and two beads on edge of top............	0–1–6	0–3–7	0–3–0	0–3–0
	Working a hollow on the edge of the under top..	0–0–4	0–1–0		
	A cock-bead round bottom of rail when straight	0–0–9	0–1–6		
	Making frame or top oval or elliptic		0–3–0	0–6–0	0–6–0

Fig. 12 — Circular Card Table

Of mahogany, the work of Jonathan Gostelowe. Note the spade feet, the tapered fluted legs and the brackets extending from the legs to the soffit of the apron.
Owned by the author.

	LONDON JOURNEYMEN 1788	PHILA. JOURNEYMEN 1795	PHILADELPHIA MASTERS 1796 Mahogany	Walnut
Table as above.........	£0–10–6	£1–8–12	£4–10–0	£3–15–0
Each inch more or less in length..............	0–0–6	0–0–6	0–0–6	0–0–6
An extra fly foot........	0–0–6	0–1–10½	0–10–0	0–9–0

The Philadelphia Journeymen's book gives a table of the comparative value of English and American money, by which the above prices may be translated into values of the time.

1 shilling —	.13 cents
2 shillings —	.27 "
4 " —	.53 "
7s 6d —	1.00 "

The journeymen of those days worked—according to their own demands in the *Book of Prices* — twelve hours, from six o'clock in the morning until six o'clock at night and were paid for the work completed at the detailed rates listed for every kind of work measured by the inch. The master had to furnish a heated and lighted shop, the materials to be worked upon, hardware, stain, and the like, in addition to the labor charge of the journeymen, "finding his apprentices", and so forth —all of which costs must be deducted from the prices named above before his profits may be computed. It seems to have made no difference to the journeyman whether he worked walnut or mahogany, but harder woods such as maple and satinwood called for extras.

It may also be interesting here to consider the comparative prices for Figure 1:

A SERPENTINE DRESSING CHEST

Three feet long (Philadelphia Masters 3′–4″), four drawers in ditto, cockbeaded, an ogee and square on the edge of the top, or the edge veneered and a string in the upper corner, square corners, on French feet, or common brackets, all solid, the drawer fronts sawed out.

	London Journeymen 1788	Phila. Journeymen 1795	Philadelphia Masters 1796 Mahogany	Walnut
Dressing chest as above.	£1–14–0	£4–13–5	£16– 0–0	£14– 0–0
Extras				
Each inch or less in length.............	0– 1–0	0– 1–4½	0– 3–9	0– 3–9
Ditto above 2′–6″ high between mouldings (2′ 8″ do. in London)....	0– 0–3	0– 1–2		
Add for swelled brackets			0–10–0	0–10–0

These are only a few of the detail quotations on which it is possible to make comparisons. Each of the original books gives a long list of various extras peculiar unto themselves.

Other Work Attributable to Gostelowe

So far we have been entirely upon firm ground, and, while some of the surmises and deductions offered may be subject to correction upon future evidence, many facts are firmly established. From the documented work of Gostelowe as a starting point, certain other pieces which show familiar characteristic details may fairly be attributed to the same maker. Thus, by gradually building up characteristics one upon another, we may at length obtain a fairly complete knowledge and estimate of the man's whole work. To judge from the great variety of articles advertised in his public announcements, a vast quantity of furniture must have been made by Gostelowe. This will be discussed in a subsequent installment.

Add to Gostelowe

THAT Jonathan Gostelowe of Philadelphia made chairs, in addition to executing other and more elaborate cabinetwork, has long been known from his advertising label attached to a serpentine chest of drawers now in the Pennsylvania Museum. Both chest and label were pictured in ANTIQUES for June, 1926, among numerous examples of Gostelowe's case work identified and discussed in Clarence W. Brazer's noteworthy study of the master's life and accomplishment. With so many impressive items thus discovered and satisfactorily ascribed, it seems strange that three years should elapse before the finding of an authenticated Gostelowe chair. Credit for that feat belongs to Joe Kindig, Jr., of York, Pennsylvania. The chair, itself, now belongs to Richard D. Brixey of New York City, by whose permission it is here reproduced. The piece is of mahogany, with pierced ladder back and straight rectangular front legs slightly molded on the outer edges. The tenons of the seat rails, right and left, penetrate the stiles. On the rear rail of the seat is glued the maker's customary label, still excellently preserved.

Fig. 4 — Serpentine-Front Chest of Drawers by Jonathan Gostelowe
Though this piece of furniture is unmarked, its close resemblance to a labeled specimen in the Pennsylvania Museum leaves no reasonable doubt of Gostelowe's authorship. (See ANTIQUES for June, 1926, p. 387.)
From the collection of Doctor and Mrs. Frank S. Hall

Fig. 3 — Ladder-Back Chair by Gostelowe
This is the first, and thus far the only, chair to be found bearing the label of Jonathan Gostelowe of Philadelphia. Its label is the same as that illustrated in ANTIQUES for June, 1926.
From the collection of Richard D. Brixey

Thomas Tufft

By Samuel W. Woodhouse, Jr.

IN the eighteenth century Philadelphia came near to realizing William Penn's ideal, which was for a "fair, green town." It was fair, and it was green, for all about was spread a lovely countryside dotted with farms. Urban Philadelphia extended but a few blocks back from the bluffs of the Delaware, and much of the traffic of the place came by water to be landed in the dock creek. In such a community there was little room for industrial gadding, and we find, accordingly, that the shops of different craftsmen in the same trade were seldom far apart. The majority of the cabinetmakers appear to have operated on Front, Second, Third, or Fourth Streets, generally between Arch and Dock.

Among the names of these men, that of William Savery is still the best known, mainly because his work was the first to be identified by its maker's label. But other names have been culled from old-time newspaper advertisements and business cards, and are — some of them — gradually coming to be associated with existing specimens of furniture. Occasionally a labeled piece turns up, and in so doing retrieves a number of unlabeled contemporaries from the long burden of anonymity.

I am not yet prepared to link this latest discovery with any series of analogues. But here is a typical Philadelphia lowboy whose design nevertheless displays points of distinct individuality. It is, furthermore, both pedigreed and labeled.

I was casually visiting a friend; the talk had drifted to antique furniture and the rarity of labeled specimens.

"That lowboy in front of you is labeled," observed my host.

You may imagine the thrill. Ever since Mr. Halsey unearthed the first Savery label, I had been searching eagerly for an equally happy find; and here it was! I pulled open the top drawer of the piece before me. In the same position as the Savery label discovered by Mr. Halsey,

DETAIL OF TUFFT LOWBOY
While typical of Philadelphia design, this lowboy displays a number of individual characteristics, notably in the treatment of the skirt and the pattern of the legs.

and in appearance similar, lay the label of a cabinetmaker hitherto unknown to fame. Its inscription read as follows:

Made and Sold by Thomas Tufft, Cabinet and Chair-Maker, Four Doors from the Corner of Walnut Street in Second Street, Philadelphia.

I lost no time in looking up this recent addition to the roll of Philadelphia's cabinetmaking craft. Imagine my disappointment to find not a single reference in any of the old newspapers. But, of course, I did discover him in the first *Directory*, published in 1785. Further hunting revealed some additional information. In 1779 Thomas Tufft first acquired property; in 1780 he bought his shop from Israel Pemberton. Judging from the fact that his witness "affirmed," Tufft was probably a Quaker.

In 1793 the widow of Thomas Tufft was administering her late husband's estate. That was the year of the plague. No doubt our cabinetmaker was one of the many victims of that calamitous contagion. He cannot have been an old man at the time; in the fifties perhaps, if we may judge from the fact that he was married in 1766. The lady of his choice is known to have been one Martha Gauff, who, in the course of twenty-five years of matrimony, presented her husband with six offspring.

Thomas Tufft was a man of some circumstances — as Philadelphia cabinetmakers seem to have had a way of being. His belongings at the time of his death included horses, cows, sheep, and dogs; a long-case clock, mahogany desk, looking-glass, pewter, a silver watch, and plate appraised at £24.12.6. The only known monument to his memory, however, is the labeled lowboy whose picture and pedigree accompany these notes. But this, let us hope, will, in due time, evoke yet other monuments, sufficient in number at least to furnish data for determining the characteristic elements of their maker's style.

PHILADELPHIA LOWBOY (*c. 1780*)

Made by Thomas Tufft. In the top drawer occurs the maker's label, reproduced in facsimile. *Privately owned.*

PEDIGREE

Believed to have been made for William and Abigail Griffith (Powel). She
was the sister of Samuel Powel. It descended to their daughter Abigail,
who married James Saunders, and through Hannah Saunders, who married Lewis, in the direct line to the present owner. Dr. Samuel Powel
Griffith, brother of Abigail, was presumed to be the heir of his uncle,
Samuel Powel, who lived in the Powel house on Third Street opposite St.
Paul's Church, the second story back room of which is now the chief glory
of the American Wing of the Metropolitan Museum.

61

Fig. 1 — Stenton (*Built 1728–1730*)
The home of Deborah Norris Logan, whose wedding gift from her mother was an outfit of furniture made by Thomas Tufft.
Photograph by Philip B. Wallace.

Early Pennsylvania Craftsmen

Thomas Tufft "Joyner"

By Clarence W. Brazer, *Architect**

THE lives of the best of our early Pennsylvania craftsmen are quite rapidly becoming known, and examples of their work are being steadily identified. Doctor Samuel W. Woodhouse, Jr. has shown us a labeled lowboy† by another hitherto unheralded Philadelphia "cabinet and chair-maker." In addition, he tells us that its maker, Thomas Tufft, was married in 1766; acquired property in 1779; bought his shop "four doors from the corner of Walnut Street in Second Street" in 1780; appears in the Philadelphia *Directory* for 1785; and that his wife, the mother of six children, was a widow by 1793. Tufft's estate included a long-case clock, a mahogany desk, and a looking-glass. We may surmise that these pieces of furniture were of his own making, and thus, in addition to the Powel lowboy, his repertoire at least includes a clock and a desk. We also have to thank Dr. Woodhouse for detailed photographs of the lowboy, which tell the story of the craftsman's style and technique more elaborately and more accurately than could any words.

Pre-Revolutionary Period

Now that the man's work is at last identified, it may be time to record some additional information that I find in my files about Thomas Tufft, and thus to assist in compiling a greater

fund of information concerning one of early Philadelphia's fine furniture makers. Tufft may, perhaps, have started his own shop about the time of his marriage in 1766; but we know that he was regularly established as a cabinetmaker prior to August 4, 1772, at which time he took Edward Lewis as an apprentice for a period of seven years, seven months, and nineteen days. In 1774, six years before the purchase of his shop, Thomas Tufft was assessed for taxes in the Walnut Ward. Probably, therefore, he may have occupied the same shop before his actual acquisition of the property. If the shop named on his lowboy label was at the address where he was taxed in 1774, then we know that it was on the *east* side of Second Street, four doors *north* of Walnut Street, because the dividing line between the Walnut and South Wards lay through the centre of Second Street; while Dock Ward included all south of the center of Walnut Street. On the same side of the street, in the square to the northward, at that time stood the shop of William Savery, now the most prominently known of Philadelphia's early cabinetmakers.

For a period of over ten years spanning the Revolution — from December 29, 1773 until February 24, 1784, to be exact — Tufft frequently worked for Mrs. Mary Norris, then the widowed second wife of Charles Norris of Fair Hill. This is attested by some thirteen separate bills, which I have seen, in Tufft's own handwriting. The first of these bills was simply for making "4 glass frames for a Coach £1-1s-6d-." On June 9, 1774, Tufft mended three tables, two chairs, a "table stairs,"* and a desk for Mrs. Norris; and on September 7, "2 window rails with pulleys." Early in February, 1774, Mrs. Norris's negro man died, and Tufft then made a "ridged-top walnut coffin" for the servant's burial.

On March 19, he sharpened a saw. April 24, he mended a cradle. In May and June he made his client some "boxis for stays and sundries." Even a "water spout" came within the circle of his accomplishments, as is shown by one of his typical bills (*Fig. 2*). Only four months later he made a "ridged-top stained coffin with silvered Handles for Negro child, 2 feet 6 inches long."

Mary Norris frequently called on Tufft for general services, such as the making of packing boxes, small picture frames, rulers and toy guns for her sons, as well as for "pulling down and putting up bedsteads." There is nothing odd in this, for most of the famous cabinetmakers, from William Savery to Duncan Phyfe, did similar odd jobs, as we shall see later when considering these men. In fact, just at this very time, April 7, 1775, Mary Norris had William Savery "bottoming and mending the back of one old fationed chair," "3 chairs and a stool" and "2 high back chairs." A chair to have been old fashioned in those colonial days must surely have been an early product!

DURING THE WAR

January 6, 1776, Tufft made a tea table for Mrs. Norris, and, on December 19, was called upon "to repair a small tea table." Perhaps children

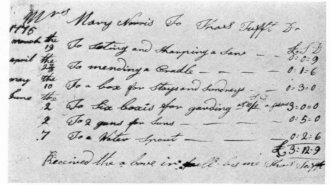

Fig. 2 — A THOMAS TUFFT BILL (*1775*)
Rendered to Mrs. Mary Norris of Fair Hill, mother of Deborah Norris Logan, for the performance of various humble commissions.

were as destructive then as now. While Tufft may have been a Quaker, as Dr. Woodhouse surmises, his series of bills was suspended, May 27, 1777, not long prior to the British occupancy of the city, which occurred in the following October.

On "the fifth of sixth month 1778," Thomas Tufft signed as witness to a bond of James Logan, Jr., who was the son of James Logan, William Penn's secretary and personal friend. Logan's town house adjoined to the southward "the first built house of brick erected in Philadelphia" which was on Second Street on the southwest corner of Lodge Alley.* This tends to support the belief that Tufft was a Quaker, as Logan, no doubt, would have preferred a near neighbor of his own faith as a witness.

STENTON

Stenton, the large mansion, named after the East Lothian English village where his father was born, was begun in 1728 by James Logan, George Logan's grandfather (*Fig. 1*). It was originally planned as a stone house, but failure of the quarries on the place necessitated a changed design from "a plain cheap, farmer's stone house" to a cheaper (!) one of brick, and the building was first occupied and furnished in 1730. The original walnut furniture, which, of course, would not have been made by Tufft, represents what we, today, call the Queen Anne style, with curved seats and backs and cabriole legs. The majestic high-back upholstered sofa illustrated in Figure 9, which was one of James Logan's original pieces, in 1730, may now be seen in the American Wing of the Metropolitan Museum. By no stretch of the imagination can it be assumed that this piece was made by Thomas Tufft, since its

Mrs. Mary Norris	To Thos. Tufft–Joyner, Dr.		
March 17	To making a mahogany Breakfast Table................	5	– –
May 29	To a Mahogany high posted Bedstead Caps & Bases.......	13	– –
	To a Scaloped Bed Cornish with Pulleys................	2– 5	–
June 1	To a Walnut Butlers Tray....................	1	– –
7	To One Mahogany Dining Table — 4 feet long...........	8	– –
	To ditto..........ditto — 3 feet 7 In. long.......	7	– –
9	To 2 Card Tables....................................	10	– –
16	To a Mahogany Bason Stand.........................	2– 5	–
28	To 3 plain Window Cornishes with Pulleys.............	1– 2 6	
July 3	To 1 plain Bed Cornish..........ditto.............	1– 2 6	
11	To 1 Mahogany Sofa...............................	20–	–
13	To 12 ditto Chairs with open Backs.................	36	– –
Sept. 17	To One pair Mahogany Drawers With fret & Dentels..... (a scrawl is drawn here rep-) & Table to suit...... resenting carving)	} 45	– –
20	To 2 Mahogany Bottle Boards.......................	12–	
	To One Roling Pin...............................	1– 6	
21	To a Bread Tray................................	11– 3	
25	To a large Pye Board...........................	17– 6	
27	To a Mahogany Knife Box.......................	15–	
29	To a Tea Board................................	1– 2 6	
	To a Pine frame Table...........................	12– 6	
	To a large Ironing Board..........................	1– 2 6	
Oct. 6	To 6 Mahogany Chairs Bases & Brackt...............	20	– –
13	To a Mahogany Skreen Table.......................	4– 10	–
17	To a Mahogany Fret Tray for Chaney................	3	– –
		£184– 19– 9	
Cr.–	June 13 — By Cash 21		
	25 — By ditto 24		
	—————		
	£45–		

Fig. 3 — AN IMPORTANT TUFFT DOCUMENT
Tufft's bill rendered to Mrs. Mary Norris for successive deliveries of wedding furniture made for Deborah Norris Logan. On the back of this bill are to be found an endorsed receipt and the words *Thos. Tufft's Account for my Daughter's Furniture, Paid Feb. 24, 1784.*

*In Stenton may still be seen what might be called a "table-stairs"— a low table, one step high, on which is superimposed a stair of two steps. This contrivance offered, in all, three steps by which one might ascend to his high bed, beneath which, during the day, the children's trundle bed found inconspicuous refuge.

*Watson's *Annals*, Vol. I, p. 437.

production must antedate that master's birth by a number of years.

Before the battle of Germantown, Stenton was taken by General Sir William Howe for his quarters. Later General George Washington occupied it with his staff. Afterwards, as President of the United States, he there became the guest of Deborah Norris Logan, Pennsylvania's most distinguished Colonial Dame.* She also entertained there, for her husband, who was a member of the Pennsylvania Legislature and of the United States Senate, Franklin, Lafayette, her cousin Charles Thompson, Thomas Jefferson, John Randolph of Roanoke, and Presidents Madison and Monroe. The portrait of Deborah Logan may be seen in the entrance hall of Stenton, above the Chippendale chair shown in Figure 8. The mansion and its beautiful gardens, at Eighteenth and Courtland Streets, has been in the possession of the Logan family, untouched by vandalism, until its recent acquisition by the City of Philadelphia and its restoration by the Pennsylvania Society of Colonial Dames, in whose custody it now is.

TUFFT'S FURNITURE FOR STENTON

Tufft did some minor work directly for Deborah Norris and George Logan, the bride and groom of Stenton, to whom he sent his bill, November 3, 1783. On the same date he addressed another bill for unimportant things to Mrs. Mary Norris. But yet another of these documents is, indeed, the most important; for from it (*Fig. 3*) we learn that Thomas Tufft made the bridal equipment of furniture for Deborah Logan, a gift from her mother Mary Norris. On the back of this bill, in what appears to be Mary Norris's hand, is written "*Thos. Tufft's Account for My Daughter's Furniture — Paid Feb. 24, 1784.*"

The year of this bill's rendering is not given; but the dates of various payments on account of this large sum of over 184 pounds lead us to believe that the debt may have been incurred

Fig. 4 — THE WHARTON MAHOGANY HIGHBOY
From Walnut Grove. This highboy shows so many points of similarity to the lowboy bearing Thomas Tufft's label, which was published in ANTIQUES for October, 1927, that its attribution to the same maker seems reasonable.
Owned by Mrs. J. Bertram (Wharton) Lippincott

a year or so before its final settlement, February 24, 1784. The making of so much fine furniture would take many months for an average shop such as Tufft's must have been. We may therefore, believe that the order was given about the time of Deborah's wedding, although delivery was not made until the respective dates named for each item, probably during the year 1783, but possibly in 1782. A long receipt in full, by Thomas Tufft, appears on the back of this bill and mentions other credits receipted for in an account book. Such an account book may now be seen in a glass case on the second floor of Stenton, but I have not had the privilege of looking through it for Tufft's receipt.

THE PRICES

The first of this furniture, delivered on St. Patrick's Day, was a little breakfast table. During the next seven months various pieces of dining-room, kitchen, drawing-room, and bedroom furniture made their appearance at Stenton. Thus the cabinetmaker Thomas Tufft, whom Mary Norris favored over William Savery for the important commission, was called upon to make not only a carved top highboy worth forty-five pounds, but also the simple kitchen equipment so necessary to a bride of those days.

Tufft's charge for a rolling pin, of one shilling and sixpence, seems high in comparison with William Savery's charge of only nine pence for a rolling pin to another customer at this same time. Tufft's charge for an ironing board of one pound two shillings and sixpence is also more than Savery's charge of one pound. That Tufft was a higher priced craftsmen than Savery is also proved by his having charged Mary Norris three pounds and ten shillings for a ridged-top walnut coffin for her negro man, while, about the same time, Savery charged another customer only three pounds for a similar coffin for a negro.

These comparisons will be further elaborated upon in a subsequent paper which will discuss some bills of William Savery. All this would indicate that Tufft had a greater reputation at the time than our heretofore most famous Philadelphia craftsman, and would explain why Mary Norris, who was one of Philadelphia's foremost women, preferred to have her finest gift made by Thomas Tufft. Such a grand country mansion as Stenton should have only new fashioned furniture brought to it

---

*Deborah Norris Logan, daughter of Mrs. Mary Norris for whom, as already noted, Thomas Tufft had done considerable work, was born at Fair Hill, the six hundred acre estate of her grandfather Isaac Norris, along the York Road in the Northern Liberties. September 6, 1781, she married George Logan, owner of Stenton.

by a new mistress who was accustomed to the very best of surroundings at her mother's home, Fair Hill.

THE DINING-ROOM FURNITURE

Imagine that high ceilinged dining-room furnished throughout in mahogany, with three tables, a knife box, a set of twelve chairs with open backs, and a fretted tray for the china! "Skreen-table" was the ancient name for what we now generally call the tilt-top table. Its top was from two to three feet in diameter, slightly dished, with a bead or more elaborate pie-crust carving around the edge. This top rested upon a bird-cage baluster supported on a tripod. The contrivance permitted the top both to turn and to tilt. Upon the square bed to which the table top was hinged, a candle-stick could be placed without fear that the wind would blow out its light, which the table top screened when adjusted to any point of the compass. Such tables could also be placed in front of the open fire to protect those at the dining table from the intense heat.

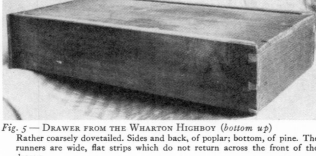

Fig. 5 — DRAWER FROM THE WHARTON HIGHBOY (*bottom up*)
Rather coarsely dovetailed. Sides and back, of poplar; bottom, of pine. The runners are wide, flat strips which do not return across the front of the drawer.

That dozen chairs with open backs must surely have been of the Chippendale pattern of the period. Whether they were of the so-called ladder-back type which appears beside the high-back sofa in the drawing-room, or like the cabriole-leg chair shown in the illustration of the entrance hall, I cannot now even guess. It is more probable that these dining-room chairs were like the other open-back Chippendale chairs with cabriole legs, priced at an average of three pounds each, of which an armchair and several side chairs have now been restored to Stenton. All three varieties of the Chippendale style of chair with open backs are to be found at Stenton, and all most probably came there as

early as Deborah Logan's wedding, for soon afterward the styles underwent a marked change. There is also still at Stenton a mahogany chair with bases and brackets in the Chippendale style, but of rather plain design. If it is one of the chairs mentioned in Tufft's bill, one wonders why he charged for them an average of three pounds, six shillings, and eight pence.

What a wonderful mahogany sofa that must have been for which he charged twenty pounds! Such pieces were, indeed, rare, and no doubt have remained in existence to the present day. It seems likely, therefore, that we may, before long, be able to identify this piece; for most of the furniture from Stenton may be readily traced, although recently a number of pieces went to one of the heirs now resident in England.

THE BEDROOM FURNITURE

How fine must have been the bride's bedroom, with the high-post mahogany bedstead with scalloped cornice and pulleys for the drawing of the curtains, a mahogany basin stand, and window cornices which may have matched the bed cornice! The *pièce de résistance* of this magnificent gift of furniture was the "pair Mahogany Drawers with fret & Dentels & (carved) Table to suit" for which Tufft charged the enormous sum of forty-five pounds. Oh, if we could only find that highboy! For such it must have been, although the description is so quaintly expressed. In those days a lowboy was called a dressing table, and, by the superimposing of a chest-of-drawers, it became a highboy.

The lowboy shown in ANTIQUES for October, 1927, has a distinctly characteristic scalloping on the skirt, or apron, such as I have seldom noted on other pieces of Philadelphia furniture.

Figs. 6 (left) and 7 (right) — COMPARATIVE DETAILS
At the left is a reprint of the lower part of the lowboy published in ANTIQUES for October, 1927, page 293, bearing the label of Thomas Tufft. *At the right* is pictured a corresponding detail of the so-called Wharton highboy, likewise attributed to Tufft by the author of the present article. The treatment of many decorative elements is precisely the same in both pieces. The fronts of the two skirts display minor differences, but major similarities.

For purposes of comparison, a detail of this lowboy is reproduced again (*Fig. 6*). An identical skirt carving does, however, appear upon a highboy that was loaned to the Sesqui-Centennial Exhibition of Chippendale furniture in Mount Pleasant, under the care of the Pennsylvania Museum. This highboy (*Fig. 4*) has the same characteristic and unusual moldings that are found upon the lowboy illustrated. It also has a fretted and carved scroll top with spiral finials over fluted columns on the corners. It has the same ball-and-claw foot and the same peculiar thin, raised, carved bead on the shank of the cabriole leg.

WALNUT GROVE

It was, no doubt, made by our friend Thomas Tufft. It bears a brass plate stating that it was formerly owned by Joseph Wharton and used at his home, Walnut Grove, at the time of the famous British Michianza in 1778. If this be so, the piece was doubtless made by Tufft before the Revolution, as its style clearly indicates. It also gives us a date before which the labeled lowboy probably was made. It seems hardly possible that this Wharton highboy can be the one made by Tufft for Mary Norris, even though it tallies with description in his bill, except for the "dentels," which do not occur in the cornice of the Wharton piece.

There are certain characteristics of this fine mahogany highboy that are similar to those discernible in pieces by Jonathan Gostelowe, and other characteristics which recall pieces by William Savery, while the small bead of the apron suggests James Gillingham. Yet, with this combination, we find also the undoubtedly individual characteristics of Thomas Tufft himself. Gostelowe, so far as is now known, did not make highboys. The cabriole leg which was necessary to this piece of furniture was distinctly a chairmaker's product, whereas Gostelowe came into cabinetmaking as a "joiner" of case-work. Anciently the two trades of chairmaker and joiner were separate and distinct; but, about Thomas Chippendale's time, they were merged, and, thereafter, both joiners and chairmakers became cabinetmakers. Thus craftsmen old enough to have been trained in the making of Queen Anne chairs introduced certain of the chair-

makers' characteristics into their cabinetwork, and produced the American highboy.

The top of this Wharton highboy is, undoubtedly, inspired by a chest-on-chest of Chippendale's, from which the carved scroll-terminals and latticed pediment are taken. Here we find the same horizontal moldings of delicate profile that were used by the well trained cabinetmakers of the time. Savery was one of several craftsmen who, so far as I know, never used this horizontal cornice under his scroll tops, and his moldings were considerably heavier. Tufft also used the same ovolo lip-mold on the face of the drawers that was used by Savery.

The workmanship, however, on this highboy does not compare with the fine and exquisite workmanship invariably found upon Gostelowe pieces. Note in the drawer construction (*Fig. 5*) that the dovetailing is coarse and heavy. The flat runner strips along the sides, cut on the mitre at the rear end, are somewhat similar to the construction used by Savery. The latter, so far as I know, always continued the same flat strip across the front. The sides of the drawers of this highboy are one-half inch thick poplar, and the bottoms are white pine. Then, as now, each master craftsman had his own ideas as to the best way in which to construct drawers, as well as case-work. Hence, certain principles were generally followed in all pieces turned out of his shop. Thus, by comparing different pieces with a known labeled piece, and by careful scrutiny of their details of workmanship in relation to their dimensions, proportions, and details of design, we are enabled to find the "earmarks" by which the maker may be known. It cannot be argued, therefore, that Thomas Tufft was influenced

Fig. 8 — ENTRANCE HALL OF STENTON
A portrait of Deborah Logan hangs above the Chippendale chair here shown. Whether or not this chair represents part of the original wedding equipment is not known.

either by Gostelowe or Savery, except in a most general way. His design is more correct than Savery's in its following of Chippendale's precedent, but, by the same sign, less originally American.

The sparse use of carved ornament on both this Wharton highboy and Tufft's labeled lowboy would rather indicate that the master did not call in a professional carver. The degree of ability displayed in this carving and its peculiar characteristics

Fig. 9 — THE DRAWING-ROOM AT STENTON

The walnut sofa, now in the Metropolitan Museum, with its curved seat and Queen Anne back, antedates the period of Thomas Tufft, and was, no doubt, part of the original equipment installed by James Logan when he built his home. The ladder-back chairs, while of the later period, may not certainly be attributed to Tufft.

would lead to the belief that it may well have been executed by the regular chairmaker of the shop, who was, perhaps, Tufft himself. Those who desire to know the characteristics of Tufft's workmanship should compare the carving and moldings of the labeled lowboy with those of the Wharton highboy (*Figs. 7 and 8*).

With this various additional evidence before us, it will probably not now be long before other specimens of Thomas Tufft's workmanship will be brought to view and identified. I note that he made long-case clocks, mahogany desks, looking-glass frames, breakfast and dining tables, ''skreen'' tables, butlers' trays, fretted trays, high-post bedsteads with cornices, window cornices, basin stands, fine sofas, open-back chairs, and chairs with

bases and brackets, lowboys, and carved highboys, as well as the most ordinary kitchen equipment, and coffins for negroes. With all this finery in his repertoire, he was not averse to the menial tasks of producing toy guns and rulers for children, making packing boxes, or even of filing and setting a saw. His charges were higher than those of the now famous William Savery, although, at this writing, I have not yet seen any furniture which is superior to that which we can now fairly attribute to that famous Quaker chairmaker. It is sufficient, however, that Tufft had a following of patrons among the best of Philadelphia's leading citizens, and that his furniture was considered good enough for the finest mansions in all Colonial America.

ADAM HAINS OF PHILADELPHIA

Master Cabinetmaker of the Marlborough School

By CARL M. WILLIAMS

AT THE SALE OF THE REIFSNYDER COLLECTION in New York in 1929 a superb Philadelphia Marlborough pembroke table was sold for $2,600. This price was apparently paid exclusively on the basis of the outward merits of the piece, for it was not catalogued as being labeled and the fact that it bore a cabinetmaker's mark was known to only one or two persons who had made an examination of its construction. Strangely enough both the mark and the maker of this important table, displayed and sold at probably the greatest sale of American furniture yet held, still remain unrecorded and virtually unknown to students and collectors.

Adam Hains, the maker of this faultless example of the Marlborough, was born February 9, 1768, the son of Heinrich and Anna Catharine Hähns. He was baptized Heinrich Adam at old Saint Michael's and Zion Lutheran Church in Philadelphia on February 28 of the same year. His father, proprietor of the Spread Eagle Tavern, was commonly known to his patrons as Henry Hains, and when Heinrich Adam came of age in 1789 he too discontinued the German pronunciation of name. He was known as Adam Hains during the remainder of his life.

To whom Hains was apprenticed has not been learned. He lived at the Sign of the Spread Eagle on the east side of North Third Street in Philadelphia, about eight or ten doors north of Race Street and on a site now lost beneath the massive supports of the Delaware River bridge. In this neighborhood and located in the streets and alleys immediately contiguous dwelt and worked a host of cabinetmakers in that day. Anyone of that group active about 1785 could have been Hains' master. A block or so away on Arch Street was the extensive cabinetmaking establishment of David Evans, who was then specializing in furniture of the Marlborough style. Evans used an incised or branded mark similar to that employed by Adam Hains and could very well have been responsible for Hains' knowledge of the basic principles of the craft. Others of that near-by group of cabinetmakers who are known to have favored the use of the straight leg in their productions were Daniel Trotter, Thomas Tuft, and John Webb of Elfreth's Alley; Josiah Elfreth, William Wayne, Jacob Wayne, and William Rigby of North Front Street. In reference to the last named I recall my purchase in Haddonfield, New Jersey, of a plain mahogany Marlborough card table. Upon examination of its drawer construction I had the pleasure of determining the maker's name: on the inside of the back board of the drawer appeared the paper label of Henry Rigby, son of the aforementioned William Rigby.

Adam Hains established his shop not earlier than the year 1788 or 1789. On September 8, 1791, the records of Saint Michael's and Zion Lutheran Church disclose the fact that "Adam Haehns and Margareta Baisch" were married. She was a daughter of Martin Baish, a cordwainer in Philadelphia, and she remained the cabinetmaker's lifelong companion. It was not until 1792 that Hains was identified as a cabinetmaker in a Philadelphia newspaper. A news item appearing in *The Pennsylvania Journal* on July 25, 1792, conveyed the alarming information that an attempt had been made "to set fire to the house of Mr. Hains Cabinet Maker in Third near Vine Street." The fire was prevented—luckily, for Hains' neighbor conducted a lumber yard! By 1797, Hains' enterprise on North Third Street had gained the significant classification of "Cabinet Manufactory," and on May 18 of that year he announced the removal of his shop from 135 North Third Street to a new location, "No. 261, south [side of] Market street" (*Fig. 3*).

On April 4, 1801, Adam Hains and his wife Margaret, sold to his brother-in-law, Christian Dannaker, their interest in the Spread Eagle Tavern, the adjoining cabinetmaker's shop, and other buildings which had been devised by Henry Hains to his children at his death in 1783. Adam Hains was then referred to as "of Philadelphia, Cabinet Maker," but soon after he and his wife conveyed their interest in her father's real estate, in 1803, Hains' name no longer appeared in local records. Continued investigation was rewarded, however, by the location of a deed from Adam Hains and his wife, who on November 3, 1815, were described as residents of Ruscomb Manor Township, in

FIG. 1—CARVED MAHOGANY PEMBROKE TABLE (*c. 1790-1795*), made by Adam Hains. *Collection of Henry F. du Pont.*

FIG. 2—ADAM HAINS' BRAND, which appears on underside of drawer of the pembroke table.

FIG. 3—ADVERTISEMENT from *The Pennsylvania Journal* for May 18, 1797, announcing Hains' removal to a new address.

Berks County, Pennsylvania. His occupation on that date was given as cabinetmaker, but a later deed, dated March 20, 1820, described him as "yeoman." It is at this point that the career of Adam Hains, so far as the collector's interest is concerned, is brought to a close. Ruscomb Manor is a small township some few miles northeast of Reading, Pennsylvania, in a fertile, elevated, picturesque region. A little more than a half-century ago, say about the year 1885, a descendant of Adam Hains named Henry Hains was living at Pricetown, the principal settlement in the township, and following the occupation of joiner.

Adam Hains' interpretation of the Marlborough style as developed in Philadelphia and illustrated in his labeled pembroke table (*Fig. 1*) presents another instance of the way in which a popular style was produced with little variation by local cabinetmakers for more than a quarter of a century, and another reminder that caution should be used in ascribing too early a date to examples of that style. In every detail the design of this table indicates an early date of manufacture. In fact, it could have been produced as early as April 1766, when Marlborough patterns were included along with various forms of the cabriole in a book of manuscript designs drawn and used in the shop of Jonathan Shoemaker, cabinetmaker of Philadelphia. Yet original manuscript evidence exists to show that Hains could not have made this table prior to 1788 and it is quite likely that it was produced between the years 1790 and 1795. This table compares more than favorably with the dozen or so of its type known to collectors. A nice detail of enrichment not found on most of the others of this group is the "toad back moulding," as the term gadrooning was quaintly described by David Evans in an entry in his account book on April 4, 1785.

The mark used by Adam Hains is the most elaborate of the incised or branded labels known to have been used by Philadelphia cabinetmakers. A printed paper label was generally used by the early members of this craft locally; however, Hains' branded mark is not unique. David Evans, Edward James, and Daniel Trotter used burned-in marks which consisted simply of their names or initials. Hains' brand (*Fig. 2*) reads *A. Hains Phila fecit*.

Although only the pembroke table here illustrated is known to bear this maker's identification, an examination of other pieces made in Philadelphia during the Marlborough period might reveal additional productions of Hains' shop.

Note: The writer wishes to acknowledge his indebtedness to Messrs. John and Benjamin Ginsburg of Ginsburg & Levy, Inc., New York, for their courteous assistance.

Aesop's Fables on Philadelphia Furniture

BY DAVID STOCKWELL

SOME YEARS AGO when the Philadelphia Museum was exhibiting the wonderful Howe highboy for the first time, I was struck by the unusual motif carved in high relief on the lower central drawer *(Fig. 2)*. It illustrates Aesop's fable, the fox and the grapes. One luscious bunch of grapes hangs from a tendril on the vine and Br'er Fox sits below, bright eyed and very bushy tailed, with his nose almost touching the fruit. Surrounding this vignette are carved lively rococo scrolls and tattered asymmetrical leafage that would place this Philadelphia Chippendale masterpiece before the Revolutionary period.

At about the same time another fable illustration in Philadelphia carving came to my attention. This embellishes the much-admired mantel from the famous Powel House ballroom, now in the Philadelphia Mu-

seum. In the frieze beneath the shelf is a framed depiction of Aesop's fable of the dog and the meat, boldly and vigorously carved *(Fig. 4)*. Under its coating of ivory paint, the wood is, as usual, white pine. The dog is shown pausing to view the reflection of his meat-stuffed jowls from a low cyma-scroll bridge, while another dog peers speculatively from behind another scroll just ahead, and a picturesque mill and wheel fill the background. This interesting scene is again surrounded by rococo scrolls and the tattered leafage so typical of Chippendale's designs. There seems certainly more than a passing resemblance between the carving of the highboy and that on Samuel Powel's pine mantel.

At this point in my observations several difficult questions puzzled me and it is only over a period of some years that the slowly unfolding answers seem to create a discernible picture. First, what cabinetmaker or carver conceived this idea of employing the fable motif? Second, what inspired the fable motif in eighteenth-century Philadelphia? Third, were there other examples than the two I had noted or were these isolated instances of some unusually imaginative craftsman's whim?

To date we have no answer to the first question. We do not know the identity of the cabinetmaker or carver. A clue to his name may some day be found in bills relating to the Samuel Powel house, bills made out perhaps to

FIG. 1—THE HOWE HIGHBOY *(Philadelphia, c. 1760)*. With carving on lower center drawer depicting Aesop's fable of the fox and the grapes. *From the Philadelphia Museum of Art.*

FIG. 2—DETAIL of the fable carving on the Howe Highboy.

Charles Steadman, who built the house in 1768. Some of these papers must be in existence among Steadman or Powel descendants.

The second question, regarding the inspiration of the fable motif, is easier to answer. Philadelphia, like other cities in the eighteenth century, made good use of fable and allegory for teaching truisms easily and diplomatically to both old and young. No less than three editions of Aesop's *Fables,* all by different translators, were printed in Philadelphia in the single year 1777—during the course of the Revolution. At least nine editions of Aesop were printed there before the turn of the eighteenth century, three of which were "for the benefit of youth"; one at the request of the Trustees of the University of Pennsylvania; one printed by Benjamin Franklin Bache, grandson of Benjamn Franklin; and one in German, apparently for the large body of Palatinate Germans then settled in the Philadelphia region. Several English editions and at least one French have been on the shelves of Philadelphia libraries since the middle of the eighteenth century. The fact that the first Philadelphia issues of Aesop's *Fables* (1777) were a few years later than we date examples of furniture and architecture on which fable motifs appear still serves to point up the enormous interest in fables. Worthy of special emphasis is the fact that many editions were illustrated with wood or copper engravngs. A wood engraving from a Caxton edition long in the Philadelphia Public Library *(Fig. 3)* is similar in general composition to the fable drawer from the Howe highboy.

It is likely that literary popularity alone does not account for the fable's becoming a carver's motif in Philadelphia furniture and architectural detail. There must have been inspiration from other sources as well. An article by Joseph Downs in the Metropolitan Museum *Bulletin* for December 1932 points out that four engravings of Aesop's fables appear in some copies of the 1762 edition of Thomas Chippendale's *Director.* One of the engravings for a mantel block, illustrated in the article, has as its subject the fable of the two pigeons, and Mr. Downs suggests that it is a likely source of inspiration for the carved drawers of the Metropolitan Museum's Pompadour highboy and matching lowboy. The fact that all four of these plates do not appear in all copies of the 1762 edition is worthy of note; also the fact that two of them appear as motifs in the silk embroidery for pole screens in the 1755 edition of the *Director.* The Library Company of Philadelphia is known to have had a copy of Chippendale's *Director* as early as 1769 and since it still has the 1755 edition this is probably the same copy. The Library Company is also listed as having the 1762 edition. It is likely that the *Director's* association of fable with architecture and, in a limited way, with furniture did influence contemporary Philadelphia designers and craftsmen. None of the *Director's* plates, however, suggests incorporating the fable motif into the carved design of case pieces of furniture, as was done in Philadelphia.

Third, concerning examples of Aesop's fable motifs in case pieces originating in the Philadelphia area, there are, counting the Howe highboy, seven in all. One is the lowboy which matches the "fox and grapes" highboy, illustrated in Plate 118 of William MacPherson Hornor's *Blue Book of Philadelphia Furniture.*

Others are the Madame Pompadour highboy and matching lowboy in the Metropolitan Museum of Art's American Wing *(Fig. 5).* Upon the streamer drawers of both pieces is carved Aesop's fable of the two pigeons, and a third animal, a sort of Chippendale dragon, carved in the scrolling on the right side of the drawer, is thrown in for good measure. This carving is more delicate and finely detailed than that on the Powel house mantel and the "fox and grapes" pieces. The pigeons are surrounded by a centralized cyma scrolling replete with tattered leafage and exquisite rococo details. Beneath the fable drawer the same sort of scrolling outlines and enhances the delicately pierced skirt. It should be noted that the drawers of these matching pieces are finished with applied beading and that the brasses are of the elaborate rosette variety, in direct contrast with the "fox and grapes" highboy and lowboy which are finished with lip-edge drawers and pierced-plate brasses. The lip-edge finish in urban Chippendale pieces is usually considered earlier and more usual than the bead.

To this group also belongs a magnificent scroll-top chest-on-chest in the Henry Francis du Pont Winterthur Museum (illustrated in ANTIQUES, November 1951, p. 425). In the pediment is a beautifully carved drawer depicting a ewe and suckling lamb surrounded by a rococo frame. Out of thousands of fables (both Aesop's and his imitators') I have not yet found one to match this interesting vignette, but the chest belongs in the category of fable-inspired Philadelphia case pieces for reasons other than the animal carving. The same exceptional workmanship and unusually careful attention to detail common to all is observable in this piece. The bead-edge drawers and exuberant carving seem to date it somewhere between the "fox and grapes" pieces and the two more delicately carved Pigeon-Pompadour items at the Metropolitan.

Another piece of Philadelphia furniture in the fable tradition is a lowboy in the Karolik collection of the Boston Museum of Fine Arts *(Fig. 6).* This beautiful

FIG. 3—WOOD ENGRAVING of the fox and the grapes in an eighteenth-century edition of Aesop's *Fables. Phila. Public Library.*

❡ The fyrst fable maketh mencyon of the foxe and of the raysyns

FIG. 4—DETAIL of carving in frieze of mantel in the Powel Room illustrating the fable of the dog and the meat. *From the Philadelphia Museum of Art.*

FIG. 5—POMPADOUR HIGHBOY. With carving on the lower center drawer illustrating the fable of the two pigeons. The same vignette is carved on the corresponding drawer of the matching lowboy. Both are finely detailed, with the vignette framed in the scrolls and tattered leafage typical of Chippendale work. *From the Metropolitan Museum of Art.*

piece exhibits fine, rather delicate carving reminiscent of the Metropolitan examples. The fable drawer in effect is almost lacy, with a magnificent swan as central motif. There are scrolls and leafage in the best Chippendale tradition and a touch of chinoiserie in the slender lantern-like columns on either side of the vignette. The fable represented is presumably the sad tale of the proud swan that made her sisters so jealous they pulled out all her fine feathers.

The seventh piece of this "fabulous" furniture is illustrated as Plate 435 in Wallace Nutting's *Furniture Treasury.* It is a highboy base displaying a finely designed drawer carved with a fanciful crane or heron. The surrounding frame is the usual Chippendale cyma scrolling and leafage. Clearly of the same lineage as the three previous examples, it exhibits the elaborately carved skirt and vine-carved corner finish also seen on other pieces. The splendid fret and the knee carving are identical to those of the lowboy in the Karolik collection.

All these case pieces of the fable family are of the finest quality. Except for the "fox and grapes" highboy and matching lowboy, all are finished with bead-edge drawers. All have the carved inset quarter columns, carved skirts, applied frets, and other details that even in the Philadelphia school place them on a plane above ordinary furniture.

Since my quest for Aesop began, I have found fables also in architectural details and in other materials than wood. Besides the Powel mantel, I know of two others and an overmantel embellished with fable or bucolic motifs. One is part of the woodwork of the superbly carved room from the Stamper-Blackwell house built in 1761 near Third and Pine Streets, Philadelphia, now in the Henry Francis du Pont Winterthur Museum. This mantel, illustrated in ANTIQUES for November 1951 (p. 429), has animal motifs carved on the frieze with vigor and restless vitality. Though I cannot trace these directly to Aesop, they seem to be fable-inspired. The left-hand panel represents dogs chasing a stag, the center panel dogs baiting a bull, and that on the right dogs chasing a wolf running away with a large plump goose.

The other mantel, of exceptionally beautiful design and quality, is not of Philadelphia origin. It is part of the original paneling from the Beekman house, Mount Pleasant, formerly located in what is today Beekman Place, New York City, and now in the New York Historical Society. The design in the mantel block depicts two swans swimming amid cattails and is apparently inspired by the oft-employed Aesop's fable of the swans mentioned before. The mantel was doubtless installed about the time the house was built in 1760.

Another architectural detail of Aesopean inspiration is the well-known overmantel panel in the great room at Kenmore, the Virginia home of Colonel Fielding Lewis and his wife, sister of George Washington. The medium here is plaster composition, not carved wood (Fig. 7). The design is centered in an oval of garlands and enclosed in a frame with crossetted corners embellished by rosettes, husks, palmettes, and other classic motifs. The oval encloses four Aesop's fables worked into a single scene. The central group with tree in foreground represents the fox, the crow, and the piece of cheese, or beware of flattery. On the right we are shown that pride goes before a fall by the two swans, one of them with sadly plucked feathers, another rendering of the fable on the Karolik lowboy. Just to the left of the tree a lamb, unable to drink in the stream that he himself has muddied, teaches the lesson that spite acts as a boomerang. And to the left of that is illustrated the fable of the mouse that freed the lion by gnawing the net, proving that patience wins where strength fails.

This composition, like the fine stuccowork ceilings in this and two other rooms at Kenmore, has been established as the work of an unidentified Frenchman, done in 1775 (ANTIQUES, January 1935, p. 16). "That French-man," as George Washington called him, also did the ceiling and overmantel in the east parlor at Mount Vernon in 1777. The discrepancy in design between the rather amateurishly composed fable panel at Kenmore and the sophisticated treatment of the ceilings supports the legend that Washington himself designed the panel for the edification of his sister's family.

I have seen a mantel carved with the fable, the wolf in sheep's clothing in a mid-Georgian house near London. There may well be other English architectural examples, but I know of no other American ones.

Another medium with an architectural connection in which the fable motif occasionally appears within the sphere of Philadelphia influence is that of cast iron. The eighteenth-century fireplace was often furnished with a cast-iron fireback, sometimes quite elaborately decorated, to reflect heat into the room. One from a South Second Street house built about 1754 has exquisitely detailed leafage and scrolling and an Aesop's fable sensitively modeled in high relief, representing the stork and the crow. It is illustrated in *The Editors' Attic,* page 555.

I have seen the fable motif used in many European decorative arts: in ceramics (delft tiles, porcelains of various origins) ; in textiles (toiles de Jouy, prints, tapestries, embroideries) ; in silver, copper, and other metals in the form of household vessels. Some tapestry on a set of French chairs is the closest approach to an example in European furniture that I have seen. The fable as suggested by Chippendale's *Director,* or merely by contemporary illustrated books, may have been used in architectural detail in several localities. I believe, however, that the unusual and delightful use of the carved fable motif in case furniture is a concept only of the Philadelphia school of craftsmen.

FIG. 6 — PHILADELPHIA CHIPPENDALE lowboy *(c. 1760-1770).* With carving on lower center drawer probably illustrating the fable of the swans. *From the Museum of Fine Arts, Boston.*

FIG. 7—OVERMANTEL in the great room, Kenmore *(1775).* Plaster composition illustrating four of Aesop's fables: the lion and the mouse; the lamb in the stream; the two swans; and the fox, the crow, and the piece of cheese. *Photograph from Wallace Nutting Pictures.*

Philadelphia via Dublin:

influences in rococo furniture

BY MEYRIC R. ROGERS, *Curator of the Garvan and related collections, Yale University Art Gallery*

Fig. 1. Tympanum detail of the "Van Pelt" high chest, Philadelphia, 1765-1780. This shows the use of a motif similar to that of Figure 2, but completely transformed in effect and feeling as part of an all-over dynamic linear pattern. *Henry Francis du Pont Winterthur Museum.*

Fig. 2. Detail of a design for a "Gothick Cloths Chest," Plate C, Chippendale's *Director*, ed. 1754. Note the closed, frame-like character of the applied carving.

JOSEPH DOWNS STATED a generally held belief when he wrote in 1952, "The sophistication of design is a striking feature of Philadelphia furniture, owing to its derivation from contemporary London books, particularly Chippendale's *Director*. Although chair backs and scrolled pediments can be traced to engraved sources, the improvisation of them in Philadelphia created wholly new interpretations in colonial furniture, unparalleled elsewhere." (*American Furniture*, p. XXVI.) This acceptance of the *Director* as the principal and immediate source of the Philadelphian interpretation of the rococo style remains largely undisputed; no source more germane and reasonable seems to have been suggested.

While the Philadelphia cabinetmaker offered no substantial addition to the basic English ornamental vocabulary, it is easily seen that he used this common visual language with a different syntax and accent. English precedent is generally apparent even where obvious differences in proportion and character exist between the English and the American products. When, however, this precedent is sought in the rococo decorations which are the unique and distinguishing feature of the fully developed high chest and its accompanying dressing table, the closest English analogue appears to be the ornament on a Chippendale rococo mirror frame. Comparison will show how essentially different in feeling the American *rocaille* (Fig. 1) is from the English (Fig. 2). Though both designs employ the same C-scroll, acanthus, and rock-shell forms, the Chippendale engraving shows them used as a framing composition, a closed pattern unit static in feeling, while the ornament on the

Philadelphia high chest is so arranged as to produce a strongly rhythmic, linear, open pattern essentially dynamic in character. The same words have been used in both cases, but to say different things.

When we leave the *Director* engravings and compare actual examples of furniture and decoration, we find the same situation. The catalogue of the 1934 exhibition *New York State Furniture* at the Metropolitan Museum of Art referred to this difference in discussing the quality of New York design at the mid-eighteenth century: "There is none of the airy chinoiserie and French rocaille spirit of Philadelphia furniture evident, but rather the sobriety of the forms evolved by the English school—a distinction, generally agreed upon, which runs somewhat counter to acceptance of the *Director* as the major source of Philadelphia inspiration—unless the *Director* is also held to reflect the essentials of the French rococo spirit.

If we turn to eighteenth-century French design, however, as a possible direct source of the playful fantasy and mobility of Philadelphia rococo ornament, we meet a like but opposite difficulty. From about 1725 the French ornamental designer was concerned very largely with the development of highly organized patterns, dynamic in character, with the vertical movement dominant and a corresponding axial control even when the arrangement was asymmetric. The result is seldom if ever thought of as all-over surface enrichment (Figs. 3, 4). There is, therefore, as much difference between the French and the American interpretations of basic rococo forms as between the English or Chippendale version and the American.

With both French and English designs apparently eliminated as the immediate inspiration of the Philadelphia craftsman at this time, where shall we find his source?

My first promising clue to this problem was some photographs of the middle phase of eighteenth-century plasterwork in Dublin. The curious linear exuberance and free dynamic quality of this ornament and its ten-

Fig. 3. Detail of carved wood panel, Hôtel de Soubise, Paris; attributed to Germain Boffrand, c. 1735. Note the highly organized and strongly axial character of the ornament. The design is *in* rather than *on* the surface decorated. *From* Vieux hôtels de Paris, *F. Contet, Paris, 1910, Vol. 1, Pl. 23.*

Fig. 4. Detail of plaster ceiling, Hôtel de Soubise, showing the characteristics of Figure 3 in a more developed, freer form. Compare with Figures 5 and 6. *From* Vieux hôtels de Paris, *Vol. 2, Pl. 30.*

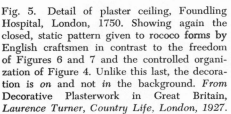

Fig. 5. Detail of plaster ceiling, Foundling Hospital, London, 1750. Showing again the closed, static pattern given to rococo forms by English craftsmen in contrast to the freedom of Figures 6 and 7 and the controlled organization of Figure 4. Unlike this last, the decoration is *on* and not *in* the background. *From Decorative Plasterwork in Great Britain, Laurence Turner, Country Life, London, 1927.*

Fig. 6. Detail of plaster ceiling, 86 St. Stephen's Green, Dublin, 1760-1765. The free, dynamic, open pattern formed here contrasts sharply with both Figure 5 and Figure 4. *From The Georgian Society,* Records of Eighteenth Century Domestic Architecture and Decoration in Dublin, *Dublin University Press, 1909-1913, Vol. II, Plate LXXXVIII.*

Fig. 7. Detail of ceiling, 42 Sackville Street, Dublin, 1760-1770. A somewhat freer treatment than Figure 6, with strongly accented, open linear rhythm. Probably by a follower or assistant of Robert West. *Georgian Society,* Records, *Vol. III, Pl. LVI.*

dency to develop as an all-over pattern appeared strangely akin to the qualities of Philadelphia ornament. Could there be a connection?

The flowering of this Dublin decorative art took place roughly between 1750 and 1770. Almost nothing has been written about it except for the publications of the Georgian Society in Dublin early in this century (*Records of Eighteenth Century Domestic Architecture and Decoration in Dublin,* Vols. I-V, 1909-1913), and a study by Constantine P. Curran, "Dublin Plasterwork," in the *Journal of the Royal Society of Antiquaries in Ireland* (Vol. LXX, 1940, pp. 1-56). Mr. Curran showed that a long native tradition of decorative plasterwork preceded the introduction of the late baroque-rococo manner probably by the Italian stuccoworkers Paul and Philip Francini about 1740. Irish craftsmen such as Robert West, strongly influenced by French teaching, incorporated these imported forms into the individual native rococo style, so different from that of England though derived from similar sources.

Emigration from Ireland to the American colonies, owing to economic and particularly to religious discrimination, had begun in the seventeenth century, encouraged by the Calverts of Maryland, and during the early 1700's it was vastly increased by the great numbers of Scotch-Irish Quakers who came to Pennsylvania. It continued throughout the century, and many Irish-trained craftsmen were among the immigrants. Well-known examples in Philadelphia are Plunket Fleeson, paper stainer, active after 1739, and Hercules Courtenay, carver, active before the Revolution (see William Mac-Pherson Hornor Jr., *Blue Book, Philadelphia Furniture,*

pp. 91, 191, and F. Lewis Hinckley, *A Directory of Antique Furniture,* p. xxvi ff.). Such craftsmen must have been the physical bridges by which Irish ideas and methods were transferred to the American colonies. Further research will undoubtedly reveal a more definite linkage through artisans, and possibly also through the importation of Irish-made objects.

A recent brief visit to Dublin made it possible for me to see a good deal of the mid-eighteenth-century plasterwork, of which an amazing amount survives. Plaster rather than wood paneling seems to have been generally preferred as an interior finish in Ireland, and the stucco-worker seems to have had much broader scope than the woodcarver. With the greater flexibility and freedom afforded by his material, the plasterer probably set the character of the prevalent decorative style. Some definite indication of the transfer of this stucco style into terms of wood during the mid-eighteenth century in Ireland is, however, a necessary link between Dublin plasterwork and Philadelphia woodwork.

By great good fortune, at least one such link was discovered on my recent visit to Dublin. It is a monumental bookcase made for the Irish House of Lords presumably between 1750 and 1760, which since 1893 has been resting on the balcony of the famous library of Trinity College. It is said that a similar case made for the same purpose is in Leinster House, now occupied by the Irish Dáil. The bookcase, strongly Burlington-Palladian in design, consists of a full Corinthian order with a heavy entablature, two cases of shelves protected by double-glazed doors on either side of the central pilaster, and a podium containing cupboards. Flanking the outer pilasters are extensions about a foot wide, and these, between cornice and podium, are faced with three vertical panels. The field of each panel is filled with applied rococo carving (Fig. 8) which is so close in form and style to that found on the best of the Philadelphia high chests (Fig. 9) and to some of the Dublin ceilings (Figs. 6 and 7) that their relationship is undeniable. This is the only time I have seen rococo ornament in woodcarving used with such surface-covering dynamics elsewhere than in Philadelphia.

In addition to this stylistic parallel, a somewhat cursory study of the mid-eighteenth-century furniture in the National Museum of Ireland produced many indications that a much closer connection existed between Dublin and Philadelphia craftsmen than has hitherto been generally recognized. Two significant parallels may be cited. The first is a type of pad or club foot, in common Irish use and also not unusual in Philadelphia, and a related type of trifid foot, found in both these areas but very rarely if ever encountered on English pieces; the distinctive feature is a socklike decoration probably derived from a much conventionalized shell. The second parallel is the accenting of the ends or ears of the bowed crest rail of a Chippendale chair with a shell or shell form, which occurs on certain Philadelphia productions and is also frequently found in Irish examples; I have seen no instance of it in English chairs. Since such features are primarily carver's embellishments we have here, in all probability, two instances of the direct influence of Irish taste and training on Philadelphia work.

Though much further research is necessary to establish or disprove the hypotheses here advanced it would seem that sufficient internal evidence is available for a productive start. The English, the Irish, and the American rococo all drew on a common reservoir of ornamental elements provided by France and Italy and secondarily by Holland and other European countries. Each used this common stock according to the demands of its particular tastes and needs, and transformed its borrowings in like manner. The suggestions offered in this essay are not intended to disqualify the *Director* and other English sources as important factors in the formation of the pre-Revolutionary decorative style of Philadelphia. That would be absurd. The stylistic data submitted, however, give strong evidence that the Philadelphia rococo drew on the independent contemporary Irish version of the style as much as on the English, if not more, and had practically no direct relationship with Continental sources. It seems indicated also that the close relationship between Irish and Philadelphia craftsmen came about by personal contact, a contact made possible and almost inevitable by extensive Irish migration to Pennsylvania during the first half of the eighteenth century.

I am greatly indebted in this exploratory quest to the Rt. Hon. Desmond Guinness, president of the Irish Georgian Society; to Dr. William O'Sullivan of the National Museum of Ireland; to Dr. Robert B. McDowell, tutor, lecturer, and junior dean of Trinity College, Dublin; and to Francis Hurst, deputy librarian, Trinity College.

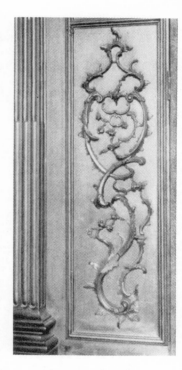

Fig. 8. Details of a bookcase made for the Irish House of Lords, Dublin, 1750-1760. This applied carving shows the transfer into wood of the plaster style of Figures 6 and 7. The free rhythmic informality of its composition should be compared with Figures 1 and 9. *Photograph by the author, by courtesy of the library of Trinity College, Dublin.*

Fig. 9. Detail of tympanum of a high chest, Philadelphia, 1765-1780. The kinship in design and feeling between this carving and that of Figure 8 and the plasterwork of Figures 6 and 7 is obvious. *Mabel Brady Garvan collection, Yale University.*

77

III Federal and Empire Styles

Both the Federal and Empire styles were characterized by the revival of interest in the arts of antiquity. The earlier, or Federal, phase of this neoclassical movement started in Philadelphia during the decade following the Revolution, and it lasted through the first decade of the nineteenth century. Archeological discoveries at Pompeii and Herculaneum in the mid-eighteenth century led interest throughout Europe in drawing artistic inspiration directly from the remains of the Classical past, instead of from Renaissance sources. In both architecture and furniture design, the works of the Adam brothers in England established some of the main characteristics which would appear slightly later in American Federal furniture. In both forms and colors, there was a new interest in delicacy and lightness. The long-favored cyma curve and cabriole leg were abandoned in favor of straight, attenuated outlines. The use of contrasting inlays and veneers gave the surfaces of furniture a coloristic, and sometimes pictorial, quality. The two most influential English design books for American Federal furniture were George Hepplewhite's *Cabinet Maker and Upholsterer's Guide,* first published in 1788, and Thomas Sheraton's *The Cabinet-Maker's and Upholsterer's Drawing Book* of 1791-1794.

Milo Naeve's article on the chairs produced by Daniel Trotter is an appropriate starting point for a consideration of Philadelphia Federal furniture, for the palmette motif on the backs of these chairs marks them as being transitional from the Chippendale to Federal styles. For the reader wishing to know more about Trotter, Anne Castrodale Golovin's article, "Daniel Trotter: Eighteenth-Century Philadelphia Cabinetmaker," in the sixth *Winterthur Portfolio* (1970), is recommended highly. The article by Marian S. Carson on Philadelphia Sheraton furniture surveys the achievements of the city's cabinetmakers in this style. It should be noted that this article, plus a loan exhibition at the Philadelphia Museum of Art in 1953, did much to publicize the works of Philadelphia'a best-known cabinetmakers in the Sheraton style, Henry Connelly and Ephraim Haines. Anthony Stuempfig's article on fancy chairs from Philadelphia presents excellent documentary materials on an often overlooked aspect of Federal furniture. Although Hornor illustrated the great pier table by Barry in 1935, forty years were to pass until Robert Trump's article expanded our knowledge about this very talented cabinetmaker.

Our current state of knowledge about Philadelphia Federal furniture still suffers from many gaps. The relationship between Philadelphia and Baltimore Federal furniture merits further study. Moreover, it is surprising that relatively few names of cabinetmakers can be associated with signed or labelled pieces. Representative of skilled Philadelphia cabinetmakers of the Federal period who merit more study is John Aitken, who made a desk and bookcase for George Washington in 1797.

The Empire style started in the Napoleonic courts, and it made its debut as an avant-garde style in New York and Philadelphia about 1810. As conceived in France, this style employed many forms and ornamental devices drawn from ancient Roman architecture, along with various eclectic elements. In general, the style reached America as it was transmitted through English interpretations. The pier table by Joseph B. Barry and Son, made for Louis Clapier between 1812 and 1816, stands as one of the earliest datable examples of the fully-developed Empire style in Philadelphia cabinetwork. It is difficult to state when the Empire style ended in Philadelphia, for some elements of its designs lasted into the early Victorian period. Certainly the greatest name of all Philadelphia's Empire cabinetmakers is Anthony G. Quervelle, whose outstanding creations are discussed in two articles reprinted here. Due to limitations of space, only the first of Robert Smith's four-part series on Quervelle, which appeared in ANTIQUES between May, 1973, and January, 1974, could be included in this book.

Daniel Trotter
and his ladder-back chairs

BY MILO M. NAEVE, Secretary, Winterthur Museum

A former Winterthur Fellow, Mr. Naeve presents here fresh biographical information he has uncovered on a Philadelphia cabinetmaker, and a group of this maker's ladder-back chairs which invite further study.

THE POST-REVOLUTIONARY cabinetmaker Daniel Trotter was the fourth generation of a Quaker family to be active in the woodworking trades of Philadelphia. This competent craftsman and original designer imparted the skills and standards of his craft to the nineteenth century through his apprentice, partner, and son-in-law, Ephraim Haines.

Contemporary documents portray Daniel Trotter as an individual and as a craftsman. The copybook of his son Nathan, in the Trotter-Newbold papers at the Historical Society of Pennsylvania, lists the date of his birth as June 13, 1747. According to Elva Tooker's authoritative history of the Trotter family, published in *Nathan Trotter, Philadelphia Merchant* (Harvard University Press, 1955), Daniel was an orphan at the age of sixteen. Neither the name of the cabinetmaker to whom he was apprenticed nor the period of his service has been determined. On November 9, 1773, Daniel Trotter married nineteen-year-old Rebecca Conarroe. Among the witnesses who signed his marriage certificate, owned by Mrs. C. Raynor-Smith, were the cabinetmakers Stephen Mayfield, David Evans, John Webb, and Josiah Elfreth, a first cousin. Daniel Trotter's literary interests are indicated by his admittance to the Library Company of Philadelphia in 1789. His adherence to Quaker discipline resulted in double taxation in 1779 for his refusal to be identified with the Revolutionary cause. Rebecca Trotter died on February 25, 1797, after the birth of their tenth child; three years later Nathan Trotter wrote in his copybook that his mother's death had been a "close trial" to his father, who died on April 30, 1800. *Claypoole's American Daily Advertiser*, May 6, 1800, noted the cabinetmaker's death after a "lingering illness" and cited him as a ". . . well known and much respected inhabitant of this city." He was survived by seven children.

Within a year after his marriage Daniel Trotter opened a shop on Water Street, and in 1783 he obtained the title to a house and lot in Elfreth's Alley. He built a new house in the Alley about 1795. Philadelphia directories list the address of his shop in 1791 as 61 North Water Street and between 1795 and 1800 as 100 North Front Street.

The relationship between Daniel Trotter and his only known apprentice, Ephraim Haines, developed in the last decade of the eighteenth century. Haines was born on October 23, 1775, and is thought to have been apprenticed to Trotter in 1791 (ANTIQUES, April 1953, pp. 342-345). He was Trotter's partner by March of 1799, the date when the craftsmen first appear as co-signers

Fig. 1. One of a set of six ladder-back chairs for which Daniel Trotter billed Stephen Girard £19/0/0 on August 29, 1786. *Reproduced from the Girard collection, Founder's Hall, Girard College, by courtesy of the Trustees of the Estate of Stephen Girard, Deceased.*

in the shop's transactions. These records are included in a receipt book now owned by Theodore T. Newbold, which was kept by Daniel Trotter from 1794 to 1800. Nathan Trotter's copybook records that Ephraim Haines married Daniel Trotter's twenty-one-year-old daughter, Elizabeth, in 1799, and that their first son was appropriately named Daniel Trotter Haines.

After Daniel Trotter's death, Ephraim Haines advertised in the *Federal Gazette,* May 8, 1800, requesting a settlement of accounts with the former partnership of Trotter and Haines and announcing that he would continue to operate the shop in Front Street and to live in Elfreth's Alley. Elizabeth Haines died July 2, 1803, after the birth of their daughter. In 1804 Ephraim Haines was listed in the Philadelphia directories as the proprietor of a lumberyard, and from 1806 to 1813 as the owner of a cabinet warehouse. In 1806 and 1807 he supplied Stephen Girard with a set of ebony furniture for which he commissioned the same carver, John Morris, and the same upholsterer, George Bridenhart, as had been employed by his former partner (ANTIQUES, April 1953, pp. 342-345). Haines was listed in the Philadelphia directories in 1813 at a new home and shop address and was described as a lumber merchant until 1833. The inventory of his estate, taken in Philadelphia, December 11, 1837, gives no indication of his occupation as a cabinetmaker.

Daniel Trotter increased his production by employing other craftsmen in addition to the assistance he may have had in his shop. The account book of John Janvier

of Cantwell's Bridge (later Odessa, Delaware), in the Delaware State Archives, records that between July 1795 and September 1796 Daniel Trotter commissioned him to produce furniture valued at £245/5/10 (ANTIQUES, January 1942, pp. 37-39; October 1956, p. 369). Daniel Trotter's receipt book records his employment of specialists in the trades allied to cabinetmaking that developed in Philadelphia in the last half of the eighteenth century. He paid John Howe and Robert Taylor for turning; John Morris and James Reynolds for carving; and George Bridenhart, Andrew Henry, Thomas Jaquett, and David Thompson for upholstering. The cabinetmaker also exchanged objects made in his shop for materials. A ledger of the Philadelphia cabinetmaker David Evans, in the Historical Society of Pennsylvania, reveals that in 1779 Daniel Trotter exchanged finished work, such as the top of a tea table, for lumber used in making coffins.

A variety of forms were sold in Trotter's shop. The administration papers of his estate, in the Baker Library of the Harvard School of Business, reveal that at his death furniture in the Trotter-Haines shop was valued at $1,571.91 and was consigned to Henry Connelly, an auctioneer. Connelly's advertisement in *Claypoole's American Daily Advertiser,* May 17, 1800, listed the following "New Mahogany Furniture" as "Being part of the stock on hand belonging to the estate of Daniel Trotter, deceased": "Bureaus, circular and square; Chairs of different patterns, hair cloth and brass nailed seats, etc.; arm and easy do.; Dining tables, card, sideboard and breakfast do. different patterns; Wardrobe and desks; Cradles, bason stands and candle do.; Field, high and low post, and trundle Bedsteads mahogany and painted; A number of well finished mahogany portable writing desks, with sundry other articles in the cabinetmaking line." A sofa is the only form mentioned in Daniel Trotter's receipt book which does not occur in the Connelly advertisement. The production of coffins is proved by

Fig. 2. Ladder-back chair attributed to Daniel Trotter by analogy with Fig. 1. This chair is No. 601 in the *Girl Scouts Loan Exhibition* catalogue, 1929. *Figs. 2 and 3, Henry Francis du Pont Winterthur Museum. Figs. 2, 3, 5, 6, 7 photographed by Gilbert Ask.*

Fig. 3. Detail of central carved ornament on stile of Fig. 2, identical with carving on chair of Fig. 1.

Trotter's account with David Evans and by a bill of 1793, in the Library Company of Philadelphia, in which the cabinetmaker charged Robert Dawson for a "Ridge Top Coloured Coffin." Trotter's receipt book records his payment to carvers for an extensive production of "stove plates" and "stove patterns," molds used in the sand-casting of iron. A group of bills owned by Theodore T. Newbold, which were rendered by the administrators of Daniel Trotter's estate against accounts that were not paid when the craftsman died, indicate that he frequently repaired furniture and that he made rockers as early as 1786, when James Carman was charged four shillings for "putting Rockers on a Chair."

The only extant furniture to be traced to Daniel Trotter's shop through documents was produced between 1786 and 1796 for Stephen Girard. The cabinetmaker's bills and the furniture of the financier have been preserved in Girard College, Philadelphia, and were published by William Macpherson Hornor in the *Blue Book, Philadelphia Furniture* (1935). The furniture at Girard College that specifically matches descriptions in the Trotter bills consists of two semicircular ends to a din-

ing table, a semicircular bureau, four bedsteads, and two sets of chairs. Most of this furniture is in a plain version of the Federal style; but one set of chairs made in 1786 (Fig. 1) is of particular interest.

These might be designated "slat-back" chairs, a term that occurs in John Janvier's accounts with Daniel Trotter. American acceptance of the form was a reflection of its popularity in England after the mid-eighteenth century. Although a document in Mr. Newbold's possession lists "1 Book Designs Cabinet work" that Ephraim Haines received from Daniel Trotter's estate, this book may not have been significant in Trotter's development of the ladder-back form. It does not appear in such popular design books as those of Chippendale, Manwaring, Hepplewhite, or Sheraton.

The 1786 Girard chairs represent an innovation in design by the Philadelphia cabinetmaker. For the design of the back, no English or American counterpart in pattern books or furniture has been established. Each stile is made from a single piece of wood from which the three horizontal divisions and the central ornament were carved. The stopped fluting on the outer two sides of the front legs, extending down from the top of the leg, as in English work, is another distinctive Trotter feature not found in the work of other American craftsmen.

On the basis of this documented example, several chairs have been attributed to Daniel Trotter in recent years. A chair in the collection of Colonel and Mrs. C. Raynor-Smith and another in the Winterthur Museum are identical. Another chair in the Winterthur Museum (Figs. 2, 3) is similar to that made for Stephen Girard in 1786 except that the front legs are straight, not tapered, and the feet are similar to those found on the

Fig. 4. One of a pair of ladder-back chairs attributed to Daniel Trotter. *Metropolitan Museum of Art.*

Fig. 5. Ladder-back chair with fretwork on the seat rail, attributed to Daniel Trotter. *Figs. 5-7, David Stockwell, Inc.*

82

Fig. 6. Ladder-back chair with a second motif in the carved ornament on stile, attributed to Daniel Trotter.

Fig. 7. Detail of central carved ornament on stile of the chair in Fig. 6, identical with carving on the chair in Fig. 8.

Marlborough leg in furniture of the Chippendale period. A pair of chairs in the American Wing of the Metropolitan Museum is almost identical with the Girard chair in the design of the back but has a straight seat rail and straight front legs without fluting (Fig. 4). Another variant is similar to this pair but has the added feature of fretwork applied to the seat rail (Fig. 5). This fretwork, which is identical with that on several Philadelphia high chests of the Chippendale period, could be the work of Daniel Trotter or of an unidentified craftsman who supplied several cabinetmakers.

Daniel Trotter did not confine this type of ladder back to side chairs. Edgar G. Miller illustrates in *American Antique Furniture* (Baltimore, 1937) a settee composed of three chair backs and an armchair, as well as a side chair, all made with backs identical with that of the Girard chair but with straight legs and straight seat rails. A variation in the design of the back occurs in two chairs in which scrolls flanking a leaf—suggestive of the anthemion motif—are substituted for the plumelike design (Figs. 6, 7, and 8); the chairs have a straight seat rail and molded, tapered front legs. Figure 8 does not have the usual back stretcher and has straight legs. A pair of chairs owned by Mr. and Mrs. Harlan Slack correspond to the chair in Figure 8 in all features except that the seat rails are serpentine.

All these versions of Daniel Trotter's design for Stephen Girard have slip seats and match the Girard chair in such construction features as the Philadelphia technique of mortising the side rails of the seat through the back legs. The primary woods are mahogany, usually of a light color. Secondary woods are generally mahogany or pine. The cabinetmaker's receipt book records his purchase of large quantities of these woods, as well as poplar and cedar. Daniel Trotter's original combination of decorative elements in these chairs forms a unique contribution to American cabinetmaking.

Fig. 8. Ladder-back chair similar to Fig. 6. *Ginsburg and Levy, Inc.*

83

Sheraton's influence in

BY MARIAN S. CARSON

Chair made in 1807 by Ephraim Haines and one attributed to Henry Connelly, showing in the feet the key to their makers' individualities. Haines used a bulbous pointed terminal, Connelly a crisp spade. *Courtesy: above, of the Board of City Trusts; below, of the Philadelphia Museum of Art.*

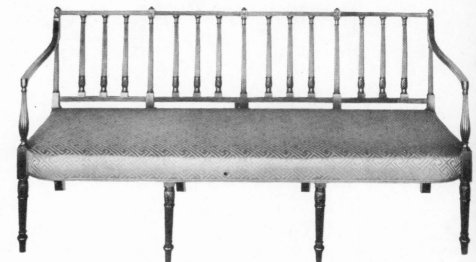

Chair-back settee of dark ebony, part of the "Front Parlour" furniture made by Haines in 1807 for Stephen Girard. *Courtesy of the Board of City Trusts.*

THE STUDY OF AMERICAN FURNITURE is no longer in the pioneer stage. We can give it a perspective. Twenty-five years ago a label of Henry Connelly, a then unknown name, was noticed on a Philadelphia Sheraton kidney-shaped sideboard. Currently an exhibition of his work and that of a contemporary, Ephraim Haines, is presented by the Philadelphia Museum of Art through the efforts of its curators and some interested members of its Board. Collectors and students may share the results of their search for the truth about two exponents of the Philadelphia Sheraton school.

Henry Connelly had indeed made several pieces of turned, reeded-leg furniture for an early Philadelphia banker, Henry Hollingsworth, who lived on South Third Street. The labeled sideboard and matching kidney-shaped side tables were recognized as important discoveries. The turnings consisted of an unusual form of

bulbous knee, tapered, reeded leg, and round spade foot. A new type was defined and hailed as characteristic of Connelly. It was in fact the basis for widespread attribution of all pieces with similar turnings, both the plain, like the Hollingsworth dining-room furniture, and those with flat oak-leaf bulb carvings later brought to attention as of the same genre as the key Connelly pieces.

The story did not long remain simplified. The *Blue Book of Philadelphia Furniture* in 1935 documented a large group of Stephen Girard's parlor furniture that had features associated with Connelly's recognized work, but the original bills, rendered in 1807, proved Connelly had nothing to do with these chairs, settees, and tables. Another cabinetmaker, Ephraim Haines, working on North Front Street, was making what at first glance seemed identical to furniture made by Connelly on Spruce Street. Thus, it seems desirable to a coterie of students that the

Philadelphia

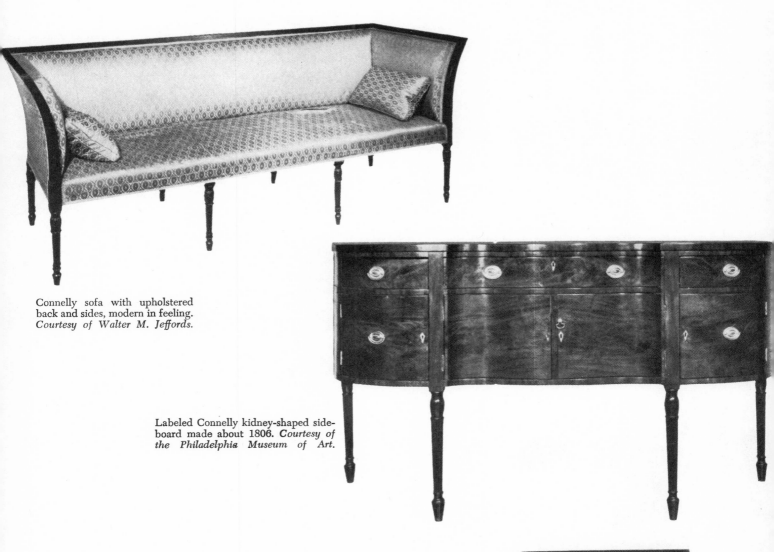

Connelly sofa with upholstered back and sides, modern in feeling. *Courtesy of Walter M. Jeffords.*

Labeled Connelly kidney-shaped sideboard made about 1806. *Courtesy of the Philadelphia Museum of Art.*

Reading or music stand on carved pedestal base, attributed to Connelly. *Courtesy of Walter M. Jeffords.*

similarities and differences of the Connelly and Haines furniture be compared and, if possible, that their pieces be related to others unsigned and unaccounted for through documentation. Indeed, to understand these two cabinet- and chairmakers closely working in the Sheraton tradition, the entire field of Philadelphia makers must be surveyed.

Between the first census in 1790 and the next one in 1810, the population of the old city and "liberties" more than doubled to close to 100,000. The establishment of the national government gave impulse to the growth of its capital. Artisans came from Europe in large numbers, and among these was the Connelly family, to whom Henry was born in either 1769 or 1770. He first appeared in the directories in 1801 and worked steadily until just before his death in 1826. Apprentices were placed in the bustling shops in this land of opportunity, and among

85

Trade card and label used by Henry Connelly about 1800-1804. Second state gives address at 44 Spruce Street. *Courtesy of Joseph J. Curran.*

Pedestal table attributed to Connelly. A popular type found in numbers in Philadelphia, but rarely of this quality. *Courtesy of Walter M. Jeffords.*

Carved dolphin base and brass paw feet are important details on this table made in 1818 for Stephen Girard by Henry Connelly. *Courtesy of the Board of City Trusts.*

Extension dining table attributed to Connelly. Paw feet similar to those on Girard's 1818 piece were used from 1795 onward in Philadelphia. *Courtesy of Walter M. Jeffords.*

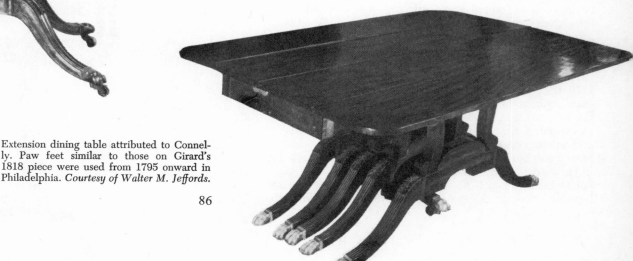

these was Ephraim Haines, born in Burlington "10th mo. 23rd 1775," as his Society of Friends wrote the date. In 1791 he was apprenticed to learn the art and mystery of the craft from Daniel Trotter, Philadelphia cabinet- and chairmaker. By 1799 he became a partner in Trotter's business and married his daughter. When Trotter died the next year, Haines succeeded to the business at 100 North Front Street.

With the dawn of the new century Connelly and Haines each had his own establishment. The former worked first at 16 Chestnut, then 44 Spruce, next South Fourth and finally at 8 Library (now Sansom) Street, according to the directories from 1801 through 1824. He became wealthy through his work for Stephen Girard, Henry Hollingsworth, Manuel Eyre, Captain John Carson, Richard Ashbridge, Charles Graff, and others, including almost certainly Hollingsworth's friends and neighbors, the Willings. His positively identified pieces are few but sufficient for a knowledge of his art. His trade card, also used as a label, was engraved by John Draper when Connelly went to 16 Chestnut Street about 1800, and altered on his removal to Spruce Street. It pictures fashionable furniture of types he presumably made at the time: a bow-front bureau, a slant-top knife box, and an inlaid console table with his monogram worked into the center—pieces not only never found, but also difficult to attribute. The discovery of one of these Hepplewhite forms with Connelly's label would indeed broaden our knowledge of his repertoire, for only by the study of actual Connelly pieces can we know his work.

The Hollingsworth furniture bears the label used after 1803. It is believed the two side tables and sideboard were made for Henry Hollingsworth upon his marriage on October 6, 1806, to Sarah, daughter of Joshua Humphreys of "Pont Reading." The style falls into the category of furniture inspired by that great English designer, Thomas Sheraton. His *Cabinet-Maker and Upholsterer's Drawing Book,* issued in sections between 1791 and 1794, contained in all 113 plates. This London publication in turn was the basis of the Philadelphia *Journeymen Cabinet and Chairmakers' Book of Prices,* 1795. Here were outlined the various basic sideboards: straight-front, round-front, serpentine, elliptic hollow on each side, or "ovalo" corners "with eliptick middle," as Connelly's Hollingsworth sideboard might well be described.

Later, the "Sideboard cellaret," as it was termed, was a standard six feet long and two feet two inches wide, and an extra charge was made for any change in these proportions, whether larger or smaller. Here the purchaser might have an even wider choice, including a straight front, pedestal end, "round front," "serpentine," "ovalo corners," or "with eliptick middle and eliptick hollow on each side," or "with eliptick middle, Ogee on each Side." In the present exhibition examples of sideboards demonstrate the variety of body outlines on what are basically similar sideboards with four or six round legs of the same general turnings, and with the addition of carvings, crossbanding, veneers that form square or oval panels, and other details. Many sideboards are in fact attributable to Henry Connelly by comparison with the Museum's labeled one.

Late in his career Henry Connelly made for Girard a commodious and, it must be admitted, cumbersome mahogany sideboard resting on large animal-paw feet. Its heavy Empire feeling is reason enough for excluding it here. Connelly followed current fashions all his working days—no doubt a reason for his success. Certainly he even made use of the twist leg among other novelties.

The year 1811 marks another epoch in the study of Connelly. In this year he first worked for Stephen Girard, whom he continued to satisfy over a period of years. In 1818 Connelly made a pair of card tables, distinguished by their lyre-shaped pedestals which are formed by dolphins, and three curving fluted legs ending in brass paw feet. The cross band of light wood surrounding the concave mahogany base is the only instance positively known of Connelly's inlaid work which was pictured perhaps as early as 1800 on his trade card. Here, too, is the first piece of brass paw-footed furniture to be traced to a Philadelphia maker.

The greatest variety of tables was undertaken in the Sheraton style—tables for every room and every use. Nevertheless it is in the sewing, dressing, and washstand tables that the imagination of designers and their interpreters went wild. Possibly no one lady would have a table like another!

While Connelly received Girard's custom beginning in 1811, he did so only because Ephraim Haines, with whom Girard had long dealt, declined his old business to operate a successful mahogany yard. Due to the preservation of their original bills, it is possible to know the work of Ephraim Haines and his one-time partner, Daniel Trotter, beginning in 1786 and for a period of more than twenty years. At first their ball-and-claw-foot furniture was in the simplest style of the Philadelphia Chippendale school. Working from English patterns, Haines nevertheless gave his later productions an originality of treatment that has led to the recognition of the Haines style identified by the swelled bulb feet.

From his bills we learn that Girard paid over five hundred dollars for the black ebony furniture used in the front parlor in 1807. It is happily all in existence, except for four missing stools. The records of this purchase reveal an extension of the specialized crafts of the last half of the eighteenth century and the beginning of mass production that was to alter the character and quality of furniture making. Barney Schumo turned the legs and quite properly charged a stiff price for cutting the dense ebony and a slight sum for the mahogany. John R. Morris had the difficult task of carving oak leaves on the knees and the splats in this notoriously hard wood, probably using Sheraton's Plate 11 dated 1794, or some drawing derived from it. George Bridenhart upholstered the furniture in crimson velvet, and then Robert Pullen (later treasurer of the New Theatre) applied "Plated Beading" or brass-headed nails probably in a festooned pattern. Each step in the making of the ebony furniture was a separate one calling upon the services of importer, sawyer, turner, carver, chairmaker, upholsterer, metalworker, yet withal it is the production of Ephraim Haines.

Connelly or Haines? Or one of literally a hundred others who had established shops in Philadelphia between 1800 and 1820? It is obvious from the *Journeymen Cabinetmakers' Book of Prices, 1795* that any workman might be called upon to frame and ornament the great variety of then current pieces. Any cabinet- and chairmaker operating a shop on the principal thoroughfares of Philadelphia, expecting the trade of the neighborhood, would have the ability to supply designs and materials from which the journeyman then wrought the furniture under the supervising eye and helpful hand of the master.

It is a dangerous oversimplification not justified by contemporary practice to attribute all turned spade feet to Connelly, and all turned bulbous feet to Haines, yet that generality is at present indicated. Until overwhelming contrary data appear, the distinguishing feature of the furniture of Henry Connelly is the round spade foot, and of Ephraim Haines the bold bulb above a long turned terminal, just as we still accept the swelled tapering foot, recognized years ago, as a sign of Duncan Phyfe.

Marble mosaic top in mahogany frame made by Haines in 1807 at the time he finished the long-famous ebony suite. *Courtesy of the Board of City Trusts.*

William Haydon and William H. Stewart

Fancy-chair makers in Philadelphia

BY ANTHONY A. P. STUEMPFIG

ADDING TO THE PUBLISHED record of cabinetmakers and related artisans, and identifying existing documented examples of their work as well as some of their patrons, is one of the most rewarding aspects of scholarship in the decorative arts. The late eighteenth- and early nineteenth-century directories of Philadelphia list vast numbers of craftsmen whose work has yet to come to light, while family records and cabinetmakers' account books reveal the complex pattern of patronage, often of several makers by many generations of the same family.

The Wistars and Haineses of Philadelphia are typical of prominent early nineteenth-century patrons in that city.

Family records and furniture still owned by their descendants show that the cabinetmakers from whom they ordered furniture include William Savery, Jonathan Gostelowe, Daniel Trotter, Jacob Wayne, Jacob Super, Duncan Phyfe, and the previously unpublished fancy-chair making firm of William Haydon and William H. Stewart. Haines family furniture made by Wayne and Super will be discussed in future issues; pieces made for this family by Haydon and Stewart are presented here.

Reuben Haines* was born on February 8, 1786, in Germantown, Pennsylvania, the son of Caspar Wistar Haines and Hannah Marshall. His ancestors included some of the first Quaker settlers of Germantown (now part of Philadelphia), who in about 1690 built Wyck, the family house into which Reuben moved shortly after his marriage. His wife, Jane Bowne, born on January 31, 1792, was descended from another prominent Quaker family and lived in the ancestral Bowne house built in 1661 in Flushing, Long Island. Reuben and Jane were married on May 13, 1813, in the Liberty Street Meeting House in lower Manhattan. After their marriage they lived for a short time at Wyck until the house they rented at 300 Chesnut (today spelled Chestnut) Street in Philadelphia was ready for them. In 1820 they moved permanently back to Wyck and gave up the Chesnut Street house. For Chesnut Street they ordered furniture which they later took to Wyck, where some of it remains today. Wyck belongs to the last living descendant by marriage of Reuben and Jane Haines.

Haydon and Stewart, who were partners from 1809 to 1814, were among the craftsmen from whom Reuben and Jane Haines bought furniture, as a study of family records shows. Haydon is first listed in the Philadelphia directories

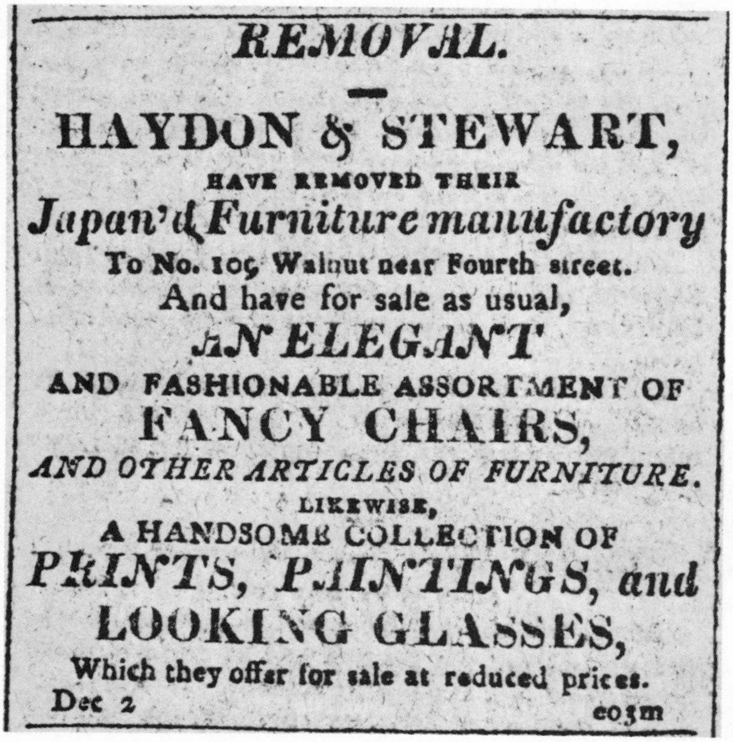

REMOVAL.
—
HAYDON & STEWART,
HAVE REMOVED THEIR
Japan'd Furniture manufactory
To No. 109, Walnut near Fourth street.
And have for sale as usual,
AN ELEGANT
AND FASHIONABLE ASSORTMENT OF
FANCY CHAIRS,
AND OTHER ARTICLES OF FURNITURE.
LIKEWISE,
A HANDSOME COLLECTION OF
PRINTS, PAINTINGS, and
LOOKING GLASSES,
Which they offer for sale at reduced prices.
Dec 2   eo3m

Fig. 1. Advertisement published on December 2, 1812, in *Poulson's American Daily Advertiser* (Philadelphia). *Pennsylvania Historical Society.*

Fig. 2.   One of two armchairs in a set of two dozen chairs made in Philadelphia by William Haydon and William H. Stewart and bought in 1812 by Reuben Haines. Maple and yellow poplar, originally painted with graining in imitation of satinwood (none of the original finish remains today), rush seat; height 32½ inches. *Except as noted, all objects illustrated are privately owned and photographs are by Cortlandt V. D. Hubbard.*

Fig. 3.   Side chair *en suite* with Fig. 2.
Height 33 inches.

in 1800 as an ''ornamental painter'' at 78 Dock Street. The following year he is listed as having a ''japann'd furniture manufactory'' at the same address. The terms ornamental painter and japanner were often used interchangeably during this period in such contexts. When Haydon took Stewart as a partner in 1809 they were listed first as ornamental painters at 77 Dock Street and the following year at the same address as ''fancy japanned chair and cornish [cornice] makers.'' They moved in 1812 to 109 Walnut Street, as they announced in a local newspaper, *Poulson's American Daily Advertiser* (Fig. 1). William Haydon after 1814 is listed variously as an ornamental

painter or a fancy-chair manufacturer at 109 Walnut Street. The city directory lists him in 1825 as a chair ornamenter at George Street above Tenth and from 1829 to 1833 as an ornamental painter at 204 Cherry Street. As he is not listed after that, it is presumed that he died in 1833. Stewart is listed after his partnership with Haydon at various addresses until 1836 as an ornamental painter, japanner and gilder, and fancy-chair maker.

A set of maple and yellow-poplar fancy chairs at Wyck (Figs. 2, 3), known to have been made by Haydon and Stewart, is documented by family records of 1812 and 1813. At that time there were seven other fancy-chair

Fig. 4. Bill dated December 12, 1812,
in Haines family papers, from Haydon and Stewart
to Reuben Haines for two dozen chairs.

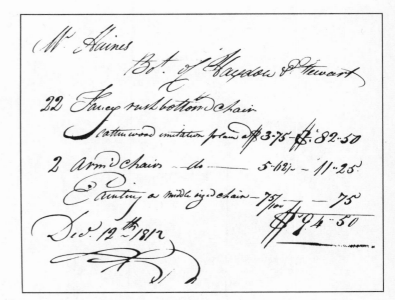

Fig. 5. Entry dated January 9, 1813,
in Reuben Haines' account book recording payment
to Haydon and Stewart for the two dozen chairs.

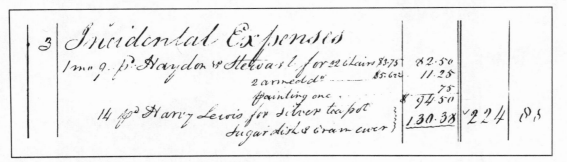

Fig. 6. Receipt dated January 9, 1813—in Reuben Haines'
book of receipts—from Haydon and Stewart
for full payment by Reuben Haines for the two dozen chairs,
noting further that the firm agrees
to "repaint the seats without charge in the spring."

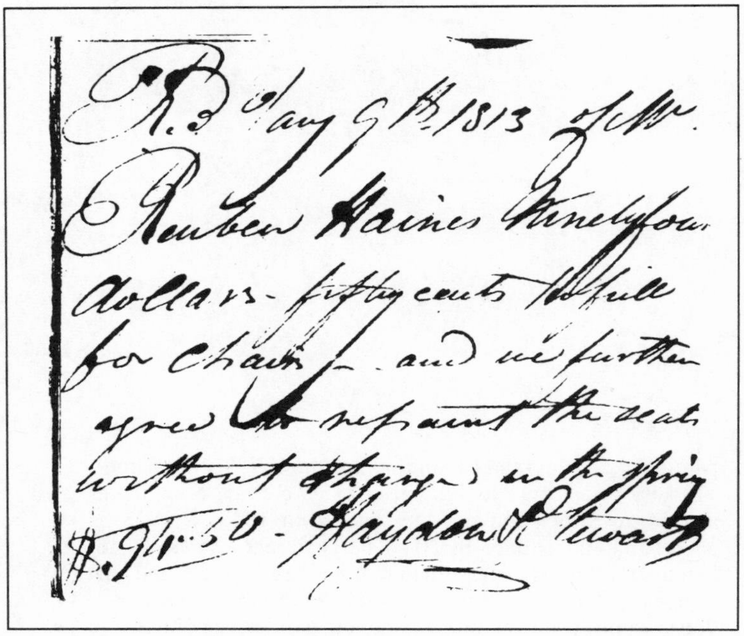

manufactories in Philadelphia, those of Bird, Burden, De-lavau, Halzel, Mitchell, Patterson and Gerro, and Rolph. Some of these were eighteenth-century craftsmen still in business, others were their sons. There were also seven ornamental painters and one japanner, all of whom were probably involved in the production and decoration of fancy chairs and other japanned furniture. The manufacturing of fancy chairs was thus a thriving craft. These chairs were used not only in nearly every room in the house but also in vast numbers in taverns and other commercial establishments. Patrons of fancy- and windsor-chair makers, such as Stephen Girard, ordered impressive numbers of chairs to be exported and sold as venture cargo in the Southern states, the Indies, and sometimes as far away as South Africa.

The set of twenty-two side chairs and two armchairs at Wyck today is referred to in a bill dated December 12, 1812, from Haydon and Stewart (Fig. 4) and in Reuben Haines' account book (Fig. 5). An advertisement in *Poulson's American Daily Advertiser* (to which Haines subscribed) dated ten days earlier announced their move to 109 Walnut Street and described their stock, which they offered at reduced prices (Fig. 1). These "Fancy rushbottomd *[sic]* chairs sattinwood imitation plain" were originally painted (the contemporary term would have been "japanned") in imitation of graining to resemble one of the most fashionable woods used by the foremost cabinetmakers of the late Federal and early Empire periods. West Indian satinwood—in color and finish not unlike the finest

90

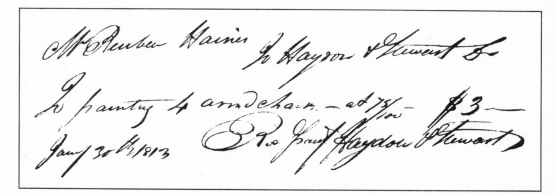

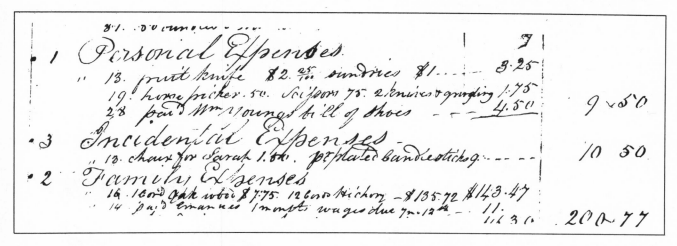

Fig. 8. Entry dated August 13, 1813, in Reuben Haines account book recording payment for a chair (Fig. 9) for Reuben and Jane Haines' first child, Sarah.

curly and bird's-eye maple—was used less extensively although somewhat longer here than in England. By about 1810 native burl ash and bird's-eye maple were beginning to be used quite frequently by American cabinetmakers. A set of twenty-four chairs of solid satinwood would have been extremely expensive. Haydon and Stewart's more economical versions were nevertheless very fashionable: the fretwork on the backs of the chairs he made for the Haines family is typical of the work found on English chairs of the Regency period. The chairs at Wyck thus represent a desire on the part of Reuben and Jane Haines to furnish their house on Chesnut Street in the newest fashion.

A receipt dated January 9, 1813, for full payment for the chairs (Fig. 6) notes that Haydon and Stewart "agree to repaint the seats without charge in the spring." Wooden seats such as those found on windsor and other plank-bottomed chairs were not the only ones that might have been repainted occasionally or frequently. The rush seats on the majority of fancy chairs were also painted in an opaque color which was generally very close to the natural color

Fig. 9. Child's chair made by Haydon and Stewart to match the set of twenty-four chairs Reuben Haines bought from the same firm the previous year. Height 29½ inches.

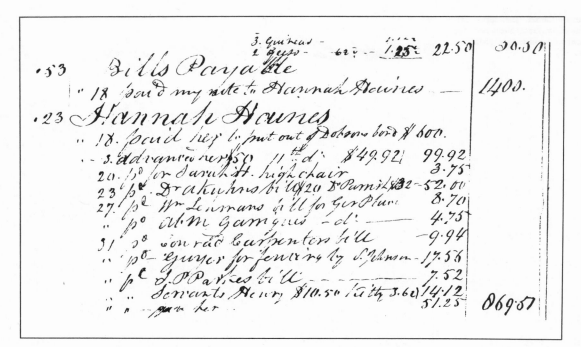

.53   Bills Payable
   " 18 pai'd my note to Hannah Haines —   1400.

.23 Hannah Haines
   " 18. paid her to put out of Dobsons bord $ 600.
   " 3. Advance week 50   11 $ d. $49.92   99.92
   20. p.d for Sarah H. high chair   3.75
   23 p.d Dr akuhns bi 20 $ Pumil $ 32 – 52.00
   27. p.d Wm Lemmans bill for Ger Plam   8.70
   "   p.d at M Gamgus – d. ——   4.75
   31 p.d con rad Carpenters bill   –9.94
   "   p.d guyer for fencing by S. Johnson –17.56
   "   p.d J.P.Parkes bill — — —   7.52
   "   "   Servants Henry $10.50 Catty 3.60) 14.12
   "   "   gave her   51.25   0696?

Fig. 10. Entry dated December 12, 1813,
in Reuben Haines' account book recording payment
for a high chair (Fig. 11) for Sarah.

Fig. 11. High chair made by Haydon and Stewart
to match the set of twenty-four chairs
Reuben Haines bought from the same firm the previous year.
Height 34 inches.

of the rush, with varnish, or (most commonly found) with
shellac which was sometimes tinted with japanning color.
The Haines chairs could have been repainted purely for
appearance, or to preserve the rush from dehydration and
deterioration, or to protect the sitter's clothes from the
roughness of the rush. Close examination of a number of
rush-seated fancy chairs in other private and public collections shows that most of them had painted seats, generally
in earth colors and in rare cases with two shades, corresponding to the rush work. In most instances the paint was
applied quite thinly and has worn away in places where
it would have been visible. On the chairs at Wyck, no
trace of the original finish remains. Research has failed
to turn up Philadelphia fancy chairs like the Haines chairs
with the original decoration, but other chairs of the period
exist with simulated satinwood decoration so that the original japanning on the Haines chairs may be easily imagined.

A receipt dated January 30, 1813 (Fig. 7), indicates that
Haydon and Stewart painted four armchairs for Reuben
Haines. These chairs are no longer at Wyck and it is not
known what type of chair they were, though they were
very probably windsor armchairs used both inside and
outside the house and thus in need of frequent repainting.

Later that year, as documented by a memorandum dated
August 13 in the Haines family records (Fig. 8), Haydon
and Stewart made a child's chair for the Haineses' first
child, Sarah (Fig. 9). Except for the front legs and the
small scale of the chair, it is identical to the other twenty-
four. On December 12, 1813, the family records (Fig. 10)

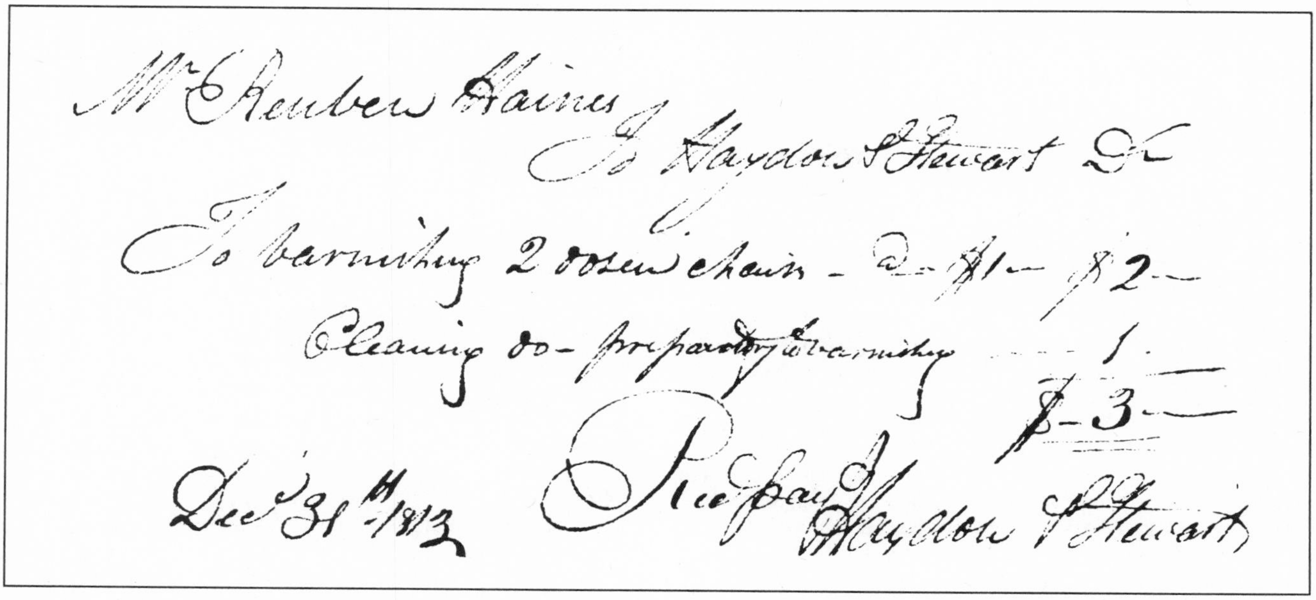

Fig. 12.   Receipt dated December 31, 1813, from Haydon and Stewart
to Reuben Haines for payment by Reuben Haines
for cleaning and varnishing two dozen chairs.

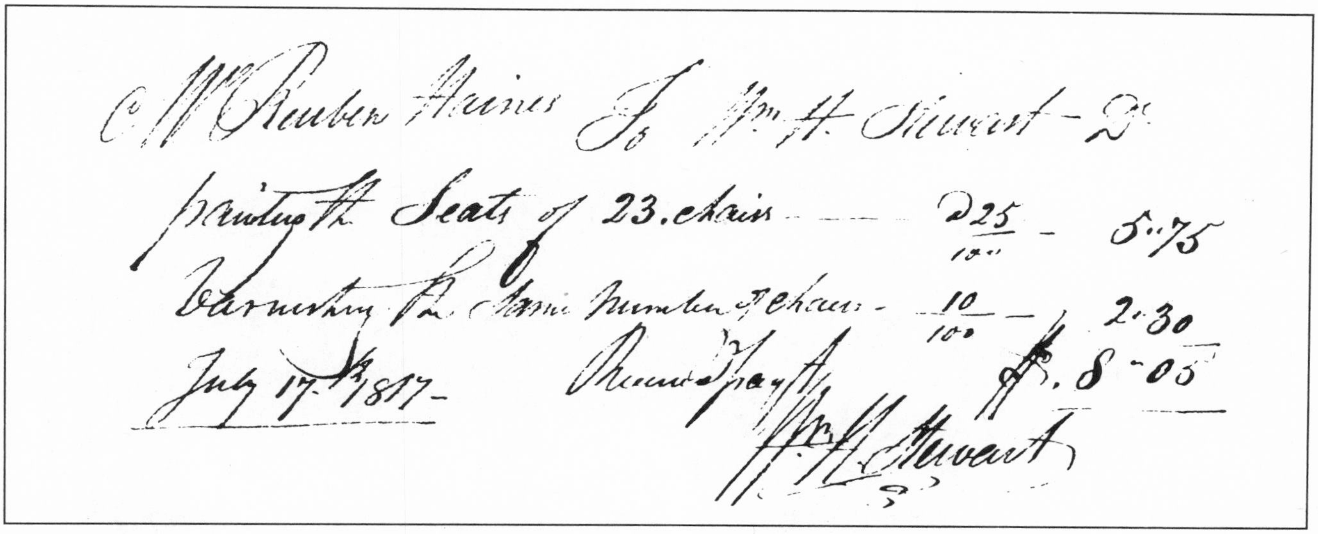

Fig. 13.   Receipt dated July 17, 1817, from William H. Stewart
for payment by Reuben Haines for painting the seats
of twenty-three chairs and varnishing the same chairs.

show payment to Haydon and Stewart for a high chair for Sarah, which matched the set of twenty-four (Fig. 11). A receipt from Haydon and Stewart dated December 31, 1813 (Fig. 12), records payment for cleaning and varnishing the two dozen chairs. As a later receipt (Fig. 13), dated July 17, 1817, makes clear, the paint was used on the seats and the varnish on the japanned parts of the chair.

Documentation of this kind can lead us to a greater understanding of our American craftsmen and the intricacies of their arts. It also adds to what we know of the cultural and social background of our forebears and their relationship to the many gifted craftsmen who produced the treasures so sought after today.

*Reuben Haines was active in a number of important Philadelphia institutions: he served as secretary of the Philosophical Society, as a founder and president of the National Academy of Science, as a founder and board member of the short-lived Philadelphia Botanical Society, as a supporter of Peale's Museum (he also lent Rembrandt Peale money to go abroad on the grand tour and commissioned Peale to paint his portrait), and participated in other artistic and civic organizations. He invested in China Trade ventures, and was a friend of John James Audubon (he attempted to find support for the printing of *Birds of America* in Philadelphia), the naturalist Charles Lucien Jules Laurent Bonaparte, the architect William Strickland (who redesigned the Haines family house, Wyck, about 1824), and was himself a scientific agriculturist and a distinguished mineralogist and botanist.

93

Joseph B. Barry, Philadelphia cabinetmaker

BY ROBERT T. TRUMP

THE CAREER of the Philadelphia cabinetmaker Joseph B. Barry, born in Dublin and trained in London, spans the era of the new republic.[1] During this period there were a number of highly trained furniture craftsmen working in Philadelphia, chief among them Barry, whose earliest trade card reads "of London." Even though an impressive number of pieces of Philadelphia-made furniture of the early nineteenth century can be attributed to Barry with some degree of confidence, we know distressingly little about his earliest years in Philadelphia. He had arrived there by 1790, the year in which the Federal Congress moved from New York to Philadelphia and President George Washington established his own official residence in the town house of Robert Morris on Sixth Street below Market. The city, with a population of about 45,000, had recently been incorporated, and the state of Pennsylvania was suffering from the disruptions of drafting a new state constitution. During this period of chaotic change and noble aspirations, Barry arrived to launch himself in trade, although whether he worked first under an established master

cabinetmaker or began a shop under his own name is not known. In James Hardie's *Philadelphia Directory and Register* for 1794, Barry is listed as a partner of Alexander Calder at 75 Dock Street.[2] The following year, at the age of thirty-eight, he became a member of the firm of Lewis G. Affleck and Company.[3] It appears from this fragmentary evidence of the 1790's that Barry moved from firm to firm and address to address during his early years in Philadelphia.

What can be learned about Barry thereafter comes largely from his trade cards, his newspaper advertisements, and most of all from his furniture. For example, an advertisement that appeared in the *Columbian Museum & Savannah Advertiser* for October 5, 1798, announced Barry's arrival in Savannah with "Lately landed from Philadelphia and for sale at Messrs. Meins & Mackay's stores . . .A most compleat Assortment of Elegant and warranted well finished MAHOGANY FURNITURE."[4] His wares included plain and "Cillender" desks, bookcases, "Sophas," chairs, wine coolers, "Side Boards . . . Dining tables . . .

Fig. 1. Pier table attributed to Joseph B. Barry (1757-1838), Philadelphia, 1808-1810, mahogany with satinwood veneer; carving attributed to William Rush (1756-1833). *Henry Francis du Pont Winterthur Museum.*

Fig. 2. Eagle carved by William Rush, c. 1810; painted pine. Details in the carving of the head, beak, and feathers correspond to the carving of the eagles shown in Fig. 1. *Philadelphia Museum of Art.*

Card and Breakfast tables . . . Wardrobes . . . Circular and plain Bureaus. . . . The terms of sale are ready payment of cash, produce, or red cedar timber of certain dimensions.'' By the time this advertisement ran, the firm of Meins and Mackay was only about ten months old. Barry's professional relationship with the firm appears to have been short lived, for less than two months later, on November 23, 1798, he advertised in the same Savannah newspaper:

FURNITURE. The Subscriber wishes to inform the inhabitants of Savannah, as he means to return to Philadelphia, the first vessel that offers, That he will dispose of his elegant Furniture on Moderate terms for cash, produce or bills on New York or Philadelphia. Joseph B. Barry, At Mein's & Mackay's Stores under the Bluff.[5]

Philadelphia was the capital of the nation from 1790 until 1800 and the capital of Pennsylvania until 1799. At the beginning of the nineteenth century, even though the machinery of the national government had moved to Washington and the state government to Harrisburg, Philadelphia was considered the cultural center of the country because of its eminent scientific institutions and philosophical societies.

Fig. 3. Pier table made by Joseph B. Barry and Son, 1812-1816, for Louis Clapier of Philadelphia. This is considered the most important piece of labeled Barry furniture. *Collection of Mr. and Mrs. T. Wistar Brown.*

Fig. 4. Label on the table shown in Fig. 3.

Fig. 5. Joseph B. Barry and Son label from mahogany breakfront bookcase in Savannah, Georgia.

Fig. 6. Warehouse and showroom of Joseph B. Barry and Son, corner of Second and Union streets, Philadelphia. The photograph was taken between 1865 and 1875. Barry built this structure about 1804, renting out portions to various organizations and using it for retail showrooms for his furniture. The building was demolished recently. *Photograph by courtesy of Historical Commission, City of Philadelphia.*

Barry next turned up in Baltimore in search of new markets; he was a seasoned craftsman by now and offered his clients "CABINET FURNITURE, of the newest London and French patterns," prominent among which were marble-topped pier tables and corner tables, through an advertisement in the *Federal Gazette & Baltimore Daily Advertiser* of February 9, 1803.[6] In another advertisement in the same newspaper on May 9, 1803, he informed the public that he had moved from No. 130 Baltimore Street to No. 3 Light Street in Baltimore, where he had "just received from Philadelphia . . . large sets of Dining tables" among other furniture.[7] We may surmise that Barry used his shops and partnerships in Savannah and Baltimore as merchandising outlets for furniture made in his Philadelphia headquarters.

As one historian has written, "From the beginning of Jefferson's severe restraints on trade, in 1807, down to the close of the war [of 1812], there was a period of eight years in which imports were more or less excluded."[8] The effect of the embargo was to place pressure on local craftsmen to make use of indigenous materials. Fine brass mounts or furniture hardware, for example, which had traditionally been imported from Paris and London, were in short supply until after the conclusion of the war. For this and other reasons, American furniture made during the Federal period took on national as well as regional characteristics which help us today to identify and attribute it.

It has not been possible as yet to identify any pieces of furniture made by Barry during his first eighteen years

Fig. 7. Sofa attributed to Barry, c. 1805-1808. The sofa was made for Louis Clapier. *Private collection.*

in this country. The distinguished examples that can be attributed to him date from 1808 to 1825. It is my contention that Barry and the noted Philadelphia-born woodcarver William Rush became allied during this period and that together they executed some magnificent pieces of furniture. Charles F. Montgomery has previously suggested Barry as the possible maker of the grandiose mahogany and satinwood pier table in the Winterthur Museum (Fig. 1).[9] When the carving of the eagles on this table is compared with that on one of Rush's eagles in the Philadelphia Museum of Art (Fig. 2), the strong similarity in the heads, beaks, and feathers corroborates the suspicion of a partnership between the carver and the cabinetmaker. During this period Barry also formed a working partnership with his son which he announced on January 19, 1810, in the *Philadelphia Aurora General Advertiser:*

Joseph B. Barry, *Cabinet-Maker and Upholsterer,* Presents his grateful acknowledgements to his friends and the public in general for the very liberal encouragement he has so long experienced. He now respectfully informs them that he has this day taken into partnership, his Son, Joseph Barry. The business will in Future be conducted under the firm of JOSEPH B. BARRY & SON, (at the old established warehouse, No. 134, South Second street,) in the same extensive manner it has hitherto been, and hopes for a continuance of their patronage. They have now in their ware-rooms a variety of the newest and most fashionable Cabinet Furniture, superbly finished in the rich Egyptian and Gothic style, which they will dispose of on the most reasonable terms.

The reference to "the rich Egyptian and Gothic style" at this date anticipates Barry's transition from the early Federal style to his supreme achievement in the famous labeled pier table which he made for Louis Clapier of Philadelphia between 1812 and 1816 (Figs. 3 and 4).[10] The label on the Clapier table is badly foxed today; it was clearer when William MacPherson Hornor reproduced it in 1935 in his *Blue Book, Philadelphia Furniture.*[11] A later version of this label with minor variations is shown in Figure 5.[12] As Hornor has pointed out, the designs for the pieces of furniture shown in Barry's labels were taken from plates in the appendix to Thomas Sheraton's *The Cabinet-Maker and Upholsterer's Drawing-Book* dated no later than July 25, 1793.[13] Although the legend is barely legible in Figures 4 and 5, Barry's label reminded his customers of his willingness to ship furniture to the "West Indies or elsewhere." After having had shops during the 1790's at 75 Dock Street, 13 Union Street, and 148 South Third Street, Barry constructed a building on the corner of Second and Union streets about 1804 for a warehouse and showroom (Fig. 6).

In addition to the labeled pier table, Louis Clapier also owned a sofa (Fig. 7) which I feel can be attributed to Barry with a degree of certainty. The dog's heads (Fig. 8) on the arm supports and the ram's heads (Fig. 9) on the back rail of the sofa are typical of the animal carving that Barry incorporated into the furniture he made before the War of 1812. In those pieces made by Barry and his

Fig. 8. Detail of Fig. 7.

son after the war, not only was there a greater emphasis on figures in the carving but also a greater sense of ornateness and imported high style. Barry made a trip to Europe in 1811; upon his return he inserted the following advertisement in the *Philadelphia Aurora* for January 12, 1812:

Cabinet Ware-Rooms, No. 134 South Second Street. Jos. B. Barry Having lately returned from Europe informs their friends and the public, that during his stay in London and Paris, He made some selections of the Most Fashionable and Elegant Articles in Their Line, which in addition to their elegant stock on hand, forms a display of furniture, well worth the attention of the respectable citizens of Philadelphia.

This trip was the watershed in Barry's career, separating the more traditional Sheraton-style designs of his early career from the French Empire and Regency styles for which he is more famous.

[1]ANTIQUES, March 1940, p. 146.

[2]Dorothea N. Spear, *Bibliography of American Directories Through 1860* (Worcester, 1961), p. 274.

[3]William MacPherson Hornor Jr., *Blue Book, Philadelphia Furniture* (Philadelphia, 1935), p. 164.

[4]ANTIQUES, March 1967, p. 366.

[5]Mrs. Charlton M. Theus, *Savannah Furniture, 1735-1825* (Savannah, 1967), p. 86.

[6]Charles F. Montgomery, *American Furniture: The Federal Period* (New York, 1966), p. 369.

[7]*Ibid.*, p. 370.

[8]John Russell Young, *Memorial History of the City of Philadelphia* (New York, 1895), p. 440.

[9]Montgomery, *American Furniture*, pp. 366-367.

[10]Hornor, *Blue Book*, pp. 234-235, 246; Pls. 432-434.

[11]*Ibid.*, Pl. 432.

[12]Also illustrated in ANTIQUES, February 1954, p. 135. The earliest known version of this label was illustrated in ANTIQUES for July 1938, p. 36, and discussed in ANTIQUES for October 1938, pp. 206, 208.

[13]Hornor, *Blue Book*, Pl. 432.

Fig. 9. Detail of Fig. 7.

Philadelphia Empire furniture by Antoine Gabriel Quervelle

BY ROBERT C. SMITH, *University of Pennsylvania and Winterthur Museum*

FRENCH ARCHITECTS, painters, and craftsmen in the decorative arts played an important role in the development of the classical style in America during the second and third decades of the nineteenth century. This is particularly true of a group of cabinetmakers who settled in New York and Philadelphia and included, among others, Michel Bouvier, Joseph Brauwers, Charles Honoré Lannuier and his successor John Gruez, and Antoine Gabriel Quervelle. The last of these men has been mentioned on a number of occasions in ANTIQUES and elsewhere but no attempt has been made to reconstruct his career in this country or to assemble a representative group of his furniture. This can now be done, at least in part, thanks to recently found documents and to several hitherto unknown pieces bearing his label, on the basis of which other furniture can be attributed.

Antoine Gabriel Quervelle was born, according to the inscription on his tombstone in Old St. Mary's Roman Catholic cemetery in Philadelphia, in Paris in 1789. Nothing more is known of his early years. Like Lannuier, he may have belonged to a family of cabinetmakers, for there was a Jean-Claude Quervelle (1731-1778) who worked at Versailles as *ébéniste du garde-meuble de la Couronne.* Antoine Gabriel received his training during the Napoleonic era and may, like other young Frenchmen, have left France disillusioned after the fall of Bonaparte. The inventory of his household furnishings, at the Philadelphia city hall, filed at the time of his death, lists several engraved portraits of Napoleon, which suggests that Quervelle may have had a long-lived admiration for the Emperor.

The young French cabinetmaker was in Phil-

Fig. 1. Labeled mahogany pier table with white marble top. Typical of Quervelle's furniture of 1825-1830 are the gadrooned moldings, the vases, and the front scroll-paw supports decorated with acanthus leaves and grapevines. They are all derived from George Smith's *Cabinet-Maker and Upholsterer's Guide* (London, 1826 [1828]). The gilt pattern around the mirror comes from Plate LXXX. *Athenaeum of Philadelphia.*

99

adelphia early in 1817 if not before, for on January 30 of that year, in Old St. Joseph's Roman Catholic church, he married Louise Genevieve Monet, also of Paris, whose father, Pierre, is listed as a "machine maker" in the Philadelphia directories of this time. The Quervelles had two sons, Pierre Gabriel and Antoine Louis, born in 1817 and 1826 respectively, both of whom were baptized in Holy Trinity Church on Spruce Street. Mrs. Quervelle died on November 22, 1847, at the age of fifty-four. Her husband, beside whom she lies buried in Old St. Mary's churchyard, subsequently remarried and had a daughter, Caroline, named for his second wife. He died on July 31, 1856, aged sixty-seven.

Anthony G. Quervelle, as he was known in Philadelphia, is listed as a cabinetmaker in the city directories from 1820 until his death. He became a United States citizen on September 29, 1823, when he was living and working at Eleventh and Lombard Streets. In 1825 he moved to 126 South Second Street, where he opened his *United States Fashionable Cabinet Ware House* or *Cabinet and Sofa Manufactory* and where he lived until 1849, when he is listed as at 71 Lombard Street.

On Second Street Quervelle was a neighbor and friend of another French cabinetmaker, Michel Bouvier (see ANTIQUES, February 1962, p. 198), who owed him $1,250 at the time of his death. This was subsequently repaid to Quervelle's estate. Both Frenchmen competed in the early exhibitions of mechanical arts of the Franklin Institute, founded in 1824, which brought together the leading furniture makers of Philadelphia of the time: Joseph B. Barry, John Graham, John Jameson, John A. Stewart, E. and John Stiles, Robert West, and Charles H. White, as well as the specialists in fancy chairs, Joseph Burden and Alexander and I. H. Leacock, about whom practically nothing is known today.

The annual reports of the Franklin Institute give an unparalleled portrayal of taste and activity in the furniture field in the 1820's and attest the important role that Quervelle played in the exhibitions. At the second, held in the autumn of 1825, he showed two pier tables, which won him an honorable mention. In 1826 he displayed a "sideboard with American marble top" that was awarded a bronze medal. The next year Quervelle earned a silver medal for the best "cabinet book case and secretary." This piece, now at the Philadelphia Museum, was judged "a splendid piece of furniture from the establishment of this excellent workman," who according to the census of 1830 employed seven assistants (Bouvier had eleven). In 1828 Quervelle received a premium for the best sofa exhibited. In 1831 he showed a dressing table and a "Ladies Work Table" which were praised along with a dressing table by Joseph Barry, himself a judge, and a "globular" worktable by Bouvier, "the design of which is new, and the workmanship exquisite." (Probably this last was like the Regency examples described in ANTIQUES for June 1957, p. 553.)

Fig. 2. Quervelle's usual label (from Fig. 1). The number in the looking glass is the street number of his shop, 126 South Second Street.

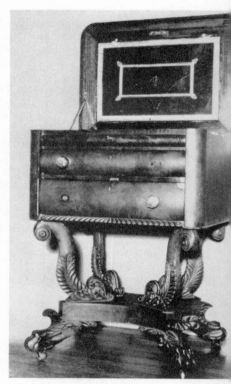

Fig. 3. Labeled mahogany worktable. This piece may have been exhibited at the Franklin Institute in 1831. It is fitted with ivory sewing utensils in ivory compartments. The inside of the top is of green leather tooled in gold. Work of this sort was done by William Tail of 225 Arch Street. *Collection of Mr. and Mrs. Robert Carter.*

Fig. 4. The rare Quervelle label engraved by Delmès (from Fig. 3).

In 1829 President Andrew Jackson furnished the East Room of the White House with lemon-color wallpaper, black and gold marble mantels, and a frieze of "24 gilded stars, emblematic of the States." The blue and gold moreen draperies, the Brussels carpet, the mirrors and lamps were purchased from the new firm of Louis Veron of Philadelphia, which between 1828 and 1837 conducted a "Fancy hardware etc. store" at 98 Chestnut Street. Veron, evidently a Frenchman, may have recommended Quervelle, who made a number of tables for the room. Five of these have survived.

It was apparently to this order that the successful cabinetmaker referred when in 1830 he advertised in the *United States Gazette* that "he has been employed as well by some of the first individuals of the city as by the general government." He thanked "his friends & the public, for the liberal patronage they have extended to his establishment" and urged them to inspect his "complete assortment of plain and elegantly ornamented Mantel and Cabinet Furniture." This he had described two years before in the *American Daily Advertiser* as including "very elegant sideboards, bureaux, sofas, dressing tables, wash stands, breakfast and dining tables mahogany and maple bedsteads." On both occasions he

solicited orders from outside the city, stating in 1830 that "orders from any part of the Union will be promptly executed on the most reasonable terms and gratefully received." He also advertised in Boston.

To prove that Quervelle grew wealthy from his work several writers have quoted a statement, which they attribute to John F. Watson's *Annals of Philadelphia,* to the effect that in 1846 he was worth upwards of $75,000, having "made his money by steady industry and strict economy." Unfortunately no such statement can be found in any edition of Watson's book. Evidence does exist, however, that Quervelle became a man of substance. When he died intestate in 1856 he owned a number of houses on Pine, Locust, and Lombard Streets, as well as a partnership in the Bristol Iron Works and a parcel of securities. He was a member of the French Benevolent and French Beneficial Societies and a stockholder in the newly founded Philadelphia Academy of Music, which in 1857 was to inaugurate a splendid opera house, still functioning in Philadelphia, designed by another Frenchman, the architect Napoleon LeBrun.

In spite of what must have been a large production, very little furniture by Quervelle can now be identified. The same situation prevails in

Fig. 5. Detail of a labeled mahogany pier table. In 1829 Quervelle made pier tables almost identical to the one at the Philadelphia Athenaeum for the East Room of the White House; the chief difference is the eagle's head set at the top of the front supports here. The same patriotic motif was originally placed above the curtains in the East Room. This and the one other surviving pier table were originally "richly bronzed and gilt." *The White House, Washington, D. C.*

Fig. 6. Labeled mahogany secretary desk. Awarded in 1827 a silver medal by the Franklin Institute, this superbly made desk, which bears no less than five printed labels, has veneered geometric ornament and a great fan-like panel which is a favorite Quervelle ornament. There are ormolu mounts, capitals, and bases, and cut-glass drawer pulls. The muntins of the glazed doors are a variant of a design in Plate 12 of the *Philadelphia Cabinet and Chair Makers' Union Book of Prices* for 1828. *Philadelphia Museum of Art; photograph by courtesy of the Newark Museum.*

Fig. 7. Labeled mahogany desk. An example even more elaborately decorated than Fig. 6, with Ionic instead of Doric columns in the lower section and exotic tapering "Egyptian" shafts above. The interior is veneered in maple. *Munson-Williams-Proctor Institute.*

Fig. 8. Attributed mahogany vertical piano. Here gadrooning is replaced by a lavish use of mother-of-pearl inlay, which originally covered the keyboard. The fall board is of rosewood and the sounding board is covered by handsomely pierced panels of ebony. The instrument is by Charles Pommer, active in Philadelphia from 1813 to 1836. Originally owned by the Hoffman family of Frederick, Maryland. *Georgetown University.*

relation to the larger establishment of his New York contemporaries, the firm of Joseph Meeks and Sons (ANTIQUES, April 1964, p. 414). Seven labeled Quervelle pieces have been located and through these a few more can be attributed. All are in the grandiose Empire style of the 1820's and early 1830's, the period of the winged-paw foot. No examples of styles popular in the 1840's and 1850's have been found. For these reasons it seems likely that Quervelle, after his initial success in the 1820's, gradually transferred his interests to real estate and other business activities, as did Bouvier, and also the Meeks brothers of New York. This would seem to be borne out by the drop in Quervelle's staff recorded in the census of 1840, from seven assistants to three. It is also possible that his later furniture was made by machine processes and therefore was never labeled.

The labeled and documented Quervelle furniture is made almost entirely of mahogany, crisply and authoritatively carved. It all reveals easily recognizable characteristics of a personal style. One of these is the use of gadrooning in prominent molding in several places on each piece. Another is the French cabinetmaker's fondness for a variety of vase and urn forms, often enriched with reeding and gadrooning and used alone or as bases for the shafts of columns. A third distinguishing mark is the red or gold painted molding set around the mirrors at the back of pier tables; a fourth is the use of a fan-shape panel of veneer on the front of a desk or the top of a table. A final characteristic is the combining of scrolls, acanthus leaves, and grapevines into a single opulent decorative member.

All but one of these pieces have the same label (Fig. 2), showing a simple dressing glass with scrolls supporting the mirror, on which appears the street number of Quervelle's shop on Second Street. One worktable (Fig. 3), however, bears a different label (Fig. 4), displaying a quite fantastically decorated dressing table, inscribed *Delmès Sculp.* There is no record in Philadelphia directories of this engraver, whose name suggests that he was still another of the French craftsmen who migrated to this country. The label indicates, however, that Delmès was not a very accomplished engraver, for the lines are neither fine nor firm and the lettering is badly placed within the frame of the mirror. The label is in fact quite inferior in technique to the worktable on which it is pasted. Since the heavy proportions and scroll feet of this table suggest a dating of 1830 or later, one is tempted to identify it and the dressing table on its label as the two pieces Quervelle displayed at the Franklin Institute exhibition of 1831.

The Delmès label is more useful, however, in attributing to Quervelle a sofa and a pier table ornamented with dolphins comparable to those on the label (Figs. 11, 12). Similar dolphins are found on a famous set of English Regency furniture commissioned from William Collins of London by John Fish and bequeathed in 1813 in memory of Lord Nelson to the governor of Greenwich Hospital, much of which is now on display at the Royal Pavilion in Brighton. Spouting dolphins were used a few years later on the base of a card table made by Henry Connelly of Philadelphia for Stephen Girard and now at Girard College, and a similar card table (Fig. 9) is owned by Mr. and Mrs. Gustave A. Heckscher. The attributed sofa (Fig. 11), has, in addition to two frilled shells like that on the label, the Quervellian feature of grapevine and fruit mingled with acanthus leaves, while the tails of the dolphin supports seem to end in leafy forms like those on the label and also on the attributed pier table (Fig. 12).

In May 1935 (p. 199) ANTIQUES illustrated a card table with the first of Quervelle's labels, but without disclosing its location. The pedestal base of this table was composed of a gadrooned plinth below cylindrical turning resembling the

Fig. 9. Labeled mahogany card table. The top, like the fronts of the desks, has a veneered fan. *Collection of Mr. and Mrs. Gustave A. Heckscher.*

Fig. 10. Documented mahogany circular pedestal table. Three tables like this were designed for the center of the East Room. The tops have depressed disks containing slabs of Italian black marble with yellow veins. Around the lower edge of the top is a gilt metal band of leaf cresting. Two of these are now in the Lincoln Bedroom, the third in the Treaty Room. *The White House.*

Fig. 11. Attributed mahogany sofa. Compare the dolphins with Fig. 12, the frilled shells with Fig. 4, the grapevine ornament with Figs. 1 and 5. *Philadelphia Museum of Art.*

103

capital and necking of a Doric column with a section of outspread acanthus foliage in the center. The design would seem to authorize the attribution to Quervelle of a tilt-top table (Fig. 13) (a rare form for this period) and a pedestal sewing table with quite similar bases, which belong to a set of furniture made for the Wetherill family of Philadelphia and recently presented to Ainsley Hall in Columbia, South Carolina. The set also includes a sofa and a pair of bow-front bureaus.

The group of fine furniture here illustrated reveals that the shop of Anthony Quervelle, aside from producing excellent carving, turned out impressive pieces in one of the most forceful and attractive personal styles of the late classical period. Most of the furniture was based on fashionable English forms which by 1825 to 1830 were current in America and which in Philadelphia, according to the *Journal of the Franklin Institute* for 1830, varied little from year to year. Thus Quervelle's pier tables (Figs. 1, 5) go back to an English model of about 1815, of which there is a good example on display in the Regency gallery of the Victoria and Albert Museum. A decade later it had become fashionable to employ a heavier version of the same forms, overlaid with a variety of foliage, as George Smith explains in his *Cabinet-Maker and Upholsterer's Guide* (London, 1826 [1828]). From this pattern book, which appears to have been the most influential source for American furniture of this period, Quervelle could have taken his formula for pier tables, including the grape carving (Plate LXIV) as well as a number of other effective elements, as the Meeks firm of New York City was to do in its broadside of 1833. For example, the eagle head added to the pier table in Figure 5 could have come from Smith's Plate XCII. Quervelle's constant use of gadrooning suggests the way Smith employed it (Plates X, XLII, LV, LXXI, LXXIV, CXIX), and several of the Quervelle vase forms recall designs in the English book. In addition, Smith illustrates frilled shells and dolphins (Plate CXV) and outspreading acanthus carving (Plate XVIII).

The way in which Quervelle combined vases with plinths and columnar shafts showed his real originality. He showed it also in his use of geometric ornament and in the grandiose fanlike forms of convex veneering applied to the desks and the attributed piano (Figs. 6, 7, 8), a heavy Empire version of an Adam device which had enjoyed favor among the Federal cabinetmakers of Philadelphia. Finally, the carving of the lion-paw feet, with its unmistakable personal quality, has a monumental character that occurs repeatedly throughout this group of furniture.

In preparing this article I received invaluable assistance from Francis James Dallett, director of the Historical Society of Newport, Rhode Island, and Berry B. Tracy, assistant curator of the American Wing of the Metropolitan Museum of Art.

Fig. 12. Attributed mahogany pier table with white marble top and gilt stencil decoration. Compare the dolphins and front feet with Fig. 4, the red painted moldings around the mirror with Figs. 1, 5, and 4, the gadrooning with Fig. 1, and the vase supports with Figs. 7 and 10. *Athenaeum of Philadelphia.*

Fig. 13. Attributed mahogany tilt-top table. Compare the pedestal with that of the labeled Quervelle card table reproduced in ANTIQUES, May 1935, p. 199. *Ainsley Hall, Columbia, South Carolina.*

The furniture of Anthony G. Quervelle

Part I: *The pier tables*

BY ROBERT C. SMITH, *University of Pennsylvania*

ANTHONY GABRIEL QUERVELLE was the outstanding cabinetmaker of the last phase of the classical revival in Philadelphia. Born in France in 1789, he emigrated from Paris about 1817, the year in which he married Louise Geneviève Monot, another Parisian living in Philadelphia. He was naturalized in 1823 and in 1825 opened his United States Fashionable Cabinet Ware House, located, as one of his advertisements states, at 126 South Second Street, "a few doors below Dock street [west side]."[1] He lived there until 1849, winning prizes at the annual exhibitions of mechanical arts of 1825 through 1828 and 1831 held at the Franklin Institute. This appears to have been the period of Quervelle's greatest activity, which brought him the success and prosperity that later enabled him to turn from cabinetmaking to amassing the considerable holdings of real estate and other property inside and outside Philadelphia which he possessed at the time of his death in 1856.

In ANTIQUES for September 1964, I published an article on Anthony Quervelle in which I illustrated a number of fine examples of his furniture, documented by two different labels advertising the South Second Street warehouse.[2] Since then many more pieces of Quervelle's work have appeared, almost a dozen of them either labeled or stamped with his name. These prove beyond doubt that he was one of the greatest furniture makers of the period in this country and one of our most distinguished wood carvers. He excelled at giving life and at the same time an air of majesty to his work, transforming the French Restoration and late English Regency patterns he employed into distinctly personal expressions.

Like his great predecessors of the eighteenth century,

Fig. 1. Three characteristic gilded stencil designs from Quervelle pier tables. The patterns are related to those of inlays used in French furniture of the Restoration period and are often repeated in Quervelle's carving. These details are taken from furniture shown in Figs. 8 and 12 and Pl. II. *Except as noted, photographs are by Robert C. Smith.*

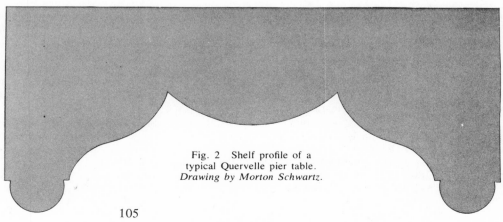

Fig. 2 Shelf profile of a typical Quervelle pier table. *Drawing by Morton Schwartz.*

Fig. 3. Pier table with paw-scroll supports. Carved mahogany and mahogany veneer. It is the smallest of the tables illustrated here. The top is black marble, the feet have a green finish with traces of overgilding, and a narrow gilded fillet outlines the sides of the scroll. Height 37½, width 41, depth 30 inches. *Photograph by courtesy of Robert T. Trump.*

Fig. 4. Pier table with paw-scroll supports. Carved mahogany and mahogany veneer. Characteristic of Quervelle are the turned forms below the Ionic capitals in the rear colonnettes (repeated in the rear feet) and the gilded, stenciled anthemion design at the corners, which resembles that of an attributed pier table with columns veneered with mahogany at Wheatland (the James Buchanan House), Lancaster, Pennsylvania. Height 39, width 42½, depth 30 inches. *Photograph by courtesy of Joseph Sorger.*

Anthony Quervelle worked for some of the foremost Philadelphia families, and from the furniture he observed in his patrons' houses may have derived his fondness for gadrooning and intricate carving of acanthus foliage. The volume of his work was enormous, so that he probably was not exaggerating when he claimed in a newspaper announcement that he had "the largest and most fashionable assortment of furniture ever yet offered for sale in this city."[3] Quervelle's tables are so numerous even today that apparently no house of distinction was complete without several examples of these masterful pedestal and pier tables, which more than any of the rest of his work must have established the Frenchman's reputation in Philadelphia.

Quervelle's furniture is preserved in quantity today, yet very little is known about its stylistic development. It appears, however, that as his distinguished countryman Charles Honoré Lannuier (1779-1819) had done in New York almost two decades earlier, Quervelle began to work in a distinctly French vein which he rapidly adapted to the British styles he found in favor here. This can be seen both in his designs for secretaries and in his handling of the pier table, a compact, rectangular, "architectural" form, made to be set in hallways or placed between long parlor windows. Developed in the late eighteenth century, the pier table played a great role in the styles of the French Empire (c. 1804-1815) and Bourbon Restoration (c. 1814-1830), as well as in the contemporary English Regency style.

When Quervelle first came to Philadelphia he may have worked in the furniture warehouse maintained at 153 South Second Street between 1819 and 1823 by Charles Nolan, who served as a character witness at his naturalization.[4] In the early years Quervelle made pier tables in the French fashion in which the shelves between the feet had either straight or elliptical edges and brasses imported from Paris were mounted on the front of the cornice below the marble top. Later Quervelle replaced these brasses with the American feature of gilded stencil painting in the form of anthemia, scrolls, and other classical devices directly related to his carving. He also applied these stencils on the front of the shelves between the legs (Fig. 1). This generally quite flat painting, which Quervelle seems to have made fashionable in Philadelphia, lacks the three-dimensional shading preferred by New York cabinetmakers, or the more subtle modeling of the Baltimore school. Quervelle also developed, as a personal feature, the use of small-scale friezes in gold or red combined with black, composed of simple shield and leaf motifs, which he set around the frames of the backing mirrors and, occasionally, along the edges of the bases.

Quervelle's fully developed pier tables, probably of the period 1825 to 1835, are all made of mahogany veneered on white pine or tulip poplar. Their mirrors rise only part

Fig. 5. Dressing table with mirror. Carved mahogany and mahogany veneer. Quervelle based this monumental piece on a pier table with paw-scroll legs. The concave and convex surfaces of the bottom drawer and adjacent sections of the case recall furniture on the labels of Joseph B. Barry of Philadelphia and the pilasters suggest those on the pier or serving table (which formerly had his label) now owned by Mrs. Wistar Brown and on loan to the Metropolitan Museum. The tapering mirror poles end in Egyptian revival capitals. The top is of poplar stained to simulate mahogany. On the shelf at the base two strips of maple veneer flank a panel of crotch mahogany. Height 91 (without poles, 43), width 45¾, depth 24½ inches. *Photograph by courtesy of Joseph Sorger.*

Fig. 6. Detail of Fig. 5. Based on French and English patterns, this leg is a superlative example of Quervelle's lively use of line and plastic carving in a synthesis of rhythmic forms.

of the distance to the bed of the top, leaving an undecorated space measuring from eight and one-quarter to as much as fourteen and one-half inches in height. The mirrors are generally flanked either by the Doric pilasters traditional in French Empire pier tables (Fig. 13) or, more frequently, by engaged columns, often with multiple necking (Fig. 4). Sometimes the shafts of the columns are combined with various vase forms having plain or gadrooned surfaces, and sometimes with a band of vigorous acanthus carving (Pl. I, Fig. 10). These classical fantasies, executed in a bold, sure, rhythmic style, are as far as I now know an unmistakably Quervellian feature.

Another peculiarity of Quervelle's pier tables is the constant use of turned rear feet. The front feet are often of bun, ball, or low vase forms topped by gadrooning. Quervelle also used the plastically carved lion's-paw feet characteristic of all forms of his furniture, sometimes with a collar of gadrooning. Since both bases and lion's paws were frequently joined by scrolls or columns in the front supports, it is not unusual to find in the pier tables one paw or one vase above another, or paws over vases, or vice versa. The effect is rich and lively and it suggests an effort by Quervelle to escape the unbroken massiveness all too common in late classical-style furniture.

Equally typical of Quervelle's vivacious spirit is the complex profile of the majority of his pier-table shelves, deeply indented by ogee curves flanking a convex projection (Fig. 2). The center of these shelves is often decorated with semicircular fillets, either inlaid or painted, which, reflected in the back mirror, appear to be full circles. In some of the most elaborate examples concentric semicircular veneers of rosewood, maple, or satinwood and crotch mahogany used in the same manner create the strong contrasts of light and dark woods that were becoming the fashion in French marquetry when Quervelle left Paris for Philadelphia.

His pier tables vary in height from twenty-seven and one-eighth to forty-four inches, with thirty-nine inches a standard height. They range in width from thirty-eight to fifty inches, most of them being forty-eight inches wide. In depth these tables extend from nineteen and one-half to twenty-seven inches, with many measuring about twenty-two inches. They can be grouped according to three major types of support—the scroll, the column, and the bird and animal form.

Of these the scroll-support tables have the best of Quervelle's masterful carving. The two front supports in the form of majestic scrolls are decorated at the top with long thin acanthus leaves, following a pattern in George Smith's *Cabinet-Maker and Upholsterer's Guide* (London, 1826), which was the source of many of Quervelle's ideas. The scrolls, which are sometimes scored below these leaves and sometimes decorated with a narrow gilded fillet, rise from noble lion's-paw feet that merge into a gauntlet of foliage, according to a formula established in France by the Jacob family of cabinetmakers at the beginning of the nineteenth century.[5] Quervelle, like Michel Bouvier (1792-1874), another French furniture maker who worked in Philadelphia in the 1820's,[6] followed the strongly plastic shapes of Georges Jacob's lion's-paws, generally permitting the toes to recede from a center point, like the elements of his typical gadroon moldings (Figs. 5, 7, 10). In the best examples each toenail is set at a slightly different angle and this careful differentiation gives the whole foot a feeling of life and movement very different from the square and inanimate paws produced by the average late classical-style carver.

Some of Quervelle's finest scroll supports have grape-vines carved on the sides in a pattern recalling the vine frieze applied to a scrolled chair back illustrated in 1817 in the influential London *Repository of the Arts*, published by Rudolph Ackermann. In one superbly carved example (Fig. 6) this vine pattern is combined with plumelike anthemion petals, both of which emerge from the scroll. Petals emerging from a scroll is a popular late classical-style convention that goes back through Thomas Sheraton[7]

to the Italian designer Giovanni Battista Piranesi, one of the principal innovators of neoclassical ornament.[8]

A labeled Quervelle pier table of the scroll-support type, with brass mounts and a straight-edge shelf, which suggest that it is an early work, appeared as Figure 1 in my 1964 article. Two attributed tables which are similar except for their curved shelves are shown here (Figs. 3, 4) together with a stately dressing table based on the same pier-table form (Fig. 5). This use of an identical scroll motif for various types of furniture[9] may also have been inspired by George Smith's book, where paired scrolls are employed several times in this manner. The practice grew during the 1830's, when very large, uncarved double scrolls became so fashionable for case pieces and tables that they were eventually applied also to sofas, as John Hall shows in his *Cabinet Makers' Assistant,* published in Baltimore in 1840.[10]

For the East Room of the White House in 1829 Quervelle provided two scroll-support pier tables with carved grapes and other fruit at the sides, a lion's paw at the base, and an eagle's head at the top of each scroll support. For each of these tables Quervelle was paid $175.[11] The model, created for President Andrew Jackson, must have been popular, for several versions of the table have appeared (Fig. 7), including one with the head, breast, and wings of an eagle (Pl. I). The latter is a sumptuously decorated table, to which is pasted an unidentified newspaper advertisement of Quervelle's business. It is unique for the number of carved and turned motifs it displays, several of them gilded or bronzed. There are foliated double cups below the gilded paws of the front supports, while the tapering shafts of the Doric columns that frame the mirror rise from superposed vases. These, it is interesting to note, have the same Oriental shapes that were popular in English and American eighteenth-century chairs.[12] As a general rule when the shelf has a straight edge (Fig. 7) the cornice is apt to also. The table in Plate I has the cavetto form

Fig. 7. Pier table with supports of the paw-scroll type surmounted by eagle's heads. Carved mahogany and mahogany veneer. With scroll legs based on those of the damaged pier tables of 1829 at the White House, this piece preserves the straight-edge shelf of the earlier tables and around the mirror and at the bases of the flanking Ionic pilasters displays gilded leaves like those painted on some of Quervelle's center tables. Height 41, width 48⅜, depth 24 inches. *Chicago Historical Society; on loan to the Art Institute of Chicago.*

Pl. I. Pier table with supports of the paw-scroll type surmounted by eagles. Carved mahogany and mahogany veneer. Glued to the frame of this table, a Quervelle advertisement from an unidentified newspaper "respectfully invites all the persons who may be in want of Cabinet Furniture to call and view the largest and most fashionable assortment of furniture ever yet offered for sale in this city. From the well known character of this establishment the public may depend upon every article being made of the best materials and workmanship which will be sold on very reasonable terms for cash or acceptance." The eagles, gadrooning, and many other details are gilded or bronzed, while the marquetry semicircle of the shelf is composed of satinwood, rosewood, and crotch mahogany. Height 41, width 44, depth 20¾ inches. *Photograph by Cortlandt Van Dyck Hubbard, courtesy of Joseph Sorger.*

Pl. II. Pier table with white-marble columns. Carved mahogany and mahogany veneer. The unusual width of this table is repeated in the handsomely carved Ionic capitals, which are gilded, as are the foliage ornament of the edge of the shelf and the gadrooning above the ebonized feet. Small gilded, stenciled friezes frame the panel above each column and define the false circle of the shelf. This table is thought to have been made for a member of the Bowlby family of Philadelphia merchants. Height 38½, width 48¾, depth 25½ inches. *Hubbard photograph, courtesy of Robert T. Trump.*

Fig. 8. One of a pair of pier tables with double-scroll supports. Carved mahogany and mahogany veneer. The gilded foliated front feet resemble the pedestals of several Quervelle center tables. The elliptical edge of the shelf is outlined in gilding and the surface has an inlaid design which, reflected in the backing mirror, produces the image of a four-pointed star. Height 39½, width 44, depth 19½ inches. *Photograph by courtesy of Robert T. Trump.*

Fig. 9. Sofa table with scroll supports. Rosewood veneered on white pine. The table, which has a top of marble mosaic, is decorated with gilded fillets and stenciled anthemia and scrolls as well as wooden bosses painted in imitation of French Restoration inlay patterns. It is stamped five times with an oval cartouche bearing the words ANTHONY G. QUERVELLE/CABINET & SOFA/MANUFACTORY/120 SO. 2D STREET/PHILAD. Height 28⅜ inches. *St. Louis Art Museum.*

111

Fig. 10. Pier table. Carved mahogany and mahogany veneer. Unusual for the height of its mirror, this table has gilded gadrooning above the feet and a gilded quarter-round molding in the front of the shelf. Penciled on the back is the name of J. L. Stellwaggon, probably the engineer whose name appears in Philadelphia directories of 1831-1833, for whom this table may have been made. Height 38⅛, width 36⅝, depth 19¾ inches. *Photograph by courtesy of Joseph Sorger.*

of cornice which Quervelle often but not always combined with his typically curved shelf. That shelf contains the grandest of his "false circles" of marquetry, a decoration which he seems to have derived from similar, full circles used in French Restoration furniture.

A pair of mahogany-veneer pier tables with lavish gilded decoration (Fig. 8) can be attributed to Quervelle because of their front feet and the resemblance of their scroll supports, rich stenciled painting, and general use of curved forms to a rosewood-veneer sofa table stamped with his name (Fig. 9).[13] All three of these tables have scroll supports like those which in coarser form became fashionable in the 1830's and ubiquitous in the 1840's. The Quervelle sofa table closely resembles one which appears as pattern 26 of the well-known broadside of 1833 advertising the furniture of Joseph Meeks and Sons of New York.[14] Since both this table and the piece by Quervelle are related to "Occasional Table II" in George Smith's book of patterns, it is quite possible that they were derived independently from this common source.

Probably created between about 1828 and 1833 (the date of the Meeks advertisement), the three Quervelle tables make abundantly clear how much lighter in its proportions and more sensitive in its rhythms was his furniture in relation to that of most of his contemporaries. Especially attractive and characteristic of Quervelle are the slightly crinkled surfaces of the water leaves applied to the vase forms of the feet of the pier tables and emerging from under the scroll supports. We shall see them again in his pedestal tables.

The Meeks broadside also illustrates pier tables carried on classical columns, an architectural formula which has sometimes been exclusively associated with New York cabinetmakers. There is, however, considerable stylistic

Fig. 11. Detail of Fig. 10. The gilt-brass mounts, probably French, are rare because they represent children wearing contemporary rather than classical clothing. Like other mounts on Quervelle's furniture they partially overlap framing fillets of brass inlaid in the wood.

112

Pl. III. Pier table with dolphin supports. Carved mahogany and mahogany veneer. Outstanding for the diversity of its carving, this large pier table has gilded dolphins, superposed acanthus leaves, and cornucopia brackets as well as a gilded, stenciled frieze forming the false circle of the shelf. Throughout the piece gadrooning is replaced by foliated carving. Height 44, width 50, depth 24 inches. *Collection of Mr. and Mrs. L. Louis Green III; photograph by Louis Schwartz.*

Fig. 12. Pier table with alabaster columns. Carved mahogany and mahogany veneer. Notable are the foliated double cups beneath the columns with gilded, stenciled friezes around their bases. A similar frieze around the mirror is framed by gilded fillets which are repeated in the false circle of the shelf. The circle is composed of rosewood, crotch mahogany, and maple veneers. Height 39, width 39¾, depth 19½ inches. *Photograph by courtesy of Robert T. Trump.*

evidence that Quervelle also made this type of table, most frequently with Doric columns of mahogany veneer and capitals and bases of minutely scored brass. The Philadelphia Museum of Art has an example of what appears to be the earlier type of Quervelle table with gilt-brass ornaments in the form of classical figures seated on klismos chairs, and a shelf with an elliptical edge which is carried on unmistakably Quervellian lion's-paw feet with gadrooned cresting. These same feet appear on another pier table of this type attributed to Quervelle (Fig. 10) which also has remarkably carved "Ionic" vase capitals flanking the back mirror and brass mounts which are unusual because the children depicted on them are dressed in contemporary clothing (Fig. 11).

Quervelle also used Doric columns of alabaster, as on a pier table attributed to him which was recently acquired by the Athenaeum of Philadelphia. It has a multiple-curve shelf with the rare feature of a semicircular center panel that is slightly raised. The foliated double-cup supports on which the columns rest and the ball feet with gadrooning are almost exactly repeated on a pier table in a private collection in Philadelphia, which has the same alabaster columns and a shelf with a simpler profile into which is set another of Quervelle's false circles (Fig. 12). In the same collection there is a pier table of unusual width (Pl. II) whose white-marble columns have a free rendering of Ionic capitals in gilded wood, between which is set a graceful decoration of long water leaves and scrolls flanking a sunburst medallion. The effect is not unlike that of an elegant early Victorian loggia or garden pavilion. Here the feet are lion's paws surmounted by gadrooning. Front feet of the same design are found on a pier table attributed to Quervelle with columns of mahogany veneer and deeply cut Ionic capitals belonging to Mr. and Mrs. H. Harold Sheaffer of Lancaster, Pennsylvania.

The dolphin was a popular nautical symbol in English Regency furniture, as well as a motif revived by French cabinetmakers in honor of the restoration of the Bourbon dynasty and the reappearance of a dauphin in the person of Charles X's son, the Duke of Angoulême. This attractive motif, which had already appeared in Philadelphia around the turn of the century in the Connelly-Haines furniture, was a favorite with Quervelle, probably because of the lively attitudes of the animal and the way its jagged fins suggest acanthus foliage. A pair of sprightly dolphins supports a mirror depicted on one of Quervelle's two known labels;[15] others appear on several of his worktables and they rise from gadrooned *tazzas* on a pier table attributed to him in the collection of the Athenaeum of Philadelphia.[16] One other such table helps establish the third category of Quervelle's pier tables, in which prominent use is made of dolphins and also of swans, another popular motif of early nineteenth-century European furniture designers, which again goes back, through Charles Percier and Pierre

François Fontaine[17] to Piranesi's book of 1769 on mantel decoration.[18]

This second dolphin table (cover; Pl. III) is the largest of all the pier tables associated with Anthony Quervelle and one of the richest of all his pieces, for not only does it have dolphins with gilded collars, but it also has four freestanding acanthus leaves of mahogany superbly carved in serpentine form, which, set one upon the other, flank the backing mirror. More leaves of this sort protrude along with fruit from two cornucopias set next to the rounded angles of the frame of the top of the table. This detail is extremely important in attributing the table because the leaves and fruit are practically identical to those emerging from baskets at the bases of the upper columns on Quervelle's great labeled secretary of 1827 in the Philadelphia Museum of Art.[19] On this table in place of conventional gadrooning Quervelle introduced moldings of ruffled foliage like those on his pedestal tables. These appear above the feet, beneath the dolphin's heads, and along the base of the frame of the top. The moldings give a special animation to what is one of the handsomest and most dramatically sculptured pieces of American Empire furniture and which, like the 1827 secretary, is worthy of comparison with some of the most finely carved examples of Philadelphia Chippendale furniture.

Very different in the smoothness of most of its carving is a pier table with monopode supports (combining parts of two or more unrelated bodies) and the unusual feature of an ogee-shape cornice (Fig. 13). This can be attributed to Quervelle on the basis of the lion's-paw feet, collared

114

Fig. 13.   Pier table with monopode supports. Carved mahogany and mahogany veneer. Entirely without gilding, this piece is notable for the animated carving of the front feet and lion's-leg-and-swan supports with their accompanying acanthus foliage. There is a semicircle veneered on the shelf, which has cross-banding of rosewood. The original marble top has been replaced by one of marbleized wood. Height 42, width 42½, depth 27 inches. *Collection of Palmer Brown.*

[1]This appears on the commoner of Quervelle's two labels. See Robert C. Smith, *Philadelphia Empire furniture by Antoine Gabriel Quervelle*, ANTIQUES, September 1964, pp. 304-309, Fig. 2.

[2]*Philadelphia Empire furniture.*

[3]From a newspaper advertisement pasted on the back of the pier table shown in Plate I. Neither the date nor the name of the paper appears.

[4]This suggestion was made by Francis James Dallett, archivist of the University of Pennsylvania.

[5]Cf. Denise Ledoux-Lebard, *Les ébénistes Parisiens, 1795-1870,* Paris, 1965, Pl. 81 (pier table by Alphonse Jacob).

[6]See Francis James Dallet, *Michel Bouvier, Franco-American cabinetmaker,* ANTIQUES, February 1962, pp. 198-200; and Donald L. Fennimore, *A labeled card table by Michel Bouvier,* ANTIQUES, April 1973, p. 761.

[7]Appendix to the *Cabinet-maker and Upholsterer's Drawing-Book,* London, 1793, Pl. 24 (pulpit stair).

[8]*Diverse maniere d'adornare i cammini,* Rome, 1769. Pls. 6, 30, 44.

[9]It is also found in two other pieces of furniture that can be attributed to Quervelle: a secretary in a private collection in Philadelphia, and a center table made for Edward Coleman of Philadelphia (ANTIQUES, February 1967, p. 236).

[10]Robert C. Smith, *John Hall, a busy man in Baltimore,* ANTIQUES, September 1967, pp. 360-366.

[11]This information, given in *First auditors' miscellaneous treasury accounts,* November 25, 1829, is taken from Kathleen M. Catalano, "Cabinetmaking in Philadelphia (1820-1840)" M.A. thesis, University of Delaware, 1972; p. 115. One of the legs of one of the White House pier tables is shown in Fig. 5 of Smith, *Philadelphia Empire furniture.*

[12]Robert C. Smith, *China, Japan and the Anglo-American chair,* ANTIQUES, October 1969, pp. 552-558.

[13]"A Philadelphia Empire table," *Bulletin of the City Art Museum of St. Louis,* May-June, 1971, pp. 8-10.

[14]Robert C. Smith, *Late classical furniture in the United States, 1820-1850,* ANTIQUES, December 1958, p. 523. See also: John N. Pearce, Lorraine W. Pearce, and R. C. Smith, *The Meeks family of cabinetmakers,* ANTIQUES, April 1964, pp. 414-420.

[15]Smith, *Philadelphia Empire furniture,* Fig. 4.

[16]Smith, *Philadelphia Empire furniture,* Fig. 12.

[17]*Recueil de décorations intérieures,* Paris, 1801 and 1812, Pls. 6, 17, 18, 19, 24.

[18]*Diverse maniere,* Pls. 8 and 42.

[19]Smith, *Philadelphia Empire furniture,* Fig. 6. The source of this design may be Pl. 16, 1-2 of Percier and Fontaine, *Recueil de décorations.*

[20]Ledoux-Lebard, *Les ébénistes,* Pl. 90. The revival of the Graeco-Roman monopode form seems to have been another of Piranesi's innovations (Cf. *Diverse maniere,* Pls. 33, 58).

with foliage like those of the dolphin pier table (Pl. III), and by the use of a second pair of paw feet resting on the shelf. These feet are part of beautifully modeled animal legs that expand like the gauntleted casing at the base of many of Quervelle's scroll supports. They end in extravagantly broad basket forms, heaped with acanthus leaves, from which seem to leap the breasts, necks, and heads of a pair of swans. Here again one is impressed by the rhythmic grace and the sensitivity of the carving, which surpasses the handling of a similar motif in a pier table by Louis Édouard Lemarchand, a celebrated Parisian cabinetmaker of the French Restoration.[20] The heads of the swans are quite like those of Quervelle's eagles and their long lithe lines recall the sweep of the water leaves and scrolls between the columns of the pier table illustrated in Plate II.

Through animated devices of this sort Quervelle conveyed to his furniture a sense of vivacious reality virtually unique at the time he was working. They helped him avoid that somnolent heaviness of form and mechanical repetition of stereotyped decoration which mar the work of so many of his American contemporaries. The unforgettable personality of ornament of this sort contributed unquestionably to Quervelle's great success, along with his outstanding ability in carving, his deep knowledge of fashionable French and English decoration, and his extraordinary feeling for good proportions and fine balance.

IV New Directions for Philadelphia Furniture

In surveying the span of articles included in this book, it is evident that, for more than half a century, ANTIQUES often has been the vehicle for publishing the latest discoveries about Philadelphia furniture. In the 1920s and 1930s, ANTIQUES published the first accounts of many of the most important Philadelphia cabinetmakers, including Randolph, Gostelowe, and Tufft. Through the years, the magazine continued to be receptive to new discoveries. The five articles in the following chapter may suggest some directions for future research and collecting in Philadelphia cabinetwork. Because all these articles appeared in ANTIQUES between December, 1971, and May, 1975, they also represent some of the newest discoveries in the field.

Donald Fennimore's article about the superb Empire card table by Michel Bouvier not only brings to public notice a hitherto unknown piece, but also helps to broaden our perspective on Philadelphia Empire cabinetwork. Seen in the context of the works of Anthony G. Quervelle, this table indicates that Bouvier's work could rival that of his better-known contemporary. In considering Quervelle, Bouvier, and their fellow craftsmen, it is evident that all were working in the milieu of a complex and rich regional school centered in Philadelphia The geographic extent of this school is implied by a sideboard signed by the Pittsburgh cabinetmaker, Benjamin Montgomery, and dated 1830; it has many of the characteristics usually associated with Quervelle's work. Information about this sideboard was first published by Lorraine Welling Lanmon in ANTIQUES in May, 1975.

Robert Smith's article about the discovery of a desk and bookcase whose design was taken in part from Chippendale's *Director* not only adds another masterpiece to the Philadelphia Chippendale School, but also reveals the influence of architectural designs on furniture. Smith's other article about finial busts on eighteenth-century Philadelphia furniture explores an otherwise overlooked area which relates to both sculpture and the decorative arts. Both Smith's articles are important in their methodology, for they go beyond the reporting of discoveries to the level of art historical analysis. If the conclusions drawn in each article may appear somewhat tentative, they can only remind the reader that scholarship very often raises more questions than it can answer at a given time.

The furniture made by the firm of George J. Henkels of Philadelphia for the Asa Packer Mansion in Jim Thorpe, Pennsylvania, was discussed by Kenneth Ames in ANTIQUES in October, 1973. This article marked the magazine's first detailed consideration of Philadelphia's Victorian cabinetwork. Whether a distinct "Philadelphia School" of Victorian furniture existed remains to be determined; certainly the Victorian period's mass-production and railroad transportation changed many of the factors which had previously influenced the development of regional schools of cabinetmaking in America. As a result of Ames's article, in May, 1974 ANTIQUES published the discovery of the first piece of furniture bearing Henkels' label.

This book's final article—on Chippendale case furniture from Lancaster, Pennsylvania—which appeared in ANTIQUES in May, 1975, may, at first thought, seem to be slightly incongruous for a book on Philadelphia furniture. This article, however, together with our growing knowledge of Chippendale furniture from Maryland and parts of inland Pennsylvania, only strengthens Philadelphia's position as the center of a large regional school of cabinetmaking. In Lancaster, America's largest inland town in the eighteenth century, the English-oriented Philadelphia style united with German baroque traditions to create a recognizable variant of the Philadelphia prototypes. The elaboration and sophistication of the best Lancaster Chippendale furniture suggests that the artistic relationship between Philadelphia and its inland is yet another field awaiting more study.

Card table by Michel Bouvier (1792-1874), Philadelphia, c. 1830. Primary woods maple, white pine (feet), mahogany (playing surface), and rosewood (cross banding in top); secondary woods white pine, tulip, yellow birch, and chestnut. Height 30 inches; width 35⅞; depth when closed, 18⅜. *Private collection; photograph by George J. Fistrovich.*

A labeled card table by Michel Bouvier

BY DONALD L. FENNIMORE, *Assistant curator, Henry Francis du Pont Winterthur Museum*

MICHEL BOUVIER, an early nineteenth-century Philadelphia merchant-cabinetmaker, had considerable success during his lifetime. Even so, a number of his contemporaries, among them Anthony Gabriel Quervelle and the Meeks family, have since received much greater attention.[1] Bouvier, born and trained in France, established himself in Philadelphia in 1815 and became an important part of the business scene there until his death in 1874. However, the full impact of his presence in the Philadelphia cabinet-making community has remained unexplored.

Until recently, only a *secrétaire à abattant* and a group of two armchairs and four side chairs have been attributed to Bouvier with any certainty.[2] His name has been tentatively associated with five stylistically related worktables, some of which have a history of Philadelphia ownership.[3] Existing records show that Bouvier did supply a variety of other forms including pieces for Henry Latimer and Charles N. Bancker, both of Philadelphia. Included among

their papers are bills for a sideboard, a set of "Northumberland" tables, a lounge, a breakfast table, two "beurough" (bureaus), a sofa, and a knife box.[4] Another bill, dated 1834, lists a music stand which Bouvier sold to a "Mr. Skerret."[5]

The card table in the color plate, a recent discovery, is the first known labeled piece of furniture by Michel Bouvier. It bears a stencil (Fig. 1) which places the address of his cabinet-and-sofa warehouse at 91 South Second Street, his location from 1825 to 1844. Previously his wareroom was at the southeast corner of Fifth and Walnut Streets except during 1823 when it was temporarily relocated to 6 South Front Street.[6] The stencil also lists "cabinet ware, mahogany, hair seating," the more important staples of his trade, and pictures a dressing table, or toilette. The possible design source for this toilette can be found in Plate 348 of Pierre La Mésangère's *Collection de Meubles et Objets de Goût*, an important and widely circulated

Fig. 1. Stencil of Michel Bouvier, Philadelphia, c. 1830, 2½ by 3¾ inches. Located in the well of the card table, it reads: *M. Bouvier, Keeps constantly on hand, Cabinetware, Mahogany, hair seating &c. At No. 91 So: 2d St. Philad*[a].

series of furniture designs published in Paris between 1802 and 1830 (Fig. 2).

Considering the possible relationship between the toilette and La Mésangère's design, as well as Bouvier's French training, it is somewhat surprising to find that the closest published design relating to the card table is in an English, rather than a French, design book. Plate 72 of Peter and Michael Angelo Nicholson's *The Practical Cabinet Maker, Upholsterer and Complete Decorator* (Fig. 3) illustrates a card table composed of the same elements organized in the same way as those on the Bouvier table. The latter varies from the Nicholson plate most noticeably in its extensive use of light-color figured-maple veneers and ebonized feet (Fig. 4), both of which were favored by French cabinet-makers during the first two decades of the nineteenth century. This is in contrast to the use of dark mahogany veneers, gilded terminals, and a profusion of surface ornament on English Regency furniture. Proof that Bouvier may have been influenced by English sources as well as French in the design of his furniture, as the table in the color plate suggests, must wait until a large body of furniture can be assigned to his shop.[7]

It is also possible that Bouvier might have derived his card table design, in large part, from the *Philadelphia Cabinet and Chair Makers Union Book of Prices*, published in 1828. Although not a picture book of designs like the Nicholsons' and La Mésangère's, this small craftsman's price guide for making furniture includes an accurate composite description of the card table in the color plate.

The predominance of elaborately figured veneers used for decorative effect, with the addition of only a few highlights of carved ornament, indicates that this table could have been made between about 1830 and 1835 to 1840. Fortunately, the earliest date can be further confirmed by two handwritten inscriptions on the table (Fig. 5). The first records that the table was a wedding gift to Susan Ross Larkin in Philadelphia in 1830. The inscriptions also name three generations of her descendants through whose hands the table passed until 1931.

This card table, with its maker's stencil and owners' inscriptions, is a fortunate survival, for it provides a useful document in the study of early nineteenth-century American furniture. With continued research its maker, Michel Bouvier, will surely prove to have been an important figure in the Philadelphia cabinetmaking trade. In a larger context, the card table adds support to the theory that Philadelphia was a major center for the creation and dissemination of high-style furniture in the early nineteenth century.

Fig. 2. Toilette.
Detail of Plate 348 from Pierre La Mésangère, *Collection de Meubles et Objets de Goût* (Paris, 1802-1830), c. 1811.

[1] ANTIQUES, April 1964, p. 414; September 1964, p. 304; July 1966, p. 69.

[2] ANTIQUES, February 1962, p. 198.

[3] Berry B. Tracy, "The Decorative Arts, Furniture," *Classical America 1815-1845*, Newark Museum, 1963; catalogue entry No. 20, pp. 43, 76.

[4] Joseph Downs Manuscript and Microfilm Collection. DMMC 52.72.10, 66x84.3, M101x22; Henry Francis du Pont Winterthur Museum.

[5] John H. Davis, *The Bouviers*, New York, 1969, between pp. 142 and 143.

[6] Philadelphia City Directory, 1824.

[7] Kathleen M. Catalano, "Cabinetmaking in Philadelphia, 1820-1840," M.A. thesis, University of Delaware, 1972, p. 61.

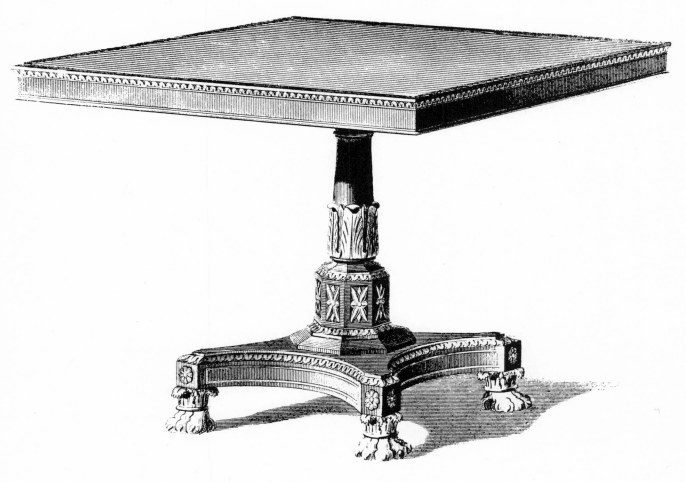

Fig. 3. Card table.
Detail of Pl. 72 from Peter and Michael Angelo Nicholson,
The Practical Cabinet Maker, Upholsterer and Complete Decorator,
London, 1826.

Fig. 4. Ebonized white-pine foot on the card table in the color plate. The carving is typically Philadelphia: the technique is loose but well controlled. This type of paw under a curled leaf with scrolls and/or leaves behind seems to be peculiar to Philadelphia furniture during the 1820's and 1830's.

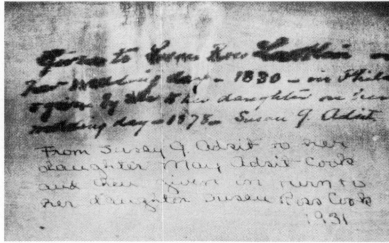

Fig. 5. Inscriptions located in the well of the card table. "Given to Susan Ross Larkin on her wedding day—1830—in Phila & given by her to her daughter on her wedding day—1878—Susan G. Adsit. From Susan G. Adsit to her daughter May Adsit Cook and then given in turn to her daughter Susan Ross Cook 1931."

121

Finial busts on eighteenth-century Philadelphia furniture

BY ROBERT C. SMITH, *University of Pennsylvania*

Fig. 1. *Desk & Bookcase.* Detail of Pl. 78 of Thomas Chippendale, *Gentleman and Cabinet-Maker's Director* (London, 1754). The richest of three Chippendale designs employing furniture busts, this pattern is reflected in Figs. 2 and 7.

Fig. 2. Detail of the trade card of Benjamin Randolph (Philadelphia, c. 1770), showing a bust similar to one of those displayed in Fig. 1.

THE ORIGINS OF American portrait sculpture in relief are found in the effigies on seventeenth- and eighteenth-century tombstones. Portraiture in the round, on the other hand, goes back to a little-known group of busts designed as finials for fine Philadelphia furniture in the last third of the eighteenth century. Almost all of mahogany, and measuring from eight and one-quarter to twelve and three-quarter inches in height, they were carved with strength and graceful vivacity and represent for the most part important literary or intellectual figures appropriate to a gentleman's library. These busts are all anonymous but the majority can be associated with the work of one of the most distinguished colonial cabinetmakers of Philadelphia.

Finial busts of this sort can be traced back, like so many other details of interior decoration, to Renaissance Florence, where around 1575 the architect Bernardo Buontalenti placed a bust in stone of the Grand Duke of Tuscany Cosimo I over a principal doorway of the Uffizi palace. Thereafter, small gilt-metal busts of famous men were used to decorate Italian luxury cabinets. In a print of about 1665 the influential French designer Jean Lepautre set a bust of a Roman military figure upon a richly sculptured cabinet, and he scattered others about the walls and chimney pieces in his designs for sumptuously decorated rooms.

The French architect Sébastien Leclerc put a bust of a young woman on a pedestal within a broken pediment on plate 152 of his *Treatise of Architecture* (Paris, 1714), which was republished in London a decade later and again in 1732. From this source as well as from the illustrations of the great Huguenot designer Daniel Marot, who was especially fond of grouping busts on a mantel, may have come the vogue for their use in English furniture and wainscot reflected in the pattern books of James Gibbs, Batty Langley, and other writers of the period 1720-1750. Their designs led directly to the extravagant composition of three finial busts atop the rococo "Desk

122

& Bookcase" of Plate 78 of Thomas Chippendale's *Gentleman and Cabinet-Maker's Director* of 1754 (Fig. 1), a pattern which seems to have been followed in colonial Philadelphia. While a number of comparable busts on Massachusetts furniture of the late eighteenth century are known, Philadelphia was unquestionably the center for this type of ornament in British America.

The link between Chippendale's plate and Philadelphia is found in the trade card engraved about 1770 by James Smither for Benjamin Randolph, who advertised that he made "all Sorts of Cabinet & Chairwork . . . Performed in the Chinese and Modern [rococo] Tastes" at the Golden Eagle shop on Chestnut Street between Third and Fourth Streets. At the upper left-hand corner of this advertisement, amidst a galaxy of that sumptuous Anglo-French rococo carving for which Randolph's shop is famous, appears the bust of a classical bearded figure (Fig. 2) almost identical with (though a mirror image of) the one on Chippendale's desk-and-bookcase (Fig. 1). The London and the Philadelphia engravings exhibit similar serpentine pedimental volutes decorated with sprigs of acanthus foliage, as well as sections of rococo diaperwork composed of intersecting diagonal lines.

Both of these features appear in one of the richest and most elegant pieces of Philadelphia Chippendale furniture, which may well be the masterpiece of Benjamin Randolph. At the top of this so-called "Pompadour" high chest of drawers (Fig. 4) there is a convex plinth bearing the bust of a lightly clothed young woman with flowers in her hair, an allegory perhaps of Flora or Spring. The pedestal is ornamented with a special sort of diaper design composed of small separate lines with a tiny dot at the point of intersection, over which hangs a carved swag of drapery.

The attribution of the Pompadour chest of drawers to Benjamin Randolph is strengthened by two elements found on the "sample" easy chair at the Philadelphia Museum of Art, one of the very few pieces of furniture traditionally considered to be by Randolph. The skirt of this chair (Fig. 3) has a diaper pattern very close to that of the Pompadour chest of drawers (though here the intersecting lines are continuous and the dots are set, like those of dice, inside the resulting compartments). Upon this pattern is carved in low relief the head of a man with deep-set eyes and open mouth that evokes a similar motif above the neo-Gothic window on Randolph's trade card, while the upraised neckcloth of this head strongly recalls the drapery on the plinth of the Pompadour piece.

Assuming the chair was made by Randolph, there is no way of knowing whether the head was carved by him personally or by some specialist engaged for the purpose, some sculptor such as Hercules Courtenay of London who in 1770 made the figures in the parlor woodwork of General John Cadwalader's destroyed house on Second Street, working along with Randolph himself, as Nicholas B. Wainwright has shown in his book

Colonial Grandeur in Philadelphia (Philadelphia, 1964). "Herclius Corteney" is also recorded as having received a payment of over £3 on December 23, 1766, in the receipt book of Benjamin Randolph at Winterthur.

Whoever this sculptor may have been, it seems unlikely that the same person made the Pompadour bust, for here the head is much rounder and the carving more superficial. Also the features of the face are more compressed, the eyes being abnormally large and the mouth correspondingly small, while the nose is markedly bulbous.

Almost the same qualities occur in a head of Franklin on the Philadelphia desk-and-bookcase shown in Figure 5, where the knotted neckcloth repeats the handling of drapery found in the Pompadour bust and on its pedestal. A third bust that appears to be by the same hand is that of a round-faced young man with a domical forehead on another desk-and-bookcase (Fig. 6), which is of particular interest because of the details of the embroidered coat and the grace of the mantle which frames it.

The convex pedestal into which this bust is set displays a simpler version of the Pompadour diaper, in which the dots are omitted, and an almost identical swag of drapery. The pedimental "trellis" has acanthus carving, as does that of the masterpiece ascribed to Randolph (Fig. 4), though the pedimental bed of the desk in Figure

123

Fig. 4. Bust of a young woman and the "Pompadour" high chest of drawers. Philadelphia, c. 1765-1775. Mahogany, 12¾ inches high. The allegorical bust flanked by draped urns from Chippendale's *Director,* the diaper fretwork, and the foliate carving constitute the richest ensemble of rococo carving in a group of stylistically related case pieces decorated with busts that seem to be by two different sculptors. *Metropolitan Museum of Art; photograph by courtesy of Ginsburg and Levy.*

Fig. 5. Bust of Benjamin Franklin on a desk-and-bookcase. Philadelphia, c. 1770-1780. Mahogany, 8¼ inches. This bust belongs to a group, including Figs. 4 and 6, which appears to have been carved by the same Philadelphia sculptor. *Collection of Mr. and Mrs. W. Colston Leigh.*

Fig. 6. Bust of a young man on a desk-and-bookcase. Philadelphia, c. 1765-1775. Mahogany, 8¾ inches. This extraordinary bust, which suggests a typical John Wollaston painting, seems to be by the author of Figs. 4 and 5. It is set in a pedestal decorated like those of Figs. 4 and 11 above a fretwork frieze closely related to those of Figs. 4, 7, 8, 10, 11, and 13. *Joe Kindig III.*

5 has plain boards in keeping with the severity of the rest of its frame. The recurring use of these details, along with the busts themselves, supports my belief that these pieces came from the same workshop, almost certainly that of Benjamin Randolph.

Seven more Philadelphia busts show facial characteristics that suggest another sculptor. This group includes the bust of a young woman on a bookcase desk (Fig. 7) which is important in relation to the one on the Pompadour high chest of drawers. In the former, which may have been inspired by the pair in Chippendale's plate (Fig. 1), the surface is more plastically sensitive and the proportions are different: the head is longer and narrower, the more attractively scaled eyes and mouth are not so close together, and there is a long commanding nose which gives an air of dignified authority to the whole countenance.

All of these characteristics are repeated in a bust on an elegant bookcase desk with mirror doors (Fig. 8), which represents the English philosopher John Locke (1632-1704), according to the Vertue engraving of Locke's portrait by Sir Godfrey Kneller (Fig. 9). In Philadelphia Locke enjoyed special esteem, for, as Edwin Wolf has shown in an article published in October 1965 in the *Pennsylvania Magazine of History and Biography*, his works on philosophy and government dominated a "parcel of books" sent out from London in 1700 by order of William Penn, while the catalogue of the Library Company of Philadelphia printed in 1741 lists his *Essay Concerning Human Understanding* as "Esteemed the best Book of Logick in the World." Locke's popularity continued in the period just before the Revolution, when this bust appears to have been carved, because it was felt that, were he alive, he would sympathize with the contemporary American grievances against the British government.

With this stately bust can be grouped one of John Milton on still another desk-and-bookcase (Fig. 10), which seems to have been derived from the William Faithorne engraving of the poet's head published in London in 1670. The bust is animated by the very fine carving of the crisp and crackling hair falling on the shoulders, a decorative tour de force comparable to the handling of rococo acanthus sprigs in Philadelphia pedimental scrolls.

Similar locks can seen in another fine bust of this group, which belongs to a chest on chest (Fig. 11). It appears to be a more youthful and spirited portrait of John Locke, based perhaps on the Wedgwood basalt bust of the great philosopher (Fig. 12). This may in turn have come from an earlier marble bust of Locke by the sculptor Michael Rysbrack, of which there are a number of versions. Using the firm chin and mouth of the Wedgwood likeness, the unknown Philadelphia carver has created a dynamic miniature head which in plastic complexity and suggestion of multiple movement goes beyond the other busts in this category.

These include the Locke of the Poulson

Fig. 7. Bust of a young woman on a desk-and-bookcase. Philadelphia, c. 1765-1775. Mahogany, 10 inches. Probably inspired by the pair of busts in Fig. 1, this piece has a facial type which identifies a second sculptor who seems also to have carved the busts of Figs. 8, 10, 11, 13, 14, and 15. *Metropolitan Museum of Art.*

Fig. 8. Bust of John Locke on a desk-and-bookcase. Philadelphia, c. 1765-1775. Mahogany, 11¼ inches. Because of the popularity of his philosophical writings Locke was a favorite subject for Philadelphia finial busts on the eve of the American Revolution. *Collection of Mr. and Mrs. Lammot du Pont Copeland.*

Fig. 9. Portrait of John Locke, engraved by Vertue from a painting by Sir Godfrey Kneller. English, 1738. The probable model for Fig. 8.

Fig. 10. Bust of John Milton on a desk-and-bookcase. Philadelphia, c. 1765-1775. Mahogany, 8⅞ inches. Closely related in spirit and style to the austere Locke of Fig. 8, the head of this bust displays superbly carved hair that clearly shows the sculptor's mastery of rococo design. *Joe Kindig III.*

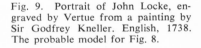

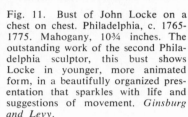

Fig. 11. Bust of John Locke on a chest on chest. Philadelphia, c. 1765-1775. Mahogany, 10¾ inches. The outstanding work of the second Philadelphia sculptor, this bust shows Locke in younger, more animated form, in a beautifully organized presentation that sparkles with life and suggestions of movement. *Ginsburg and Levy.*

Fig. 12. Bust of John Locke. English, late eighteenth century. Wedgwood ceramic basalt, 7 inches. Probably derived from an earlier Locke bust by Michael Rysbrack, this may be the model for Figs. 11, 13, and 14. *Buten Museum of Wedgwood.*

family bookcase desk (Fig. 13), which offers a somewhat softer version of the Wedgwood type, and another on the Chew family desk-and-bookcase (Fig. 14), where the treatment of the hair is heavier and the face somewhat broader, although the mouth, nose, eyes, and creased eyebrows are unquestionably those of the carver of the rest of these distinguished busts. With them can be placed an attractive and quite realistic representation of Benjamin Franklin (Fig. 15). It has the same breaking up of the surface into many plastic planes and the same paneled base as are found in the busts of Figures 8 and 13.

This portrait of Franklin (like a similar one in walnut 10½ inches high belonging to Ginsburg and Levy) seems never to have been affixed to furniture, for the base shows no trace of dowel marks. The same is true of a mahogany bust of George Washington believed to be of Pennsylvania origin (Fig. 16). This, however, is very different from the Philadelphia busts already presented because its flat, diagrammatic treatment gives it a stiffness that seems provincial and suggests that it may have been made in Lancaster or some other Pennsylvania German center.

The pieces of furniture associated with the second group of Philadelphia busts offer some interesting analogies among themselves as well as with other "Randolphian" furniture. The trellis of acanthus volutes in the pedimental area of the chest on chest to which Figure 11 belongs is almost identical with that of the desk with the bust of Milton (Fig. 10). The desk which carries Figure 13 and on which the plinth is carved with leaves and berries that recall the flowers and foliage of the Pompadour high chest of drawers (Fig. 4), has glazed doors with a pattern of mullions precisely like that of a desk at the bottom

Fig. 13. Bust of John Locke on the Poulson family desk-and-bookcase. Philadelphia, c. 1765-1775. Mahogany, 8½ inches. Another version of the second Locke portrait type, this bust must be by the same unknown sculptor. Illustrated in ANTIQUES, November 1970, p. 771. *United States Department of State.*

Fig. 14. Bust of John Locke. Philadelphia, c. 1765-1775. Mahogany, 9 inches. Still another presentation of the second Locke formula, which has a slightly broader face that makes the head seem smaller. It possesses the same animation as Figs. 11 and 13. The desk-and-bookcase to which it belongs is illustrated in ANTIQUES, December 1959, p. 536. *Collection of Mr. and Mrs. Samuel Chew.*

Fig. 15. Bust of Benjamin Franklin. Philadelphia, c. 1770-1780. Mahogany, 9 inches. This bust has the same sophisticated modeling as Figs. 7, 11, 13, and 14, and a sufficient similarity to justify its attribution to the same Philadelphia sculptor. *Collection of Mrs. Joseph Carson.*

Fig. 16. Bust of George Washington. Pennsylvania, c. 1785-1800. Mahogany, 11½ inches. Traditionally considered a Pennsylvania piece, this Washington has a flat, formalized character that suggests the stylization of Pennsylvania German folk art. *Michael Arpad.*

of the trade card of Benjamin Randolph, while the plinth of the chest on chest (Fig. 11) is decorated with the same dicelike diaperwork as is used on the skirt of the Randolph sample chair (Fig. 3). A careful study of all this furniture, which seems always to have had its present busts, from the standpoints of proportion, dimensions, and construction could well reveal further important resemblances linking it with the shop of Benjamin Randolph.

Everything indicates that this cabinetmaker, who, as is evident in his advertisement, borrowed so many ideas from Chippendale's *Director,* took over also the theme of the finial bust. This then became a specialty of his shop, along with case furniture to go with it, just as Thomas Affleck's shop seems to have become famous for chairs and tables with Marlborough legs. The making of the busts appears to have been left to two or more as yet unidentified carvers. One of these, who could have been Hercules Courtenay, may also have made the head on the Randolph sample chair in the Philadelphia Museum and the figure on the Cadwalader console table now at the Metropolitan Museum, which is known from *Colonial Grandeur in Philadelphia* to have come from the Golden Eagle, Randolph's shop on Chestnut Street.

A Philadelphia desk-and-bookcase from Chippendale's *Director*

BY ROBERT C. SMITH, *University of Pennsylvania*

VERY FEW DESIGNS for American furniture of the colonial period were taken directly from plates in Thomas Chippendale's *Gentleman and Cabinet-Maker's Director*, although the general influence of this book was almost universal. Now a mahogany desk-and-bookcase of great significance has appeared (color plate). The lower section is based directly upon one of the handsomest of Chippendale's designs, Plate 78 of the 1754 edition, and the upper section shows the influence of two other English design books. The bookcase displays an unparalleled amount of fine architectural carving and the whole piece may be related to the work of the great Philadelphia cabinetmaker Benjamin Randolph, active from about 1760 to 1791. With these points to recommend it, the desk assumes a rare position in American furniture history.

It is extraordinary that a piece of such importance should have remained unrecorded for so long. It came to my attention through my article *Finial busts on eighteenth-century Philadelphia furniture.*[1] I received a photograph from Mrs. Robert R. Dunn Jr. of La Jolla, California, of a finial bust of a young woman similar to several of those presented in the article. It belongs to a desk-and-bookcase (Chippendale's term for this form) in the collection of the Dunns. Mr. Dunn knew only that he had inherited it from his mother, who in turn had received it from a relative, the Reverend Edward Craig Mitchell (1836-1911), a Swedenborgian pastor, originally from Philadelphia.

Upon examination by myself and a prominent New York dealer the desk-and-bookcase revealed a frame of long-grained pine, while white oak is used in the lining and sides of the smaller drawers. Tulip poplar, the conventional secondary wood for Philadelphia colonial case furniture, appears in only one of the minor drawers, which because

Mahogany desk-and-bookcase, Philadelphia, c. 1755-1760 or 1770-1775. This majestic piece of furniture probably originally had looking glasses in the doors of its bookcase section. Hitherto unrecorded, it has never before been published. Height to bust, 107 inches; width 47½; depth 24½. *Collection of Mr. and Mrs. Robert R. Dunn Jr.; photograph by Waggaman/Ward.*

of its very slender dovetails must have been remade at the end of the eighteenth century. In spite of its atypical construction, there is no reason to believe that the Dunn desk-and-bookcase was made in England or anywhere but Philadelphia. It has the generous proportions, the rich and stately appearance characteristic of the furniture of that city and much of its ornament, including the handsome bust, is unmistakably Philadelphian.

Plate 78 of the 1754 *Director* is the most elaborate of Chippendale's six designs for desks-and-bookcase (Fig. 1). It has the unusual feature of a pair of carved doors flanking the three drawers in the lower section. The two almost identical busts of young women that serve as lateral finials in Chippendale's plate are reflected directly in a mahogany bust on a Philadelphia desk-and-bookcase in the Metropolitan Museum of Art,[2] and indirectly in the bust on the Pompadour high chest of drawers in the same museum.[3] The latter is a masterpiece of Philadelphia rococo carving which has analogies with the little that is known of the style of Benjamin Randolph. The Greco-Roman bearded figure, which is Chippendale's central finial in Plate 78, is seen in reverse on Benjamin Randolph's trade card of about 1770 (Fig. 2). For these reasons I proposed in my article on finial busts that Randolph's shop, the Golden Eagle, was the probable source for most finial-bust sculpture.

The bust on the Dunn desk-and-bookcase (Fig. 3) has a coiffure not unlike that found on the Pompadour high chest. The hair is gathered into a tail-like braid which falls lightly on the left shoulder. The eyes, however, are narrower and the face, neck, and especially the pleats of the bodice are carved with more dexterity and precision. The spirited expression on the girl's face suggests that this was an actual portrait such as those William Rush was to make in Philadelphia in the early nineteenth century. The cylindrical pedestal that supports the finial bust is an early Victorian replacement.

For his trade card Benjamin Randolph selected not only Chippendale's bust of an ancient but also the desk from the *Director*. It appears at the foot of the advertisement in the center of five other pieces of elaborately carved rococo furniture (Fig. 2), suggesting that Randolph intended that the card should illustrate his finest work as a

Fig. 1 "Desk & Bookcase," Pl. 78 from Thomas Chippendale, *Gentleman and Cabinet-Maker's Director* (London, 1754). This is the source for the lower section of the Dunn desk-and-bookcase, and of the desk on Benjamin Randolph's trade card. *Photograph by courtesy of the Henry Francis du Pont Winterthur Museum.*

cabinetmaker. However, the door of the bookcase in the trade card has muntins and glazing in place of the looking glass of the Chippendale design. An enormous cartouche and what may be a pair of urns have replaced the finial busts. The bookcase in Randolph's trade card again conforms to Chippendale's design in the use of two pendants of carved foliage flanking the door. There is decoration of this type on certain very rich Philadelphia chimney breasts, such as that in the Stamper-Blackwell parlor now at Winterthur, which has been attributed to Randolph by some authorities.

Plate 78 of the *Director* also inspired the lower section of the Dunn desk-and-bookcase (Fig. 4). This is the only instance of the use of this splendid pattern in any known surviving piece of American colonial furniture. Following a practice of the time, Chippendale offered two alternative schemes of decoration for the lateral sections of the desk-and-bookcase. The maker of the Dunn desk chose the richer of the two. The panels on either side of the drawers have the popular Anglo-French rococo device of paired, foliated C scrolls, while gadrooning with pendants, scrolls, and acanthus leaves decorate the ogee feet. Actually, the Dunn desk surpasses Chippendale's design in the amount of its ornament. The carving of the ogee-shape decorative panel above the drawers is richer, and the cabinetmaker has added an extra bead-and-reel molding just above the base, and a thin foliate band above the doors and drawers, which provides a link with similar decoration in the bookcase section (Fig. 5).

The proportions of the Dunn desk-and-bookcase are almost exactly the same as those noted on the Chippendale plate. The height of the desk section is forty-three and one-half inches, while that of the corresponding part in Plate 78 is given as forty-three and three-quarters inches. The case of the Dunn piece, measuring forty-seven and one-half inches in width, is one and one-half inches broader than that in the design. Because of this considerable width and the resulting weight, the fall front of each desk rests upon two plain drawers pulled out for support rather than on the more common narrow runners or lopers. This arrangement is also found in the Waln and Sharples desks-and-bookcase, the only examples which have it among the numerous Philadelphia desks illustrated in William Mac-Pherson Hornor Jr.'s *Blue Book Philadelphia Furniture*.[4]

The writing area of the Dunn desk reveals still another extraordinary feature. Flanking the door of the center compartment, which is entirely plain as in most Philadelphia desks of the Chippendale period, are two wide pilasters whose shafts are decorated with fretwork taken from Plate 151 of the 1754 *Director* (Fig. 6). The lower drawers on either side of the central compartment have serpentine fronts, while the shells carved on the drawers of the upper tier have a series of parallel knife strokes (Fig. 7). This was probably intended to enliven the surface but actually gives it a somewhat informal, if not unfinished, appearance.

The upper section is at once the enigma and the chief glory of the Dunn desk-and-bookcase (Fig. 8). It differs from all other known bookcases of this type and offers one of the finest existing ensembles of architectural carving on Philadelphia furniture. The usual Philadelphia Chippendale bookcase sections either terminate in acanthus-scroll pediments like the one in Plate 78 of the *Director*, accompanied by a baroque-rococo shell or cartouche with ornamental grasses, or in a light broken triangular pediment often set above a fretwork frieze.

The Dunn bookcase, however, has a heavier broken

pediment overlaid with rich academic foliated carving and moldings. The ornament suggests the furniture style of William Kent, which was popular in England in the 1730's and 1740's. The Kent style produced in Philadelphia the cabinet for Governor John Penn's air pump (Fig. 9), which was made for the Library Company in 1739 by the State House carpenter John Harrison.[5] This piece of furniture, entirely of pine, has the same very deep cornice with the ornament carried through the pedimental aperture, exactly as in the upper section of the Dunn desk. The latter, however, has no less than six different moldings, twice as many as the Harrison pump case, including two bands of leaves, a "wall of Troy" molding, egg and dart, and two minute geometric designs. The effect is like that of William Buckland's great Palladian room cornices at Gunston Hall, Mount Airy, and the State House in Annapolis. This decoration, however, has nothing to do with conventional Philadelphia furniture of the 1770's when the Dunn desk was probably made, although it could have been executed a decade earlier.

The stately architectural treatment continues in the pair of pilasters framing the doors of the bookcase section. These doors probably originally contained looking glasses like those in the Chippendale plate and in the Willing-Cadwalader desk-and-bookcase, a typical Philadelphia piece with rococo instead of architectural carving.[6] The Ionic pilasters on the Dunn piece were used on New York and Boston Chippendale furniture but not on any other known Philadelphia piece of this period. Yet there are no other mannerisms of these northern schools to suggest that the Dunn piece was made elsewhere than in Philadelphia. The

Ionic capitals are unusually elaborate with tiny pineapple-like motifs between the foliated and paneled volutes, beneath which are minute architectural moldings. It is important to note that their carving, like that of the rosettes in the frieze above them, has the same sharp parallel lines found in the shells on the upper tier of drawers inside the desk. This would suggest that both desk and bookcase were carved by the same person and that they were designed as a single composition in spite of the difference in style. This difference is not as great as it first might appear, because the small tufts of foliage atop the bookcase doors are closely related to the rococo carving on the doors of the desk section. Both have the same bead-and-reel and leaf moldings.

The designer of the Dunn desk-and-bookcase showed the same disregard for Greco-Roman architectural correctness that led the builders of Philadelphia's Christ Church to combine an Ionic frieze with Doric pilasters both inside and outside the chancel. The opposite occurred on the

Fig. 2.   Trade card of Benjamin Randolph, Philadelphia, c. 1770. Engraved by James Smither, it shows a desk and a bust taken from Pl. 78 of the 1754 *Director*. The Doric frieze in the background is related to that on the Dunn desk. *Photograph by courtesy of the Library Company of Philadelphia.*

Fig. 3.   Finial bust on the Dunn desk-and-bookcase. This mahogany bust of a girl is outstanding among a number of such statuettes used as finials on Philadelphia Chippendale furniture. Height 7⅞ inches. *Except as noted, photographs are by Robert C. Smith.*

131

Fig. 4. Lower section of the Dunn desk-and-bookcase. The brasses, though old, are not original. The carved doors enclose compartments for the vertical filing of ledgers and papers.

Fig. 5. Detail of the ornamental panel.

Fig. 6. Pl. 151 of the 1754 *Director*.
The center design provided the pattern for the fretwork seen in the writing compartment of the Dunn desk.

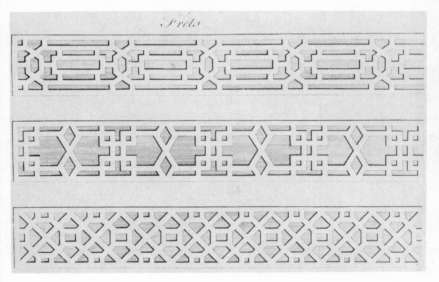

132

desk-and-bookcase. There the Ionic pilasters carry the Doric frieze, which is a hallmark of fine Philadelphia eighteenth-century architecture. There are correctly cut triglyphs and guttae, a few of which are now missing. The metopes are decorated with rosettes (almost exactly like those carved by Edmund Wooley for the doorcase of the tower of Independence Hall) which have at their centers the added extravagance of a bunch of berries. Possibly pomegranates without their husks, these berries may have been suggested by Plate 4 of Abraham Swan's *The British Architect* (Fig. 10), where the metopes of a Doric frieze have what appear to be pomegranate fruits encased in fronds of acanthus. Plate 3 of this popular pattern book, which first appeared in London in 1745, may also have suggested the introduction of a wall of Troy molding and another of leaf forms just above the Doric frieze of the Dunn bookcase (Fig. 8). In addition to these conventional European architectural enrichments the frieze of the Dunn bookcase has two other special features. The triglyphs are allowed to project with the cornice out over the pilasters. At each end of the frieze are a number of spirited small husks and scroll forms recalling ornament from Batty Langley's *The City and Country Builder's and Workman's Treasury of Designs* of 1745.[7]

These small motifs are in keeping with the spirit of the festoons of flowers, leaves, and berries ending in fluttering tassels, which are tied to the central plinth by ribbons from which hang a pendant of husks (Fig. 11). Here the carving—crisp and precise but carefully contained—is in sharp contrast to the free-moving naturalism of the ornament on the doors of the desk.

These contrasting styles of ornament, always of the highest quality, give the Dunn desk-and-bookcase its unique personality and pose the difficult question of why this was done. There are two possible answers. One, that the desk was made before the typical Philadelphia Chippendale pieces, perhaps in the late 1750's, and represents the final development of an architectural style first seen in the Library Company's cabinet, to which new motifs from the *Director* were added. This would account for the predominance of decorative details in the taste of Langley and Swan on the bookcase section and the subdued carving on the ornamental panels flanking the drawers of the desk.

There are two objections to this theory. First, no similar piece can be cited to suggest that such a transitional style ever existed in Philadelphia case furniture, although we find something approaching it in a few richly carved chairs in the Queen Anne style. Secondly, the elegance of the carving seems too advanced for the period 1755 to 1760. This is especially true of the bust, which is equal to, if not superior to, the other busts made for later furniture.

The second theory is based on the assumption that the bookcase section of the Dunn desk was out of style at the time it was made, probably around 1770. Benjamin Randolph's trade card may lend some support to this theory. Despite all its rococo novelties, the card contains one important survival from the age of William Kent in the Vitruvian scroll on the card table at the right of the card. This suggests that elements from the older style were still in use at the Golden Eagle in the 1770's, and we know that fine furniture in the Queen Anne style was still being made in Philadelphia at the end of the eighteenth century. There is also the Doric colonnade with tasseled drapery in the background of the trade card. Could this architectural theme which appears in the bookcase (and in the wainscoting of Independence Hall in the 1750's and in Cliveden, Mount Pleasant, Port Royal, and other Philadelphia houses of the 1760's) have been combined with the desk on the trade card by some ambitious cabinetmaker to create a tour de force that was never again attempted? Was this work done in Benjamin Randolph's shop, as the presence of the superbly carved bust might indicate? Did Randolph, to whom are attributed a number of sample chairs thought to demonstrate the variety of his decorative devices, design the Dunn desk-and-bookcase as a sample for case-furniture ornament to be found in his own advertisement?

Fig. 7. Interior of the Dunn desk. The central compartment with its undecorated door is typical of Philadelphia desks and has the unusual feature of pilasters ornamented with fretwork.

Fig. 8. The bookcase design is the richest reflection in furniture of the architecture of contemporary doorcases on the public buildings and private houses of Philadelphia. The Doric frieze is almost exactly like that on the south portal of Independence Hall.

Fig. 9. Top of the case of Governor Penn's air pump, made by John Harrison, Philadelphia, 1739. Pine painted white. This cabinet is an earlier version of an architectural style of which the Dunn bookcase seems to be the culmination.

George Henkels,
nineteenth-century Philadelphia cabinetmaker

BY KENNETH AMES, *Assistant professor, Franklin and Marshall College*

Fig. 1. Lithographed trade card of George J. Henkels (1819-1883), 1850-1857, showing late classical and rococo revival furniture. *Library Company of Philadelphia.*

Fig. 2. Henkels' premises on the northwest corner of Thirteenth and Chestnut streets, Philadelphia, 1867-1874. Henkels, wearing a top hat, stands by the left-hand column. The site is now occupied by the John Wanamaker store.

GEORGE J. HENKELS is one of the best-known Philadelphia furniture makers of the middle of the nineteenth century. The numerous writings by or about him are important and often consulted sources not only for information about the tastes of the period but about the techniques of making and selling furniture as well.

Henkels was born in Philadelphia, the son of Peter David Henkels, who manufactured firearms for the United States government during the War of 1812, and who helped to erect the first steam-powered factory in Philadelphia. George Henkels was trained as a chairmaker and first appeared in Philadelphia business directories in 1843, when he was listed at 371 South Third Street. During the next six years Henkels changed his address almost annually. In 1850 he succeeded Crawford Riddell, a fashionable cabinetmaker, and moved into Riddell's premises at 173

Chestnut Street, "opposite the State House," as Henkels noted in his trade card (Fig. 1). This store was demolished by fire in 1854 but Henkels rebuilt it and remained there until 1857, when he moved to 524 Walnut Street. In 1862 he moved again, this time to 809-811 Chestnut Street. By 1867 he occupied the former Fotteral mansion (Fig. 2) on the northwest corner of Thirteenth and Chestnut streets, and was there briefly in partnership with George S. and B. W. Lacy, and then, briefly too, with a relative, John A. Henkels. It was at the last two Chestnut Street addresses that in the years immediately following the Civil War Henkels carried on the most extensive trade of any furniture house in Philadelphia.

In 1874 he bought from the YMCA what was known as the German Club House at 211-215 South Twelfth Street. There he remained until 1877, when he apparently

Fig. 3. Fig. 197 from Samuel Sloan, *Homestead Architecture* (Philadelphia, 1861), showing library furniture from the warerooms of George Henkels. *Eleutherian Mills Historical Library.*

Fig. 4. Fig. 198 from Sloan, showing library furniture from the same suite as that illustrated in Fig. 3. *Eleutherian Mills Historical Library.*

retired from active business. In his moves Henkels followed the expansion of Philadelphia from the colonial part of the city to the section ten blocks west that was fashionable when he was at the peak of his career. Henkels died a widower at the age of sixty-four leaving thirteen children. His last residence was 507 South Ninth Street.

Throughout his life Henkels was a prolific writer. As a Democrat of the "old school" he wrote many articles for Philadelphia newspapers on political and economic matters, usually under the pseudonym "Mechanic." He also wrote a series of articles about billiards, a game which he played expertly. He was devoted to his country, his city, his family, and the Catholic church. His humanitarian acts during the Civil War were mentioned in most of his obituaries: when the wounded were brought to Philadelphia by the shipload in the early stages of the war, Henkels

met them at the docks with ambulances he designed himself and made at his own expense. These consisted of spring beds and mattresses placed in his furniture vans. Because they were the most comfortable, Henkels' ambulances were reserved for the most seriously wounded.

Of Henkels' writings the most important for furniture historians are the catalogues and booklets he wrote for his customers. A small *Catalogue of Furniture in Every Style* was published while he was located at 173 Chestnut Street between 1850 and 1857. This pamphlet provided prices and occasional comments on well over one hundred pieces of furniture. Prices ranged from $350 for a rosewood cabinet *étagère* or a rosewood high-post bedstead with cornice and canopy to $3 to $7 for caned-seat parlor rocking chairs and 75 cents to $1 for windsor chairs for the bedroom.

Fig. 5. Walnut bookcase in the library of the Asa Packer Mansion. Height 10½, width 10 feet. The standing figures are 19½ and 21½ inches high. *Borough of Jim Thorpe; photograph by Cortlandt V. D. Hubbard.*

Another early work was *An Essay on Household Furniture*, a sixteen-page booklet with illustrations, published in Philadelphia in 1850. It included a brief history of furniture, a discussion of woods, marbles, and construction techniques (including such curious bits of information as: "Buhl-work, it is said was first practiced in a town of the same name in Germany; though others have it that its inventor was named Von Buhl"), a treatment of the furniture appropriate to each of the main apartments of the house; and a description of his establishment reprinted from an unidentified Philadelphia magazine of the same year. While Henkels' historical information was sometimes vague or inaccurate, his description of then current furniture practices and his indications of changing fashions are generally reliable and thus helpful to historians. For example, he suggested that interest in grotesque furniture

might have developed from an admiration for its whimsical quality; he noted that native walnut was joining the list of fashionable cabinetmaking woods; and he declared that his best marble came from Spain and Italy. On the other hand, Henkels' illustrations must be treated with caution. While they may accurately represent furniture in his warerooms, the woodcuts are copied from other sources, primarily the Paris publication *Le Garde-Meuble Album de l'exposition de l'industrie, 1844*, which is a useful compendium of the best contemporary French design.

In both of these early publications Henkels described his premises at 173 Chestnut Street. These consisted of two main buildings, each four stories high. The workshop, or factory building, measured fifty-two by fifty feet. The cellar was used for storing lumber, mostly imported, and held the furnace. The first floor contained woodworking

Fig. 6. Walnut table in the Packer library.
Height 30, width 43, length 62½ inches.
Borough of Jim Thorpe; Hubbard photograph.

Fig. 7. Walnut high-back armchair
in the Packer library.
Height 51½ inches.
*Borough of Jim Thorpe;
Hubbard photograph.*

machinery, including lathes, while the second floor was a general workshop. Carving took place on the third floor and varnishing on the fourth. During the summer the roof was used for drying finished furniture.

The much larger main building was about 180 feet long and twenty-seven feet wide. The showrooms were located on the first and second stories, with the principal one on the second floor. In the cellar were two furnaces, the clerks, bookkeepers, and salesmen, and stockpiles of veneer and lumber. The third floor housed seamstresses, enamelers, the foreman's office, and storerooms for hardware and looking-glass stock. The fourth floor was used for varnishing, upholstering, and storage. Above the fourth floor was a single room in which the hair used for upholstering was stored. Stonecutting, marble polishing, and related activities were carried on in adjacent buildings. In 1850 Henkels employed about 180 people, all of whom, he made a point

of noting, were adults.

In 1850 *Godey's Lady's Book and Magazine* publicized Henkels' shop and its contents, and other Philadelphia magazines contain references to him. However, by far the best-known presentation of his furniture appears in *Homestead Architecture*, by Samuel Sloan, Philadelphia's leading architect in the middle of the nineteenth century. By including furniture in a book about architecture, Sloan might have been emulating Andrew Jackson Downing, whose *Architecture of Country Houses* of 1850 contained illustrations of furniture by Edward Hennessey, George Platt, and Alexander Roux. First published in Philadelphia in 1861, *Homestead Architecture* included twelve wood engravings of furniture available at Henkels' warerooms. These are particularly valuable documents of the taste of 1861.

Sloan may have been responsible for the furniture section

138

Fig. 8. Walnut drop-front desk in the Packer library. Height 56½, width 43, depth 24 inches. *Borough of Jim Thorpe: Hubbard photograph.*

Fig. 9. One of two identical walnut chairs in the Packer library. Height 33½ inches. *Borough of Jim Thorpe: Hubbard photograph.*

of his book, but it seems more likely that Henkels wrote it himself. Both the subject matter (woods, fabrics, and so on) and the style of writing resemble those in publications known to be by Henkels. Henkels' contributions of signed articles on economics, labor relations, and the familiar subjects of furniture woods and fabrics to Sloan's *Architectural Review and Builders' Journal,* which appeared between 1868 and 1870, suggest a continuing relationship that might well have been established already in 1861 with the publication of *Homestead Architecture.*

Much of the more elaborate furniture depicted in the wood engravings survives in the Asa Packer Mansion in Jim Thorpe, Pennsylvania. Packer became the wealthiest man in Pennsylvania by mining and transporting coal. He was elected to Congress for two terms and in 1869 he was the Democratic candidate for governor. He served in 1876 as a commissioner for the Centennial. Packer's greatest

philanthropy was Lehigh University, which he founded in 1865.

The Packer mansion was built about 1860 and is now owned by the borough of Jim Thorpe and maintained by the local Lion's Club. Of the furniture that can be attributed to Henkels the most spectacular is in the library. Sloan devoted two plates to this suite of library furniture (Figs. 3,4), which was described as "what is called *Renaissance* in France and *Antique* in this country." Clearly the major source was the sixteenth century, from which the Renaissance revival borrowed all manner of vigorously carved animal, human, and grotesque details. The style was popularized in France in the 1840's by such cabinetmakers and designers as Alexandre and Henri Fourdinois, Charles Joseph Lemarchand, Michel Liénard, and Auguste Emile Ringuet Le Prince. It was thought to be especially appropriate for libraries and dining rooms.

139

Fig. 10. Fig. 191 from Sloan,
showing a suite of
drawing-room furniture
by George Henkels.
*Eleutherian Mills
Historical Library.*

Fig. 11. Rosewood sofa in the parlor at the Packer mansion.
Height 55½, length 79 inches.
Borough of Jim Thorpe: Hubbard photograph.

Fig. 12. Rosewood side chair and armchair from the Packer Mansion.
Height of side chair, 45½; height of armchair, 53½ inches.
Borough of Jim Thorpe; Hubbard photograph.

140

Fig. 13. Rosewood *étagère* at the Packer Mansion. Height 105 inches. *Borough of Jim Thorpe; Hubbard photograph.*

The largest piece of furniture in the Packer library is the bookcase (Fig. 5). It is about ten and a half feet high and ten feet wide and like all the furniture in the suite, is made of walnut. What appears to be a drawer just above the kneehole drops to reveal pigeonholes and a writing surface. Rich and elaborate carving and a variety of planes create the visual complexity and intricately balanced composition typical of the best productions in this style. Projecting from the pediment is a carved stag's head, a recurring motif on large case pieces in the Renaissance style. Below it stand two figures, nearly two feet in height, dressed in armor and bearing spears and shields. Portrait heads, dragons, caryatids, grotesque heads, and bold moldings are among the applied carvings.

The library table (Fig. 6) exactly matches the description in Sloan. Grotesque heads serve as drawer pulls, as they

do on the bookcase, two to a drawer. *Homestead Architecture* noted that this had not always been the case: "The cut should have two heads on each drawer for handles; this improvement has been made since the artist sketched it for this book." At each end of the table a lion's head projects emphatically from between panels of foliage.

To the right of the bookcase in Sloan's plate is the large carved armchair shown in Figure 7. The lioness's claws and heads of the table reappear on the chair. The high back depicts a stag being hunted by ferocious dogs and *putti* armed with bows and arrows and spears. The carving is a bit crude and not too finely finished.

The secretary (Fig. 8) uses the same decorative vocabulary as the previous pieces. Caryatids, such as those prominent on the front corners, were used widely by French cabinetmakers after 1840. The front of the secretary drops

141

Fig. 14. Fig. 195 from Sloan, showing a suite of bedroom furniture by George Henkels.

Fig. 15. Walnut chest of drawers with ebonized trim in one of the bedrooms of the Packer mansion. Height 94 inches. *Borough of Jim Thorpe; Hubbard photograph.*

Fig. 16. Bed of bird's-eye maple with rosewood trim at the Packer mansion. Height of headboard, 72 inches. *Borough of Jim Thorpe; Hubbard photograph.*

142

to reveal a writing surface and small compartments. In the Packer mansion there are two chairs (Fig. 9) like that on the left in Figure 4. *Homestead Architecture* comments that the chair was a recent ''importation from one of the best establishments in Paris,'' thus raising questions about which of the articles sold by Henkels were actually produced by him.

The parlor at the Packer mansion contains a superb suite of rosewood furniture identical to that in Figure 10. According to the text, ''the style is now called the 'Napoleon' and is a near approach to the 'Elizabethan.' '' Today it might be included under Renaissance revival, for its verticality and agitated outline are certainly characteristic of the style that succeeded the rounded rococo-derived style of the mid-century. The settee and two chairs (Figs. 11, 12) have turned rather than cabriole legs and elaborately

Fig. 17. Washstand of bird's-eye maple with rosewood trim at the Packer mansion. Height 40 inches. *Borough of Jim Thorpe; Hubbard photograph.*

Fig. 18. Armoire of bird's-eye maple with rosewood trim at the Packer mansion. Height 106 inches. *Borough of Jim Thorpe; Hubbard photograph.*

Fig. 19. Trade card George Henkels used at the Centennial. *New-York Historical Society.*

Fig. 20. Reverse of the card illustrated in Fig. 19 showing Henkels' "Centennial Sofa Bed." *New-York Historical Society.*

shaped upholstered panels. The *étagère* (Fig. 13), said in *Household Architecture* to be in a new pattern, has many motifs that can be traced back to sixteenth-century armoires and dressoirs.

Two of the bedrooms also contain suites of Henkels' furniture (Figs. 14-18). The major pieces in both rooms are identical except that one suite is made of walnut with ebonized trim; the other is of bird's-eye maple with rosewood trim. The description in Sloan's book indicating that this style too was a new one helps to date the moment when this angular version of the Renaissance mode was deemed appropriate for bedroom furniture. The pediment broken by a cartouche that appears so modestly on these pieces became the focal point of bedroom case pieces and beds during the 1870's, particularly in the work produced by the growing firms of Grand Rapids. Each of the bedroom suites at the Packer mansion contains a bed, chest of drawers, wardrobe, washstand, nightstand, table (not shown or mentioned in Sloan), and several small chairs with upholstered spring seats.

Other rooms at the Packer mansion contain furniture that is probably by Henkels. A dozen dining chairs without arms and one with arms match models published in Sloan, but the rest of the suite has vanished, probably in a remodeling of the dining room late in the nineteenth century. In the bedrooms are pieces of furniture which do not resemble designs in Sloan but which are of high enough quality to have been made by Henkels and are of the right period. In all, the Packer mansion has a handsome collection of some of the finest furniture made in America around 1860.

Part of George Henkels' success stemmed from the fact that he never lost an opportunity to promote his goods. He advertised frequently and widely; he exhibited at trade fairs in Washington, Boston, and at the Franklin Institute in Philadelphia; his wares appeared in the New York Crystal Palace Exposition in 1853 and at the Centennial in 1876 (Fig. 19), where he showed bedroom furniture made of maple from a tree that grew in Independence Square.* He also showed sofa beds, a kind of furniture that was becoming popular as more Americans began to live in apartments. Henkels' "Centennial Sofa Bed" (Fig. 20) sold for $35 in 1876. It was perhaps inspired by a seventeenth-century sofa at Knole in Sevenoaks, England, which had been illustrated in Charles Locke Eastlake's influential *Hints on Household Taste* (1868).

No labeled or stamped Henkels furniture has yet been found, but it is evident from the furniture at the Packer mansion, which must have been made by Henkels, that his goods were of the highest quality and that he fully deserved the reputation he had at the time of his death ninety years ago.

The author gratefully acknowledges financial aid from Franklin and Marshall College in the preparation of this article which incorporates the notes of Robert C. Smith, University of Pennsylvania. The author would be delighted to hear from readers who have additional information about George Henkels.

Carved Chippendale case furniture from Lancaster, Pennsylvania

BY JOHN J. SNYDER JR.

LAST YEAR in this magazine I suggested that many pieces of carved Chippendale furniture from Lancaster County, Pennsylvania, which had been erroneously attributed to John Bachman II actually originated in the town of Lancaster.[1] This article, based largely upon new discoveries, will trace the development of a recognizable regional school of cabinetmaking in the Chippendale style which flourished in Lancaster from the late 1760's until about 1810.

The land now encompassed by Lancaster County was separated from Chester County in 1729, and in the following year the county seat, Lancaster, was laid out.[2] The town was not only the administrative, social, and economic center of a large county, but also emerged as the major center for trade between Philadelphia and the interior. By the time of the Revolution Lancaster, with a population not exceeding five thousand, was America's largest inland town not located on a navigable river.[3] The prominence of its artisans, including gunsmiths, silversmiths, coppersmiths, the young Benjamin West, and the pewterer Johann Christian (or Christoph) Heyne, has been well established; only its woodworking craftsmen have been overlooked.

Lancaster had many carpenters and joiners before the advent of the Chippendale style there in the 1760's, but a scarcity of tax lists and family papers for the first three decades of the town's existence has hindered the recognition and documentation of William and Mary and Queen Anne furniture produced there.[4] By the 1760's, when the third edition of Thomas Chippendale's *The Gentleman and Cabinet-Maker's Director* (1762) was making an impact in the Colonies, Lancaster possessed the prerequisites for becoming the center of a regional school: numerous and specialized craftsmen, wealthy patrons, the accessibility of design sources in Philadelphia, and the taste-setting influence of prominent Philadelphians who had removed to Lancaster.

Among these taste setters were the former Philadelphia mayor Edward Shippen (1703-1781), the attorney and Signer of the Declaration of Independence George Ross (1730-1779), and the attorney and later judge Jasper Yeates (1745-1817).[5] Yeates' papers, many of which have survived, document his patronage of both Philadelphia and Lancaster joiners and cabinetmakers in the decade before 1775. Although Yeates employed various Lancaster joiners for building work, repairs, coffins, and utilitarian furniture, the only local man from whom he purchased quality furniture between 1765 and 1775 was John Mears (1737-1819), a Quaker who trained in Philadelphia and who worked in Chester County, Reading, and Lancaster during this decade.[6] Before 1777, Yeates' Philadelphia suppliers included the Elliotts for looking glasses, Benjamin Randolph for chairs, and the upholsterer Plunket Fleeson for a sofa and an easy chair.[7]

Fig. 1. Base of an end tower on the Burkhart organ case shown in Pl. II. *Except as noted, photographs are by Helga Photo Studio.*

The Chippendale style in Lancaster was initiated by Germanic craftsmen working for Germanic patrons, under the influence of Philadelphia-oriented taste setters between the 1760's and 1810. These conditions caused the unique blending of Philadelphia rococo with the older German baroque which formed the major stylistic strain of Lancaster Chippendale. The earliest piece of Lancaster Chippendale case furniture that exhibits these regional characteristics is the organ case (Pl. II) at the First Reformed Church (first called the German Reformed Church) which originally contained works by David Tannenberg (also Tanneberger; 1728-1804). Although this case has been published previously in relation to Tannenberg, the identity of its maker has only recently been established. On April 2, 1771, the Lancaster joiner George Burkhart billed the congregation £50 for "making the organ case."[8] This sum did not include the cost of the wood, and may not have included the cost of the carving, which Burkhart probably subcontracted to a specialist. On February 27, 1769, Tannenberg was commissioned to make an organ of fifteen stops, and Burkhart probably began work on the case soon afterwards. The organ was first played on December 23, 1770; several days later the (Philadelphia) *Pennsylvania Gazette* noted that it was "worth the attention and notice of the curious who may happen to pass this way."[9]

In selecting Burkhart, the First Reformed congregation was not only employing a loyal member of the church, but also honoring the person who, on the evidence of tax lists and his apparent style of life, appears to have been the most prosperous joiner in Lancaster before the Revolution. Although both Alsace and Switzerland have been claimed as his birthplace, his homeland is not known for certain. He may be the "Hans Jurig Burghart" who arrived in Philadelphia in 1739.[10] He first appeared in Lancaster in July 1750 at the age of twenty-nine, when he bought a lot on the northwest intersection of Duke and Orange streets, where he built his house and shop.[11] On April 28, 1753, he married Mary Doll (1731-1812), who bore five children who survived their father.[12] In 1764 he built a large stone house at the corner of his lot which was surpassed by no other joiner's house in Lancaster at that time.[13] Burkhart died there on February 17, 1783.[14] His estate inventory again testifies to his pre-eminence, for it lists "tools and other work not finished" worth £30, "walnut boards" at £5 and, unusual for Lancaster, "Mahogini boards" valued at £20.[15]

Although Burkhart's organ case has been repainted and has wings which were added between 1883 and 1885,[16] its important elements testify that by 1769 his workshop was proficient in the production of carved furniture in the Chippendale style. The shell-like motifs with flanking vines at the bases of the three towers (Fig. 1) resemble shells on the drawers of lowboys and highboys made in Lancaster (see Fig. 11). The rather heavy, stylized vines flanking the shell-like motifs on the organ, and the complex foliate carving of the canopies of the towers (Fig. 2), approximate the carving on the pediments of Lancaster pieces. The most surprising element in this carving is the bellflowers which adorn the six paneled pilasters (Fig. 2). Their stylized leafage, separated by dots and terminating in an S curve, match corresponding elements in the design for an organ case that appeared in the 1762 edition of Chippendale's *Director* (Fig. 3). Although it cannot be proved that Burkhart owned a copy of the *Director*, this close relation of work to printed source can only indicate that he or some close associate had access to the book.

Fig. 2. Detail of an end tower on the Burkhart organ case illustrated in Pl. II, showing the carved canopy and pendent bellflowers on the paneled pilasters.

These pendent bellflowers constitute the earliest firmly datable appearance of even a remotely neoclassical design on a piece of American cabinetwork. Burkhart's organ case predates by six years the small desk with inlaid keyhole escutcheon made by Benjamin Randolph in 1776 for Thomas Jefferson, which has hitherto been regarded as the earliest piece of American furniture showing any neoclassical influence.[17] Unless Burkhart used the neoclassical bellflowers by sheer chance, it is reasonable to speculate that there may have been Philadelphia pieces of the same date showing an even stronger neoclassical influence.

The congregation of the Lutheran Church of the Holy Trinity in Lancaster had completed its grand brick church in 1766, and they were not to be outdone by the new organ at the First Reformed Church, two blocks away. On July 21, 1771, the congregation agreed to raise by subscription the funds for Tannenberg to make an organ of twenty stops.[18] Peter Frick, a native of Germantown,[19] was commissioned to make the case for this organ. Frick was perhaps trained in Philadelphia, although by the mid-eighteenth century Germantown had joiners proficient in English styles from whom he could have received training.[20] By October 1770 Frick was in Lancaster, where he married Barbara Breidenhardt.[21] He was listed as a joiner in Lancaster tax lists in 1772 and 1773.[22] Most of the work on the organ case took place in 1774 and the instrument was

Fig. 3. Center section of a chamber organ in Plate CIV of Thomas Chippendale's *Director* (1762 edition). *Photograph by the author.*

consecrated on December 26, 1774.[23] However, not until July 17, 1777, did Frick receive full payment of £160 for making this masterpiece of American Chippendale cabinetwork (Pl. I).[24] About that time, Frick moved to Baltimore, where, after a prosperous career in business and politics, he died in 1822.[25]

Although Frick's organ case was enlarged by the addition of a tower at each end in 1893, it remains the only substantial element of the church's interior to survive mid-nineteenth-century renovations.[26] The staggering profusion of light, rococo carving on the organ case would have been accentuated by the original white and gold paint, which matched that of the entire interior (see Fig. 4).[27]

The high cost of the organ case was due not only to its scale, but also to the great amount of carving. In view of Frick's Philadelphia County background, it seems likely that some of the carving was done in Philadelphia and brought to Lancaster.[28] The total cost of the case, including Frick's large bill, the wood, nails, painting, and other joiner's work, was at least £210/5/8,[29] making it probably the most expensive single piece of cabinetwork created in the Colonies on the eve of the Revolution.

A comparison of the carved details of the Frick and Burkhart organ cases highlights major stylistic differences between Philadelphia and Lancaster carving. The central tablet of the Frick case (Fig. 5) has the light, open carving, the close relation of shape to ornament, and the sense of refined delicacy which characterize the best Philadelphia rococo carving on furniture and ornamental woodwork. By contrast, the carving on the Burkhart organ case (Figs. 1, 2) has complex stylized vines, the baroque sense of mass, and the containment of carved ornament which characterize the mainstream of Lancaster furniture in the Chippendale style. Whereas the Frick organ case may be the ultimate example of Philadelphia taste transplanted inland, the Burkhart case is the earliest example of a distinct Chippendale school in Lancaster.

Although no carved case furniture for domestic use by either Burkhart or Frick has yet come to light, two pieces signed by members of the Lind family of Lancaster have recently been located. Both are of the type formerly attributed to the Bachman family. Michael Lind (1725–1807), reputedly of Swedish origin, arrived in Philadelphia in 1752 and set up a joiner's shop on Orange Street in Lancaster the following year.[30] Of his seven children, Michael Jr., Conrad, and John[31] became joiners. Conrad worked as a joiner on East Orange Street as late as 1830. Early in his career, probably between 1770 and 1790, he signed the walnut desk in the Chippendale style shown in Figure 6. When I discovered the signature (Fig. 7) two years ago, this was the first piece of carved Chippendale case furniture made in Lancaster whose maker could be identified. The only notes of elaboration are the shell-carved prospect door and the flanking document drawers decorated with devices resembling vertical baseball bats, which are encountered frequently in Lancaster work (Fig. 8). The shell is one of the simplest types found on Lancaster furniture. The stippled rays and deeply incised perimeter are typical of Lancaster County techniques. Formerly owned by the Kready family in northern Lancaster County, the desk may have been owned by earlier generations of that family in Manor Township, southwest of the town of Lancaster.

A far more elaborate example of the work of the Lind family is a richly carved cherry highboy (Fig. 9) on which in October 1974 I discovered the red chalk inscription *M (?) Lind* (Fig. 10). If the partially effaced initial before Lind is *M,* as it appears to be, the highboy could have been made by the elder or the younger Michael Lind (1763–1840). The fact that both handmade and very early cut nails were used suggests that the highboy was made sometime between about 1780 and 1800. Before being presented to the United States State Department recently, it had been for three generations in a noted family of collectors in Connecticut. No record of its original or early ownership is known.

The two carved drawers (Figs. 11, 12) reveal one of the Lancaster school's most ambitious types of shell. The foliate carving applied to the center of the skirt is edged with double stippling and is unusually animated (Fig. 11). The relief carving in the tympanum of the pediment is notable for the crispness of its overlapping, entwined vines (Fig. 12). In its over-all design, the design and placement of its carved motifs, its carved moldings, and twelve-pointed rosettes this highboy is closely related to an unsigned Lancaster County highboy illustrated in my article last year.[32] The two pieces differ only in the details of the shell and pediment carving.

The tenacity of the Chippendale style is shown by the organ case made by Conrad Doll of Lancaster in 1807 for Peace Church in Hampden Township, Cumberland County, Pennsylvania, about forty miles northwest of Lancaster (Fig. 13). The contract for this organ, dated July 6, 1807, stated that Doll was to "erect, build, set up, and finish one Organ with six complete stops . . . according to the best of his art and skill" within five months for $466.67.[33] The wording indicates that Doll made both the works and the case. Doll's versatility is in fact documented by an 1805 deed in which he is called "joiner and cabinetmaker" and the Lancaster borough tax lists where, from 1799 to 1814, he is termed "spinnet and organ maker."[34] In addition, Doll was the organist at Lancaster's First Reformed Church, and in 1798 published what is generally considered to be the earliest dated German-American music book, *Sammlung Geistliche Lieder nebst Melodien.*[35]

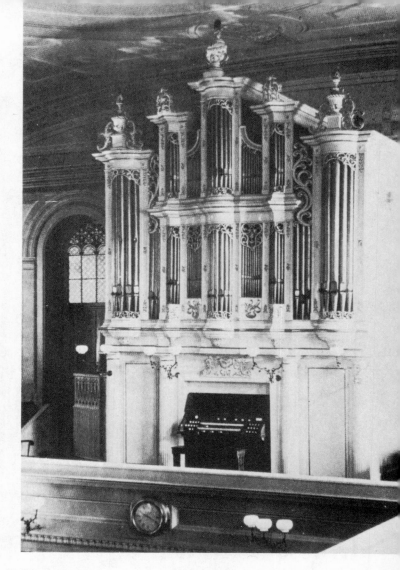

Fig. 4. Peter Frick organ case (see Pl. I) before the addition of the present end towers in 1893. This photograph, probably by Saylor, 1880-1890, may suggest the original white and gold paint. *Lancaster County Historical Society, Lancaster, Pennsylvania.*

Fig. 5. Carving on the applied tablet at the base of the central tower of the Peter Frick organ case (see Pl. I). In both execution and design this carving is so reminiscent of Philadelphia work as to suggest that it may have been done there.

Fig. 6. Desk signed by Conrad Lind (1753-1834) of Lancaster, probably 1770-1790; walnut, with hard pine and tulip the chief secondary woods. The top drawer is divided inside into two sections, each with a separately dovetailed frame. *Collection of H. B. Hartman; photograph by the author.*

It seems likely that Doll received his cabinetmaking training in the shop started by his uncle George Burkhart,[36] for Burkhart's son and namesake continued to operate the workshop until he moved to Bedford County, Pennsylvania, in 1791.[37] If this is so, the Burkhart-Doll family continued to produce some of Lancaster's richest pieces in the Chippendale style for nearly half a century.[38]

Doll's organ case at Peace Church, although actually relatively small, achieves a certain monumentality thanks to the broken pediment. The carved canopies of the towers and the other foliate carving remain firmly in the Chippendale tradition, untouched by neoclassical influence. The case was recently painted stark white, although no documentary proof has been found to indicate whether the original finish was white paint or dark wood graining.

There are some indications that the workshops of the Linds, Burkharts, and Doll were associated: all three families attended the First Reformed Church; all lived within a space of two blocks, and the estate of George Burkhart records transactions with ''Michael Lind'' between 1783 and 1791. The history of ownership of the Conrad Lind desk by the Kready family suggests that the rich farmers and landowners who came to Lancaster, the chief market town, patronized these workshops. In this connection, it is intriguing to note that Michael Withers, the original

owner of the great Lancaster desk-and-bookcase now in the Henry Francis du Pont Winterthur Museum,[39] twice figures in the accounts of the Burkhart estate in the 1780's.[40]

Documentary evidence associates the wood carvers of Lancaster only with ornamental work on buildings which no longer survive, but it is reasonable to conclude that the Linds, Burkharts, Doll, and their contemporaries also resorted to these carvers to ornament woodwork and furniture. According to the minutes of the county commissioners, in 1750 Michael Stump agreed ''to carve, paint, and afix in ye Court House . . . ye King's Coat of Arms of Great Britain.''[41] If this carving escaped destruction in the Revolution, it surely was lost when the first brick courthouse burned in 1784. Sometime between 1787 and 1792, the County paid one Christian Myer £54 for ''Carved work'' at the second brick courthouse.[42] Between 1796 and 1799 Jacob Flubacher and Michael Lind's son John built an elaborate steeple for the courthouse.[43] During those same years a man variously called Daniel or David Hostetter submitted bills totaling £112/10 for ''Ornaments . . . Carver's Work . . . and Carving ornaments'' for the steeple. In the same period Hostetter was also paid £26/5 for ''Carving Pillars in the Court House.'' The pillars themselves were made by John Lind and Flubacher.[44] That

Hostetter should have carved woodwork constructed by Flubacher and Lind indicates that neither carpenter could execute the carving himself. Unfortunately, Lancaster borough tax lists of the second half of the eighteenth century list no carvers, carpenters, or joiners. The division of labor between joiner and carver, although common in the eighteenth century, has not been suggested before for Lancaster cabinetwork.

The Lind highboy shown in Figure 9 has two distinct types of dovetailing (Figs. 14b, 14c), suggesting that it was worked on by two persons. The dovetailing shown in Figure 14b is closely related to that shown in Figure 14a, which is found in a highboy and a desk-and-bookcase illustrated in my article in this magazine last year.[45] On the other hand, the dovetailing shown in Figure 14c is markedly similar to that on the Lind desk (Fig. 14d). This structural evidence might be interpreted as an indication that the highboy and desk-and-bookcase illustrated last year were built in the Lind family workshop. However, the evidence cannot support a conclusive attribution, for even the dovetailing on a signed piece could be the work of an apprentice or journeyman who moved from shop to shop.

The five pieces discussed here are the only known examples of Lancaster County carved case furniture in the Chippendale style whose makers can be identified. They point to Lancaster as the center of a regional school and to the fact that many pieces once called ''Bachman'' actually are products of this town. However, it would be premature to attribute much Lancaster furniture to the Linds, Burkharts, Doll, or Frick, for it is only reasonable to suppose that others of the more than 160 woodworking craftsmen in Lancaster from 1760 to 1810 made elaborate pieces which have yet to be identified. Moreover, some carved pieces were probably produced by joiners in the small towns of Lancaster County, within twenty or even thirty miles of the county seat.

Fig. 7. Tracing of the signature of Conrad Lind that is inscribed in pencil on the bottom of the right-hand section of the top drawer of the desk illustrated in Fig. 6.

Pl. I. Case of the organ at the Lutheran Church of the Holy Trinity, South Duke Street, Lancaster, made by Peter Frick (1743-1822), 1774. The pointed towers at each end were added in 1893. When consecrated in December 1774, this was the largest organ in America. The present colors do not follow the originals. Fig. 4 shows the organ before the towers were added.

Fig. 8. Shell-carved prospect door and the document drawers of the desk illustrated in Fig. 6. *Author's photograph.*

Fig. 9. Highboy signed by a member of the Lind family of Lancaster, c. 1780-1800; cherry, with tulip the secondary wood. Some of the brasses are original; the finials are very old replacements. *Diplomatic Reception Rooms, Department of State, Washington, D.C.; photograph by E. Irving Blomstrann.*

[1]ANTIQUES, May 1974, pp. 1056-1065.

[2]Franklin Ellis and Samuel Evans, *History of Lancaster County, Pennsylvania* (Philadelphia, 1883), p. 360.

[3]Jerome H. Wood, *Conestoga Crossroads: The Rise of Lancaster Pennsylvania 1730-1789* (Brown University dissertation, 1969), pp. 99-159.

[4]No complete tax lists before 1750 for Lancaster borough are known, and the most important groups of family papers for this town date after the mid-1750's.

[5]Ellis and Evans, *History of Lancaster*, p. 226.

[6]For biographical information on Mears, see John G. Freeze, *A History of Columbia County, Pennsylvania* (Bloomsburg, 1883), pp. 104-105; Margaret Berwind Schiffer, *Furniture and Its Makers of Chester County, Pennsylvania* (Philadelphia, 1966), p. 157. For a record of Yeates' patronage of Mears, see Jasper Yeates Account Book, p. 34, in the Lancaster County Historical Society, Lancaster; and Yeates Papers, Business, Bills, Receipts—particularly 1767 and 1768—in the Historical Society of Pennsylvania, Philadelphia.

[7]Jasper Yeates Account Book, pp. 36, 38, 40. For Yeates' patronage of Elliott, see Joseph Shippen of Philadelphia to Jasper Yeates of Lancaster, July 3, 1776, Balch Papers, Shippen Vol. 2, p. 31, in the Historical Society of Pennsylvania. For his patronage of Randolph, see Randolph to Yeates, October 25, 1775, in Yeates Papers.

[8]Translation of German bill from George Burkhart to Reformed Congregation in Lancaster, April 2, 1771. Records of First Reformed Church, Reformed Church Archives, Philip Schaff Library, Lancaster.

[9]William H. Armstrong, *Organs for America—The Life and Work of David Tannenberg* (Philadelphia, 1967), pp. 28, 67.

[10]*Pennsylvania Archives,* series 2, Vol. 17, p. 193.

[11]Lancaster County deed XX-16, Lancaster County courthouse, Lancaster.

[12]Marriage records of First Reformed Church Lancaster, Reformed Church Archives. Lancaster County will D-1-288, Lancaster County courthouse.

[13]The house was demolished in 1902, but photographs of the exterior are preserved at the Lancaster County Historical Society.

[14]Tombstone inscription, south wall, First Reformed Church, Lancaster.

[15]George Burgart estate inventory, 1783, Lancaster County Historical Society.

[16]W. Stuart Cramer, *History of First Reformed Church Lancaster Pennsylvania 1736-1904* (Lancaster, 1904), p. 120.

[17]Charles F. Montgomery, *American Furniture, The Federal Period* (New York, 1966), pp. 9, 133.

[18]Armstrong, *Organs for America*, p. 94. George W. Leonard, "Brief History of the Organs, Organists, and Choir Leaders of Trinity 1734-1962," unpublished and undated typescript, Trinity Lutheran Church, Lancaster, p. 2.

[19]Frederick A. Virkus, *The Abridged Compendium of American Genealogy* (Chicago, 1925), Vol. I, p. 919.

[20]Such a joiner of Germanic lineage who worked in a thoroughly English style was Jacob Knor, the master carpenter for building Cliveden. See Margaret B. Tinkcom, "Cliveden: The Building of a Philadelphia Countryseat 1763-1767," *Pennsylvania Magazine of History and Biography.* 1964, Vol. 88, pp. 3-36.

[21]Marriage records, Trinity Lutheran Church, Lancaster.

[22]Lancaster Borough Tax Lists, Lancaster County Historical Society.

[23]Armstrong, *Organs for America*, p. 94.

[24]Translation from German receipted bill, Peter Frick to Trinity Lutheran Church, July 17, 1777, Trinity Lutheran Church, Lancaster. Frick's bill and accounts list some of his assistants on the organ case. These included the joiner Gottlieb Nauman and the turner Adam Hart, both of Lancaster, and the Moravian joiner Augustus Milchsack (1723-1789), also of Lancaster, who was Frick's chief assistant. Early in 1774 Frick was working in company with the Lancaster joiner Frederick Mann (but not on the organ case) at the Lutheran parsonage on North Duke Street (see Trinity Lutheran Church Account Book 1754-1782 for the year 1774).

[25]Virkus, *The Abridged Compendium*, Vol. 1, p. 919; Dieter Cunz, *The Maryland Germans—A History* (Princeton, 1948), p. 177.

[26]Leonard, "Brief History," p. 30.

[27]Armstrong, *Organs for America*, p. 30.

[28]According to the Account Book of Trinity Lutheran Church 1754-1782, at the church, and a bill there dated January 20, 1774, Frederick Schaeffer was paid £3/10 for hauling wood or wooden parts from Philadelphia for the organ.

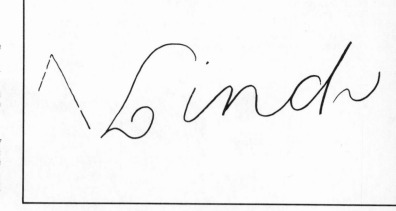

Fig. 10. Facsimile of the red-chalk signature on the bottom of a long drawer in the upper section of the highboy shown in Fig. 9. The partially eradicated initial letter may be *M. Blomstrann photograph.*

Fig. 11. Detail showing the carving on the skirt and central drawer of the lower section of the highboy illustrated in Fig. 9. *Blomstrann photograph.*

[29] The total is based on translations from German in Trinity Lutheran Church's Account Book 1754-1782 and bills of 1774-1775, all at the church.

[30] All birth, marriage, and death dates for the Lind family are based on records of the First Reformed Church, Reformed Church Archives. For Lind's arrival in America, see Ralph B. Strassburger and William J. Hinke, *Pennsylvania German Pioneers* (Norristown, 1934), Vol. 1, p. 496. For the location of the Lind property, see Lancaster County deeds KK-114, KK-116, and F-6-284, Lancaster County courthouse. The contention that "six fine Queen Anne chairs in one of America's greatest collections were made in 1753 by Michael Lind, Swedish cabinetmaker of Lancaster" (Carl Drepperd, *The Primer of American Antiques*, 1944, Ch. 5, p. 12) can neither be confirmed nor challenged.

[31] In 1783 John Lind (1761-1823) married Susanna Gonter, a sister of the gunsmith Peter Gonter.

[32] ANTIQUES, May 1974, p. 1057, Fig. 2.

[33] The contract is in the Hamilton Library and Cumberland County Historical Society, Carlisle, Pennsylvania, the gift of the Reverend John Rupp Albright.

[34] Lancaster County deed 3-363, Lancaster County courthouse, Lancaster Borough tax lists, Lancaster County Historical Society.

[35] A. Stapleton, "Early German Musical Publications in Pennsylvania," *The Pennsylvania German*, Vol. 7, No. 4 (July 1906), pp. 174-176. Robert B. Brown and Frank X. Braun, *Tunebook of Conrad Doll*, separate from *The Papers* of the Bibliographical Society of America, Vol. 42, 1948.

[36] According to Charles Edward Doll III, *300 Years of the Doll Family 1672-1972* (Mount Clemens, Michigan, 1972, pp. 4-5), George Burkhart's wife was a sister of Conrad's father John Doll (1736-1807). The marriages and death dates given in this source have been checked against the records of Lancaster's First Reformed Church, Reformed Church Archives. The death date of 1820 for Conrad Doll is based upon the date of his estate inventory at the Lancaster County Historical Society.

Fig. 12. Pediment of the highboy illustrated in Fig. 9. *Blomstrann photograph.*

Index